Ezekiel

Westminster Bible Companion

Series Editors

Patrick D. Miller
David L. Bartlett

Ezekiel

RONALD E. CLEMENTS

Westminster John Knox Press
Louisville, Kentucky

Book design by Publishers' WorkGroup
Cover design by Drew Stevens

First edition

Published by Westminster John Knox Press
Louisville, Kentucky

This book is printed on acid-free paper that meets the American National Standards Institute Z39.48 standard. ∞

PRINTED IN THE UNITED STATES OF AMERICA

96 97 98 99 00 01 02 03 04 05 — 10 9 8 7 6 5 4 3 2 1

Library of Congress Cataloging-in-Publication Data

Clements, R. E. (Ronald Ernest), 1929–
    Ezekiel / Ronald E. Clements. — 1st ed.
        p.   cm. — (Westminster Bible Companion)
    Includes bibliographical references and index.
    ISBN 0-664-25272-9 (alk. paper)
    1. Bible.   O.T.   Ezekiel—Commentaries.   I. Title.   II. Series.
BS1545.3.C58   1996
224′.4077—dc20   96-4358

Contents

Series Foreword

This series of study guides to the Bible is offered to the church and more specifically to the laity. In daily devotions, in church school classes, and in listening to the preached word, individual Christians turn to the Bible for a sustaining word, a challenging word, and a sense of direction. The word that scripture brings may be highly personal as one deals with the demands and surprises, the joys and sorrows, of daily life. It also may have broader dimensions as people wrestle with moral and theological issues that involve us all. In every congregation and denomination, controversies arise that send ministry and laity alike back to the Word of God to find direction for dealing with difficult matters that confront us.

A significant number of lay women and men in the church also find themselves called to the service of teaching. Most of the time they will be teaching the Bible. In many churches, the primary sustained attention to the Bible and the discovery of its riches for our lives have come from the ongoing teaching of the Bible by persons who have not engaged in formal theological education. They have been willing, and often eager, to study the Bible in order to help others drink from its living water.

This volume is part of a series of books, the Westminster Bible Companion, intended to help the laity of the church read the Bible more clearly and intelligently. Whether such reading is for personal direction or for the teaching of others, the reader cannot avoid the difficulties of trying to understand these words from long ago. The scriptures are clear and clearly available to everyone as they call us to faith in the God who is revealed in Jesus Christ and as they offer to every human being the word of salvation. No companion volumes are necessary in order to hear such words truly. Yet every reader of scripture who pauses to ponder and think further about any text has questions that are not immediately answerable simply by reading the text of scripture. Such questions may be about historical and geographical details or about words that are obscure or so loaded with meaning that one cannot tell at a glance what is at stake. They may be about the fundamental meaning of a passage or about what connection a particular text might have to our contemporary world. Or a teacher preparing for a church school class may simply want to know: What should I say about this biblical passage when I have to teach it next Sunday? It is our hope that these volumes, written by teachers and pastors with long experience studying and teaching the Bible in the church, will help members of the church who want and need to study the Bible with their questions.

The New Revised Standard Version of the Bible is the basis for the interpretive comments that each author provides. The NRSV text is presented at the beginning of the discussion so that the reader may have at hand in a single volume both the scripture passage and the exposition of its meaning. In some instances, where inclusion of the entire passage is not necessary for understanding either the text or the interpreter's discussion, the presentation of the NRSV text may be abbreviated. Usually, the whole of the biblical text is given.

We hope this series will serve the community of faith, opening the Word of God to all the people, so that they may be sustained and guided by it.

Introduction

WHEN EZEKIEL LIVED

The book bearing Ezekiel's name contains a series of dates that extend from the fifth year of the exile in Babylon of King Jehoiachin (Ezek. 1:2) to the twenty-seventh year (29:17). The latter is a relatively minor prophecy, but a major one is dated two years earlier, in the twenty-fifth year (40:1). These dates have aroused much discussion among scholars, but we may confidently take them as genuine and as coming from the prophet's own hand. When set against a reliable ancient chronology, they place his activity between the years 593 B.C., when he received his call to prophesy, and 571 B.C., about twenty-two years. In fact, Ezekiel's prophetic ministry falls into two very clearly defined periods. The first lasted for six years (593–587 B.C.) and was predominantly one of warning and preparation for disaster; this is covered in Ezekiel 1—24. The second period lasted for at least sixteen years (587–571) and was more centered on a message of hope; it is largely covered in Ezekiel 33—48. In between, in chapters 25—32, come a variety of prophecies addressed to nations outside Israel.

The year of the prophet's call is also identified as "the thirtieth year" in 1:1. A possible explanation is that this was his age at the time, although this interpretation is far from certain. It is not, however, unreasonable; Ezekiel appears to have been married by this time (his wife's death is recorded in 24:18), and he had almost certainly been active as a priest in Jerusalem. This would explain why, at the time of his call, he was living in exile in Babylon: In reality he was a kind of political hostage, since he was forced to live in a crude settlement camp with others of his fellow countrymen from Judah. Exiled prisoners of war would normally have been sold off as slaves.

The circumstances that led up to Ezekiel's being in Babylon were part of the political history of his people. The Babylonian armies had captured

Jerusalem after a short campaign in 598 B.C.; having plundered the city, they deported the king and many leading citizens to Babylon. Ezekiel was among them, which indicates that his family members, and probably he personally, were regarded as significant and influential figures whose removal to Babylon would serve as a lesson. They would also provide a lever by which the imperial power of Babylon hoped to force King Jehoiachin's replacement in Jerusalem, Zedekiah, to remain loyal and subservient. Ezekiel's priestly upbringing and training are reflected in his prophecies on every page.

The hope of forcing the kingdom of Judah to remain loyal, however, proved to be a vain one. The new puppet king, Zedekiah, uncle of the exiled ruler, quickly succumbed to the temptation to join, with other petty rulers of the region, in resisting further attempts at control from Babylon. In particular this meant withholding the payment of annual tribute gifts, but it seems evident that further restrictive measures were imposed on all subject nations by the mighty Babylonian ruler. Behind the regional attempts to resist further intervention from Babylon was the southern power, Egypt, with obvious reasons of its own for wanting to encourage its northern neighbors to oppose allowing Babylon free access to its frontiers.

All this is relevant for understanding Ezekiel's prophecies, since the central focus of his message concerns the ruinous consequences that will follow upon a further attempt at rebellion by Jerusalem. The prophet's divine message is that, against the wishes and expectations of his fellow exiles in Babylon, there will be further rebellion in the homeland, which will bring horrific consequences to Judah. Among the many catastrophes foretold is the destruction of the temple itself, a sanctuary regarded as so holy that its ruination and profanation were taken to be unthinkable. Ezekiel insists that this is not the case but is in fact a spiritual necessity.

History tells us that these fearful prophetic forebodings were realized; the events Ezekiel foresees happened and marked the effective end of the old kingdom of Judah. For the prophet himself, however, these events were only the beginning of his ministry. In their aftermath, his work became increasingly one of bringing hope to a despairing people and of preparing his fellow exiles to see themselves as fulfilling a central place in this hope. They would one day return to the homeland and rebuild the temple. They would establish a new people of Israel, purged of the follies and sins of the past. They would be responsible for bringing to fruition all the frustrated hopes and expectations that had been Israel's since its earliest beginnings with the great ancestral figures of Moses and David! Fittingly, therefore, the word of God that we hear through Ezekiel at the close of his active days is filled with a vision of hope. It was bent on urging the people to wait for and seek renewal. Israel would be born anew— a nation spiritually resurrected from the graves of those who suffered when the old nation collapsed.

THE PROPHET'S MESSAGE AND ITS THEMES

What God has to say through the prophet Ezekiel is readily understood as a product of the calamitous age in which he lived. It is strongly colored by the prophet's own thought world, which was itself the result of his upbringing as a priest in Jerusalem. Why had all this happened? In foretelling the future, the prophet's word also interprets the present and remembers the past. We might expect Ezekiel to direct his sharpest criticism toward Zedekiah, the puppet king in Jerusalem, and the hotheaded advisers and counselors who encouraged him to embark on a further series of rebellious acts against Babylon. Judah had already suffered brutally in the events that carried Ezekiel into exile, and behind them lay more than a century of further unwilling subjection to the earlier Mesopotamian superpower of Assyria.

Yet in fact Ezekiel's message contains little overt condemnation of the policies that brought about the calamitous events of 588–587 B.C. Instead, his word focuses on the religious shortcomings of the people, singling out idolatry as the greatest of Judah's sins. This reflects a distinctively priestly way of understanding the situation, although idolatry was undoubtedly symptomatic of Judah's wavering commitment to traditional faith in the Lord as God. One-sided as such an explanation for asserting the intensity of God's anger with the people may appear, it was nevertheless a salutary way of interpreting events. In particular it held the people as a whole responsible—both those who were suffering with Ezekiel in Babylon and those remaining in the homeland. It avoided picking out scapegoats; even the vacillating king is more pitied than condemned. Also, it avoided any concession to the belief that God was powerless in the face of a hostile world situation that Judah had neither sought nor directly provoked. Ezekiel asserted the meaningfulness of events, even when so many felt themselves on the edge of despair.

Besides being both prophet and priest, Ezekiel was also a pastor, taking responsibility for the lives of those around him, fully aware that what once encouraged complacency could readily lead to despair when its emptiness was uncovered. So the theme of judgment, which is hammered home as the core of the message throughout the first phase of Ezekiel's ministry, had a more ultimate value. Once the low point of Judah's fortunes was reached, it was possible to build hope on the conviction that the time of testing and trial was passing and a new beginning would shortly dawn. Radical as are the prophet's sweeping condemnations of Israel's past, so are his words of hope for the future equally and uncompromisingly assured and confident.

In all this we hear, reflected in God's word, the thinking of a priest drawing heavily and almost monotonously from three central themes: God's holiness, God's wrath against all human sin—abomination is one of Ezekiel's favorite words to describe this—and God's unimaginable glory and power to shape and guide human destiny. In particular we find in Ezekiel's sayings the message of a prophet who anticipated with an evangelical fervor the emphasis upon divine sovereignty that came to characterize a major stream of Christian theology. New life, born of repentance and offered as the prize of loyalty to God, is seen as an empowering by the divine spirit. Even holiness, with all its dangerous overtones of fear and wonder, is viewed by Ezekiel as a gift that is conferred on earth by the divine presence.

EZEKIEL AMONG THE PROPHETS

Ezekiel's prophetic ministry left its spiritual legacy in the book that bears his name. This occurs as the third of four great written collections of prophecy that constitute the latter prophets of the Old Testament. The earlier parts of these books had begun to take shape more than one and a half centuries earlier, with Amos and Hosea. Their work marked the first signs of the collapse of the sister kingdoms of Israel and Judah in the face of the threat posed by the imperial expansion of Assyria to the west. That initial threat, which dominated the second half of the eighth century B.C., had passed by the end of the seventh century and saw the end of the old Northern Kingdom of Israel. Judah survived, but almost immediately the earlier threat was replaced by a new one from Babylon. So the prophets of the Assyrian period of Israel's misfortunes—Amos, Hosea, Isaiah, and Micah—came to be followed by further prophets of the Babylonian period.

These later prophets were primarily Jeremiah and Ezekiel. While these two were contemporaries , they had markedly different temperaments.

Jeremiah was a sensitive and highly poetic spokesman, brought up among a family of priests in the small town of Anathoth, who began his ministry more than thirty years ahead of Ezekiel. Ezekiel, in contrast, was from a privileged priestly family of Jerusalem but did not begin his active prophetic work until he found himself in exile in Babylon.

Despite Jeremiah's earlier activity, it is the prophets' different perspectives, reflected in their words about the events and personalities of Judah's last days before the catastrophe of 587 B.C., that make a comparison between them and their books so full of interest. God's word is conveyed not in vague abstractions but as a disclosure of truth, mediated through very distinctive human personalities. Nor is it simply the prophets' personalities that contrast so strikingly, but the way in which their words and actions reflect their differing situations. Jeremiah, for example, was well aware of the developing political situation in Judah when Zedekiah was enticed into rebellion against his Babylonian overlord. Ezekiel, on the other hand, heard only whispers of this situation, but his prophecies strive hard to warn of unforeseen dangers to come. For both men, the tragedy of 587 B.C. was a turning point. For Jeremiah it came toward the close of a long ministry. For Ezekiel it came early and provides the background against which his later and more sustained message of hope needs to be understood.

In his earliest preaching Ezekiel addressed a frustrated people who were hoping, even expecting, shortly to return to their homeland. He had to convince them that they would be lucky to find any homeland left. Only penitent waiting could open the way to an eventual—and distant—return to rebuild the ruined temple and cities of Judah. So his words of hope and renewal are more varied than Jeremiah's and are spread over a longer period. Yet for both men it cannot be too strongly emphasized that the events of 587 B.C. were the fulcrum on which everything turned.

THE MAKING OF
THE PROPHETIC BOOK OF EZEKIEL

No reader of the book of Ezekiel can fail to notice its highly distinctive style. The prophet uses words that would have been common enough on the lips of a priest but that sound stilted and cumbersome to the unfamiliar ear. His manner of expression is distinctive. While it lacks the verbal artistry that characterizes Isaiah and Jeremiah, it nevertheless achieves a

poetic effect in a very different way. It is full of dramatic images, sometimes repeated extensively, in which basic metaphors, such as the vine, the
shepherd, and the cedar tree, are exploited to the full. Furthermore,
Ezekiel practiced a kind of street theater, acting out with gestures and
signs events he wished to declare as imminent.

While it is not difficult with many of the prophets to feel we can "hear"
how they preached, even though in highly condensed and abbreviated
form, with Ezekiel this is less possible. Instead we have brief reports telling
us what God told him to do or say to the people; we are left to infer that
he actually did so. This strongly suggests that the prophet himself wrote
down short reports of his messages, which provided the core of the book
that now carries his name. It is likely that, as a priest of a major temple, he
would have been skilled in the art of writing. Probably he could have
found adequate writing materials in his place of exile, so we may conclude
that he himself took the first steps toward compiling his work into a book.
The careful dating of many of the more important prophecies would also
be the mark of a priest, for whom time has a deep religious meaning. His
calling made him a person who was familiar with the skills needed for precise reporting and accounting.

There are clear signs in the book that the prophecies have been
grouped in series; the four great vision sequences—chapters 1—3, 8—11,
37, and 40—48—in particular bear this out. With other prophecies also
there are clear indications that suitable short "collections" were made. In
addition, some of the prophecies are in the form of lengthy allegories, or
parables, which reveal a carefully thought-out structure. All this indicates
that a process of shaping and editing took place, and there is no reason to
doubt that the prophet himself began the task.

Yet it seems unlikely that the book in its present form is from the hand
of the prophet. Some sections must certainly have been added at a later
stage. This is especially true of Ezekiel 38—39, which can be identified as
a very late revision of the perspective regarding God's future plans for Israel given in the main part of the book. In other parts also, even in the case
of prophecies where hopeful and reassuring endings follow stern beginnings (as in chapters 16 and 20), a process of revision and editing provides
us with the best explanation for this confusion.

The most convenient analogy to use in understanding how the scroll of
Ezekiel acquired its present form is that of a great person's collected pa-
pers—including notes and diary entries—that have been edited after their
author's death. Indeed, it may well have been the case that, while the orig-

inal prophet was still alive, the vital spiritual contact with his living voice made any movement toward compiling a scroll of the divine word given through him appear unimportant. Only the great man's passing would have brought the necessary impetus to ensure that future generations would have the real if less personal contact provided by the written word.

1. The Prophet's Call and Commissioning
Ezekiel 1:1–3:27

Each of the longer prophetic books of the Old Testament—Isaiah, Jeremiah, and Ezekiel—contains an account of how the prophet was called to his high task. It is reasonable to conclude that every prophet became aware in some distinctive fashion of a divine summons to proclaim God's message to the nation he served. This gave the indispensable assurance that the message came from God and was not simply something the prophet had personally thought up. It also remained a point of conviction and strengthening, since each of these outstanding prophetic leaders came to have an awareness of being burdened with the necessity to say things that aroused strong opposition. They were speaking against the tide of popular opinion and expectation and were themselves objects of abuse, ridicule, and attempted refutation. Prophets spoke out against official policy, against the widespread popular feeling that God is always bound to look after the interests of the nation, and against a general complacency that events would be sure to work out for the benefit and preservation of Israel and Judah, in spite of many obvious national shortcomings. The popular view of a prophet was of a person bound to see to the best interests of God's people without interfering too much in national affairs. God was expected to serve the people, instead of the people serving God!

Accordingly, remembering and recording an experience of divine call and commissioning were important to Ezekiel, and to the others, because it justified his activity and made him resolute in the face of strong opposition. It was also important to let such experiences be known to the prophet's audience. This demonstrated the prophet's integrity and sincerity and, from the outset, explained that the message being delivered was authentically "from God," even though it was not what ordinary citizens were expecting to hear. The call was both the prophet's claim to have been given a special authority from God and a public declaration that such authority was real and provided the basis for an intelligible interpretation of events that were shortly to overtake the nation.

It is important to bear in mind both the public and the private understanding of the formative role of an experience of call. This explains why it mattered to write it down for later generations to read. During the time of active ministry, the deep sense of a divine commission kept the prophet going, often in the face of grave physical threats and difficulties. Even after the prophet's death, when the tensions and trials of active ministry lay in the past, it was still valuable that others reflect upon the pain and shock this ministry had aroused. The record of the call thereby served as a kind of seal of divine authority on the fuller account of the prophet's words, showing that they brought a truth that was unexpectedly new, that this truth was of God, and that it had significantly shaped the way in which the past was to be understood and the future planned. Written prophecy could then become not simply a basis for interpreting a painful past, as it so clearly was in Ezekiel's case, but also a charter for pressing forward in the sure hope that God had planned and charted a new beginning for the people.

The event that overshadows the entire book of Ezekiel is unquestionably the prolonged siege of Jerusalem by the Babylonian armies in the years 588–587 B.C. and the collapse of the city's defense, with its subsequent ruination, including the destruction of the temple. Beyond this destruction, however, which Ezekiel presented as the work of God's hand in judgment, was the hope of rebuilding and renewal, summed up in the idea of new life. As God had judged Jerusalem, so would that judgment be turned into blessing, once the people repented.

Yet because Ezekiel experienced his call to be a prophet not in Jerusalem, where the judgment was to fall, but in Babylon, it required a very special conviction to accept that God had brought his word about Jerusalem's fate not to those who were still resident in the city but to a former priest of the temple who had been unfortunate enough to have been deported, along with many others, including the ex-king of Judah and his household. It is possible that many still clung to the belief that this exiled ruler was the rightful king of the nation. So Ezekiel's call is presented with high drama, taking the form of an astounding vision of God's arrival in Babylon, seated on a magnificent heavenly throne chariot and summoning Ezekiel, against his will and personal desires, to become a messenger to the nation.

This feature occupies the whole of the call and commissioning section of the book of Ezekiel, extending through 3:27. It falls into four separate parts, or episodes, which provide the prophet's credentials to become the messenger of God. Chapter 1 is largely taken up with describing the heavenly throne chariot, providing the assurance that it is indeed God who has visited and taken hold of the prophet. Chapter 2 reports the resistance Ezekiel feels to such a task and his shrinking from it. However, God's insistence overrules all human feelings and inadequacies, so the task is accepted. Chapter 3:1–15 then marks an act of commissioning in which Ezekiel receives, in symbolic visionary form, the message he is to convey to the people. Its judgmental nature and saving character are signified by the fact that, when eaten, the message is "as sweet as honey" (3:3).

The responsibility of being a prophet is then spelled out by comparing it to that of a city watchman or sentinel (3:16–21), and a final picture of the prophet, reeling with alarm and amazement at the high task that has been given him, is presented in 3:22–27. Throughout, there are ample hints that the message God is to give through Ezekiel will be unwelcome and unpalatable. Nevertheless, in spite of the fearful nature of the task, a deep assurance runs throughout that the message—and, with it, the messenger—will prevail. Because God has set a divine seal upon both, no human resistance can hold them back or thwart them.

THE VISION OF THE CHARIOT
Ezekiel 1:1–28

1:1 In the thirtieth year, in the fourth month, on the fifth day of the month, as I was among the exiles by the river Chebar, the heavens were opened, and I saw visions of God. 2 On the fifth day of the month (it was the fifth year of the exile of King Jehoiachin), 3 the word of the LORD came to the priest Ezekiel son of Buzi, in the land of the Chaldeans by the river Chebar; and the hand of the LORD was on him there.

4 As I looked, a stormy wind came out of the north: a great cloud with brightness around it and fire flashing forth continually, and in the middle of the fire, something like gleaming amber. 5 In the middle of it was something like four living creatures. This was their appearance: they were of human form. 6 Each had four faces, and each of them had four wings. . . .

15 As I looked at the living creatures, I saw a wheel on the earth beside the living creatures, one for each of the four of them. 16As for the appearance of the wheels and their construction: their appearance was like the gleaming of beryl; and the four had the same form, their construction being something like a wheel within a wheel. . . . 19 When the living creatures moved, the wheels moved beside them; and when the living creatures rose from the earth, the wheels rose. . . .

22 Over the heads of the living creatures there was something like a dome, shining like crystal, spread out above their heads. . . .

26 And above the dome over their heads there was something like a throne, in appearance like sapphire; and seated above the likeness of a throne was something that seemed like a human form. 27 Upward from what appeared like the loins I saw something like gleaming amber, something that looked like fire enclosed all around; and downward from what looked like the loins I saw something that looked like fire, and there was a splendor all around. 28 Like the bow in a cloud on a rainy day, such was the appearance of the splendor all around. This was the appearance of the likeness of the glory of the LORD.

When I saw it, I fell on my face, and I heard the voice of someone speaking.

Ezekiel's call is initiated by a vision of God that came to him in his place of exile in Babylon and marked the beginning of his career as a prophet. The vision of the throne chariot includes some of the most detailed and impressive descriptions of the divine world to be found in the Old Testament. It goes so far as to affirm that the prophet "saw" God clothed in glory. Many scholars, both ancient and modern, have examined minutely the language of the description in order to find out more about what God and the surrounding heavenly beings look like. But it is quite difficult to put together a clear picture of what is being described; some features are confusing, even allowing for difficulties of translation, and have defied explanation. This is true, for instance, of the living creatures with "four faces" (but not four heads) of verses 1:5–14 and their connection with the living "wheels" of verses 15–21. The precise manner of their movement (always straight ahead), described in verses 14 and 17, is also puzzling. All in all, no wholly satisfactory explanation for the different features of this heavenly throne chariot has been forthcoming to enable a clear visual picture to emerge. Consequently, artistic attempts to portray its appearance have seldom been more than partially effective, usually omitting or reinterpreting some of the description's basic assertions.

A number of significant points can help account for our difficulty in forming a mental picture of what the prophet describes. First and foremost is the fact that the central point of his vision is the knowledge that God in person has appeared to the prophet in Babylon. It is the divine presence that gives the prophet his authority to speak and provides assurance that neither he nor his fellow exiles have been abandoned by God. The felt reality of God's presence is more important than how it should be mentally pictured.

The confusing complexity of the vision indicates clearly the prophet's recognition that he cannot describe the Indescribable One! The imagery is therefore deliberately hesitant and contrasts with everyday experience in certain of its details. Divine realities overreach the boundaries of human images and ideas, as the prophet's vision demonstrates.

We are faced with a description of an awesome but mysterious chariot, different from but not altogether unlike what a human king would use. It is drawn by living creatures. Elsewhere in the Bible (Psalm 18:10), God is described as riding "on a cherub" and on "the wings of the wind." The throne on which God is seated here is located above a "dome" or platform (v. 26), which is likened to the "dome" or firmament of the sky (Gen. 1:7 uses the same Hebrew word). When we reach the point where the prophet is to describe the divine Being, his language becomes extremely hesitant, and all he can say is that he saw "something that seemed like a human form" (v. 26). God is beyond all human sight and apprehension, so ordinary words cannot describe the divine appearance! The report intentionally hides as much as it reveals and warns us off, just when it seems to be inviting us forward to discover what God really looks like. Verse 28 asserts categorically that God has been seen by the prophet, but hedges by calling it "the appearance of the likeness of the glory of the Lord." No human being can see God (see Exod. 33:20), and so no human words are adequate to describe an infinite Being! Word pictures and symbols may nonetheless point us in the right direction. We must conclude that our inability to portray what exactly Ezekiel says he saw in his vision is a consequence of his intentionally complex and restrained language.

We can deduce from Ezekiel's vision, however, that God can be known and the divine presence felt and recognized without our being in possession of the mental pictures that would define God in "our" kind of language. God is "there," but not as an object open to human examination, like a researcher's animal on a dissecting table.

Ezekiel's description shows a desire to affirm a fundamental spiritual truth in highly visual word pictures without submitting the details to precise pictorial definition. As with certain categories of painting, it intentionally blurs and contrasts the clear-cut shapes and sounds of everyday experience. To show that God's presence is a reality in Babylon, the account is suggestive and mysterious, filled with a vision of immense power and vitality but nonetheless refusing to yield to precise definition. This is equally true of the wheels (vv. 15–21) and of the throne above the well of the chariot (vv. 22–26). Some commentators have suggested that the complexity of the descriptions is a result of the efforts of later scribes to fill out the prophet's original simpler account in order to generate a fuller understanding of the divine world; in the process, the picture has become confused. This may be part of the truth, but the main point is that the prophet's vision was never intended to give clear pictures of a reality that must, by its very otherworldly nature, defy all human language. Such word pictures can, as doors of perception, let in a little light, but they cannot let in all of it without overwhelming the human capacity to see.

As a young priest in training in Jerusalem, Ezekiel would have grown up with his mind filled with the sights and sounds of the temple there (note especially the attention to the roaring sound in v. 24). The elaborate carvings and symbolism on the temple walls (see 1 Kings 6:29) would have filled his mind with deep impressions of a divine world where cherubim, palm trees, and strange creatures of mixed human and animal form abounded. Babylonian temples and palaces, which Ezekiel must have seen too, were also elaborately decorated with symbols of the heavenly world. So at the base of Ezekiel's description of God's heavenly throne chariot we find traces of an elaborate pictorial symbolism about the divine world in which Israel and the ancient Near East abounded.

Yet the prophet does not leave us with any static and rationally explicable symbolism of the kind that enables us to say that "this" figure means "that" truth. Rather, his vision comes to life and is woven into an exciting and vigorous portrayal of great splendor. It is bound up in a whirring and roaring wonder of majesty, which has no sharply defined mental shape and form. It is slightly out of focus, as it must actually have appeared to the prophet's senses. It was an experience that was inseparable from the awareness of being summoned by God to become a messenger to the Jewish exiles in Babylon (2:1–3:15). The prophet uses this personal sense of the overwhelming reality of God's presence to make a major statement about the certainty of this divine reality for all his fellow exiles in Babylon. This vision portrait of God, so rare and unusual among Old Testament descriptions, fills the gap left by the loss of a familiar place and comforting routine of worship. God answers with a vision the question: How can one whose temple stands in Jerusalem come to a people in Babylon?

In order to understand the unique importance of Ezekiel as a prophet, it is essential to grasp the central place that the visual aspect of faith plays in his life and message. He is the most visually descriptive and vision-oriented of the prophets. Among the books of the Old Testament, only the later book of Daniel, where visions and allegories become even more intricate and complex, develops this visual aspect as extensively. Mental pictures become the basis of insight, and truth has to be "seen" in order to be accepted fully. For Ezekiel, seeing is believing; truth can only be sure when it can be pictured. This helps to explain his vital bridge-building role as architect of a new dimension of faith. Not only for him personally, but for all the people of Judah, the spiritual world was one that had been given visual shape and meaning through the symbols and features of the Jerusalem temple, This was the world's center, its highest location (Psalm 48:1), because nearest to God. Its furnishings were signs and pointers to a mysterious other world of divine power. Space and time were marked by the sights and festivals of worship. So the temple and its services provided a spiritual map through which the world could be interpreted.

Only someone brought up, like Ezekiel, as a priest in Jerusalem could hope to translate and reinterpret this spiritual map of the world for a large community of people who had been uprooted from their spiritual home. They had lost their mental map, so Ezekiel was called upon to provide them with a new one in which the words of prophecy replace the sights and sounds of a sacred building. So the revelation to Ezekiel presents a great reinterpretation of the symbols of faith, as every true revelation of the divine world has to be. A special gift was given to him with the gift of prophecy: The translation of the visual symbols of an age-old tradition of worship into ideas and affirmations written in a book. This marks a shift from the symbolism of formal worship to the imagery and written word of prophecy. God is greater than Jerusalem, greater than Babylon, greater even than any human symbol or language can grasp. Yet for such truth to be understood, the bridge between seeing and knowing has to be crossed. Ezekiel is the guide across such a bridge, more than any other prophet representing the sights and sounds of ancient religious symbolism and ritual in truths written on a scroll.

So Ezekiel communicates and describes the truth of this overpowering presence of God. To do so, he uses the features and figures of the temple symbolism with which he grew up in order to insist upon its reality. This visual side of Ezekiel controls and directs the message of his entire book. Even sin is something that can be seen; psychological attitudes such as despair, faith, and hope are also given a pictorial quality. Where our modern spiritual world is usually made up largely of abstract thoughts and words, Ezekiel's was constructed of pictures. Ezekiel learned to think with his eyes, so that his prophecy has a wonderful visionary quality.

More important than the concern to satisfy intellectual curiosity about the appearance of God, Ezekiel's message served to reawaken hope and faith among Jewish exiles in whom such feelings had almost withered away. They felt God had abandoned them when the city of Jerusalem was captured by the armies of Babylon and they were uprooted from their homes. Because they felt personally defeated, they were inclined to believe that God had been defeated! To counter such despair, and in place of the Jerusalem temple that was now inaccessible to them, Ezekiel reveals the grand vision of the living and true God made present and active through the prophetic word.

THE CALL AND COMMISSION
TO PROPHESY
Ezekiel 2:1–3:15

2:1. . . . And when he spoke to me, a spirit entered into me and set me on my feet; and I heard him speaking to me. [3] He said to me, Mortal, I am sending you to the people of Israel, to a nation of rebels who have rebelled against me; they and their ancestors have transgressed against me to this very day. . . . [6] And you, O mortal, do not be afraid of them, and do not be afraid of their words, though briers and thorns surround you and you live among scorpions. . . .

[8] But you, mortal, hear what I say to you; do not be rebellious like that rebellious house; open your mouth and eat what I give you. [9] I looked, and a hand was stretched out to me, and a written scroll was in it. [10] He spread it before me; it had writing on the front and on the back, and written on it were words of lamentation and mourning and woe.

3:1 He said to me, O mortal, eat what is offered to you; eat this scroll, and go, speak to the house of Israel. [2] So I opened my mouth, and he gave me the scroll to eat. [3] He said to me, Mortal, eat this scroll that I give you and fill your stomach with it. Then I ate it; and in my mouth it was as sweet as honey.

[4] He said to me: Mortal, go to the house of Israel and speak my very words to them. [5] For you are not sent to a people of obscure speech and difficult language, but to the house of Israel. . . . [7] But the house of Israel will not listen to you, for they are not willing to listen to me; because all the house of Israel have a hard forehead and a stubborn heart. [8] See, I have made your face hard against their faces, and your forehead hard against their foreheads. . . . [14] The spirit lifted me up and bore me away; I went in bitterness in the heat of my spirit, the hand of the LORD being strong upon me. [15] I came to the exiles at Tel-abib, who lived by the river Chebar. And I sat there among them, stunned, for seven days.

The vision of God riding on a heavenly chariot leads to a report of Ezekiel's call and commissioning to prophesy. The report contains themes that are familiar from similar call narratives in other prophetic books. The prophet who is the subject of the call appears weak and fearful and needs to be given strength by God for the task that is set before him (2:2). His task will demand unflinching courage and resolution (2:6). Most emphatically noted throughout is the very black and threatening portrait of the people to whom the prophet must speak (2:3–7). Because they are people of a rebellious nature, they will give him a very hostile reception (especially v. 6). Like a king's loyal messenger carrying a final appeal to a gang of dangerous rebels, the prophet will encounter a threatening and negative response. Yet he must not turn aside or shrink from carrying his mission through to its conclusion. This conclusion is impressively described as knowing "that there has been a prophet among them" (2:5). Acknowledging the message bearer is assurance that a true message has been sent!

Other prophetic call narratives tell of comparable fears and forebodings of rejection and personal threats. Yet even Jeremiah does not outstrip Ezekiel's grim anticipation of implacable hostility from his hearers. Such earlier prophetic experience must have remained fresh in Ezekiel's mind (the "briers and thorns" of v. 6 seems to echo Isaiah's parable of the vineyard in Isa. 5:6, and the sweetness of the taste of honey (in 3:3 reminds us of Jeremiah's words about the pleasantness of eating the words of God referred to in Jer. 15:16). There may even be a touch of irony, with the prophet goading his hearers into believing his message by insisting that they are, by nature, incapable of responding to its truth. Throughout, there is an inescapable link between the painful nature of the message (2:10) and the popular rejection of the message bearer in order to deny its truth.

Even allowing for a touch of irony, the truth is that Ezekiel paints a very dark picture of what is in the minds of those to whom he is sent. They are rebellious and stubborn. It is especially noteworthy that the prophet reports the hard truth that the problem does not lie in the inability to hear (3:5–6) but in the willingness to do so (3:7). The message challenges the popular self-pity and rigidity of thinking that cannot face up to a greater truth. His hearers cannot bear the pain of accepting responsibility for their own part in the mistakes and rebelliousness of the past. Nor can they accept the challenge that there cannot be any effective future for them until they give a whole new level of priority to their loyalty to God. So the prophet sees his commission to speak on behalf of God as putting very clear alternatives to the people (3:11). One way or the other, the people cannot escape the challenge that facing up to the word of God is the central issue for their lives. There can be no real future for them without it.

We find the same remarkable picture quality in this act of divine commissioning that we noted in the vision of the divine throne chariot. It pervades the entire book. What went on as the divine word took shape in the prophet's mind is painted with extraordinary word pictures; he describes himself as living in the midst of a wilderness of "briers and thorns" that abounds with "scorpions" (2:6). God's authorization to speak takes the visible form of a hand presenting a scroll written on both sides (2:9–10), just as Jeremiah's prophecies had been written on a scroll (Jeremiah 36). Perhaps Ezekiel actually witnessed what happened to Jeremiah's scroll thirteen years earlier (Jer. 36:23–24). To have heeded the warning then would have spared Judah the political disasters that followed. It is a cruel paradox that, even though the scroll contains a message of "lamentation and mourning and woe" (2:10), it tastes "as sweet as honey" (3:3). Better to know the truth and face up to it than go on living with an illusion!

Finally, with a roar and a rushing sound, the vision ends and Ezekiel is left stunned and shocked as he takes stock of what has happened to him (3:12–15). A full seven days elapse before Ezekiel can come to terms with the task he has been given. Apparently, too, only after he has had time to let the scale of his commitment take hold of his entire person can he begin to tell others what has happened and start to explain the message he has to bring (3:15). God's work is no occasion for self-display or cause for self-congratulation. It is a cause for alarm and deep reflection, before its implications can be accepted and acted upon. Only those who have taken it in themselves can pass it on to others!

Ezekiel is now set to begin a ministry as a prophet of God, already aware that his words will often appear painful and hurtful before they can become reassuring and hopeful.

THE PROPHET'S INNER LIFE
Ezekiel 3:16–27

3:16 **At the end of seven days, the word of the LORD came to me:** [17]**Mortal, I have made you a sentinel for the house of Israel; whenever you hear a word from my mouth, you shall give them warning from me.** [18] **If I say to the wicked, "You shall surely die," and you give them no warning, or speak to warn the wicked from their wicked way, in order to save their life, those wicked persons shall die for their iniquity; but their blood I will require at your hand.** [19] **But if you warn the wicked, and they do not turn from their wickedness, or from their wicked way, they shall die for their iniquity; but you will have saved your life. . . .**

[22] **Then the hand of the LORD was upon me there; and he said to me, Rise up, go out into the valley, and there I will speak with you.** [23] **So I rose up and**

went out into the valley; and the glory of the LORD stood there, like the glory that I had seen by the river Chebar; and I fell on my face. [24] The spirit entered into me, and set me on my feet; and he spoke with me and said to me: Go, shut yourself inside your house. [25] As for you, mortal, cords shall be placed on you, and you shall be bound with them, so that you cannot go out among the people; [26] and I will make your tongue cling to the roof of your mouth, so that you shall be speechless and unable to reprove them; for they are a rebellious house. [27] But when I speak with you, I will open your mouth, and you shall say to them, "Thus says the Lord GOD". . . .

Two further admonitions are given to the prophet after the seven days in which he reflects and broods upon the task before him. In the first of these (3:16–21), he is warned that his work as a prophet will make him a "sentinel" (v. 17), or lookout, for the people of Israel. The metaphor is a military one, as are quite a number of the most telling word pictures by which Ezekiel portrays the work of a true prophet. As the guard on duty in a city or fortress carries responsibility for the lives of all the people who have appointed him to his task, so the prophet carries equal responsibility. If he fails to give a proper warning, he will afterward have to answer for it. However, if he does give proper warning but people do not listen to him, the responsibility for their inaction and complacency rests on their own heads.

At a first reading, the comparison of a prophet to a sentinel sounds rather cold and seems to indicate someone trying to fend off personal responsibility if things go wrong. Yet this is certainly to misread the situation. It is simply one of a number of occasions where Ezekiel's rather coldly reasoned argument hides the real intensity of his feeling. His aim is certainly to point out, most emphatically, that there is a responsibility in hearing as well as in speaking. If the word of God sounds dull, the fault may not lie with the speaker but with the dull and unresponsive attitude of the listener!

Almost certainly, the message here reflects the fact that, ten years earlier, Jeremiah warned of coming disaster but none of those in authority listened. Ezekiel's own warnings cannot sound any more convincing, nor can they be put any more persuasively, than in Jeremiah's prophecies. He can simply repeat the message God gave him and trust that some, at least, will give it the attention it deserves. Perhaps only later generations will really benefit from the lookout's role that the prophet plays. Probably Ezekiel was well aware that his hearers were now more ready to believe the truth of the warnings written on Jeremiah's scroll than King Jehoiakim, father of Jehoiachin, had been at the time.

Although the warning that the prophet is a sentinel appears as an addendum to Ezekiel's commissioning, it is more an admonition to the hearer and reader than to the prophet himself. Of course the prophet must be faithful and unflinching in fulfilling his job. Yet even when the prophet is utterly faithful, his hearers also carry a great burden of responsibility. Unless they listen and react positively to the message that is given them, it will have been given in vain. The true prophet must not only be faithful himself but must call for faithful hearers. He must declare the truth given to him, but he must also be as skilled as possible in the art of persuasion, if he is to achieve all that a prophet is called upon to do.

There is a fuller picture of the prophet's role as a sentinel in Ezekiel 33:1–9, so we must either conclude that this aspect of the prophet's task was repeated to him more than once or has been brought forward to be included with his commissioning at this point because of its importance. Most likely in the case of this, as in all Old Testament accounts of how a prophet is called and commissioned by God, a good deal of later reflection has been woven in. It shows how the prophet has come to see his task in the light of experience. There is good reason why the admonition is repeated at the beginning of chapter 33, since this point marks a turnaround in the message, to include a primary emphasis on hope and reassurance instead of the warning that has earlier prevailed.

The second warning, in 3:22–27, has occasioned a great deal of discussion and still leaves us with much uncertainty. Ezekiel is told that he will be bound with cords and will be unable to go about among the people (v. 25). For a time he will even be dumb and unable to speak (v. 26), which sounds an almost impossible limitation for a prophet! The reference to cords may be understood either as a symbol (he is to be tied up like a prisoner—as his hearers were prisoners in Babylon) or as a restraint (his opponents will endeavor to silence him), but the most probable explanation lies elsewhere.

There are several indications in the book that Ezekiel suffered at times from severe nervous and physical disabilities. His task was very stressful and debilitating. There are signs too that his personality was vulnerable and easily overstrained. Clearly this point may easily be exaggerated, but it seems to contain at least part of the truth about him. So we may understand the language of 3:25–26 as pointing to the temporary paralysis and dumbness of an overstressed personality. If so, it is a most remarkable testimony to Ezekiel as someone whose work as a prophet absorbed his whole being. Even a seemingly cruel and overpowering disability, which left him without speech or strength to move for long periods, could become part of the message of God to him and, through him, to the people of Israel.

2. The Message of Judgment upon Israel
Ezekiel 4:1–7:27

After the account of Ezekiel's call and commissioning, we are presented in 4:1–7:27 with a summary overview of his message relating to the first five years of his activity. It is consistently a message of doom and judgment, with only the merest glimpses of anything beyond. The central revelation is that the land of Judah and the city of Jerusalem will soon face another military attack and suffer further destruction and devastation, such as happened in 598 B.C. The message is simple and straightforward: Jerusalem will again face a terrible siege; it will again be overthrown; and a great many of its citizens will be plunged into the horrors of death by either the sword or famine or, only a little less terrifying, be scattered "to the wind." The events of just a few years earlier, which Ezekiel witnessed and which sent him to Babylon, will shortly repeat themselves.

Essentially, we find in these four chapters only repetitions of the same message. The surprise lies in the recognition that Ezekiel is not actually among the citizens of Judah, who were to be most directly affected by these events. Instead, he is at a seemingly safe distance in Babylon. Yet what happened in Judah was of the most direct concern to the prophet and his hearers in their pitiable state of exile. They had to learn to think of their situation differently—to stop envying those who remained behind in Judah and to give up their mistaken hope of a speedy return to the homeland. Moreover, the sheer terror and frightfulness of what was to happen again to Judah needs to be understood. Only one word can possibly describe it: judgment! God is still angry with the people. Only when men and women recognize the cause of that divine wrath in their long history of national failings can that anger be turned aside and a new beginning occur.

THE PROPHETIC DRAMA
OF JERUSALEM'S COMING FATE
Ezekiel 4:1–5:4

4:1 And you, O mortal, take a brick and set it before you. On it portray a city, Jerusalem; 2 and put siegeworks against it, and build a siege-wall against it, and cast up a ramp against it; set camps also against it, and plant battering rams against it all around. 3 Then take an iron plate and place it as an iron wall between you and the city; set your face toward it, and let it be in a state of siege, and press the siege against it. This is a sign for the house of Israel.

4 Then lie on your left side, and place the punishment of the house of Israel upon it; you shall bear their punishment for the number of the days that you lie there. 5 For I assign to you a number of days, three hundred ninety days, equal to the number of the years of their punishment; and so you shall bear the punishment of the house of Israel. 6 When you have completed these, you shall lie down a second time, but on your right side, and bear the punishment of the house of Judah; forty days I assign you, one day for each year. 7 You shall set your face toward the siege of Jerusalem, and with your arm bared you shall prophesy against it. 8 See, I am putting cords on you so that you cannot turn from one side to the other until you have completed the days of your siege.

9 And you, take wheat and barley, beans and lentils, millet and spelt; put them into one vessel, and make bread for yourself. During the number of days that you lie on your side, three hundred ninety days, you shall eat it. 10 The food that you eat shall be twenty shekels a day by weight; at fixed times you shall eat it. 11 And you shall drink water by measure, one-sixth of a hin; at fixed times you shall drink. 12 You shall eat it as a barley-cake, baking it in their sight on human dung. 13 The LORD said, "Thus shall the people of Israel eat their bread, unclean, among the nations to which I will drive them." 14 Then I said, "Ah Lord GOD! I have never defiled myself; from my youth up until now I have never eaten what died of itself or was torn by animals, nor has carrion flesh come into my mouth." 15 Then he said to me, "See, I will let you have cow's dung instead of human dung, on which you may prepare your bread."

16 Then he said to me, Mortal, I am going to break the staff of bread in Jerusalem; they shall eat bread by weight and with fearfulness; and they shall drink water by measure and in dismay. 17 Lacking bread and water, they will look at one another in dismay, and waste away under their punishment.

5:1 And you, O mortal, take a sharp sword; use it as a barber's razor and run it over your head and your beard; then take balances for weighing; and divide the hair. 2 One third of the hair you shall burn in the fire inside the city, when the days of the siege are completed; one third you shall take and strike with the sword all around the city; and one third you shall scatter to the wind, and I will unsheathe the sword after them. [3] Then you shall take from these a small number and bind them in the skirts of your robe. [4] From these, again, you shall take some, throw them into the fire and burn them up; from there a fire will come out against all the house of Israel.

Ezekiel's commissioning as a lookout for the people of Israel draws attention to the fact that the prophet is acutely aware of the need to get his message across. So we now have, as an opening section summarizing his prophetic message from the time of his call to the time of his wife's death (24:15–18), four sign actions—a form of mime, or street theater—that dramatically portray what he has to declare. The placing of these actions at this point demonstrates their importance as a summary of what his message at this time consisted of. It was a declaration that once again, and against all expectation, Jerusalem would be placed under siege and would suffer terrible deprivation, and its inhabitants would then be brought to ruin and disaster, with great loss of life. No other Old Testament prophet makes greater use of this dramatic and memorable technique than does Ezekiel. It fits in completely with his attention to the visual side of proclaiming truth. The people must see in order to believe.

In the first sign action, Ezekiel portrays, in a kind of model war game, a siege set against a brick, representing the city of Jerusalem (4:1–3). In the second, he lies effectively bedridden for long periods (v. 5 mentions three hundred and ninety days, v. 6, forty days) in which he will "bear the punishment" (i.e., for sin) of the people of Israel and Judah. He is to look toward Jerusalem as a sign of the period in which the city will be under siege (v. 8). The third sign action (4:9–17) consists of the eating of the sparse rations of a people under siege. The fourth and last of the mimed actions (5:1–4) is the cutting off of his hair with a sharpened sword. One-third is to be chopped up with this sword, another third is to be scattered to the wind, and the final third is to be burnt. Only some of the hair scattered to the wind will be kept (5:3), signifying the small number of the survivors. All this dramatic theater is to portray the fate that is to befall the people in Jerusalem.

The message is straightforward enough, and repeating it in this elaborate fashion shows how central it was for the prophet. It does, however, raise many questions. First, we may wonder why Ezekiel so favors this kind of street theater. It may simply be his awareness that truth has to be seen to be believed, but it may also reflect his concern to tease the minds of hearers, so as to get their attention before they take hold of his full meaning. The atmosphere would be one of onlookers saying, "What is he up to now?" Once their attention was won, Ezekiel's strange actions would unfold to disclose his unpalatable truth: Jerusalem, their home and symbol of all their hope, was to suffer yet again the horrors of siege and destruction.

This desire to attract an audience before disclosing the message may well explain Ezekiel's strange mode of preaching. The second of his sign actions—lying, apparently bedridden, for long periods—may simply have been forced on the prophet. If he did experience a stressful illness, as I have suggested, it is not at all unlikely that he should have pressed this unfortunate handicap into the service of God. Lying inactive for many days could itself become a form of preaching, indicating how Jerusalem would be inactive and imprisoned by siege. He was to become a channel of God's word. Accordingly, not only his mind and lips but his body, hands, and his entire being were to become vehicles of the divine message. The length of time in which Ezekiel experienced this disability (4:5–6) has occasioned a great deal of comment and perplexity but may simply represent the prophet's attempt to give his suffering an additional meaning as a punishment for the wrongdoing of Israel and Judah.

Two further questions require answers if we are to understand adequately the meaning of Ezekiel's strange prophetic behavior. Why does the fate of Jerusalem matter so much to him and his hearers, since they are already in exile in Babylon? Should we not expect such a message about a forthcoming siege to have been given to the people who would be most directly caught up in it: the inhabitants of Jerusalem? The reason it matters that Ezekiel's hearers know about Jerusalem's fate is that it will change their whole pattern of thinking and shake them out of their despair. They have envied the people in Jerusalem; they felt sorry for themselves and believed they had received the harsher judgment of God. They felt frustrated that they could not return to Jerusalem at the earliest possible moment and even hung on the lips of prophets who told them this would happen soon (see Jer. 29:15, 21).

Ezekiel's hearers had to reorient their thinking totally. They were the fortunate ones, compared with those they envied in Jerusalem. They were bearing their punishment in Babylon, whereas for those in Jerusalem the punishment of torment and disaster was still to come! Moreover, these hearers, by coming to terms with the devastation that was soon to be wrought upon their homeland and cherished city, could see the importance of their own part in Israel's future hope. So both Ezekiel's dramatic punishment (4:5–6) and the sign of the few hairs preserved in the skirts of his robe (5:3) indicate that God's plan for Israel's future is to take effect through a penitent remnant. Although the precise word "remnant" is not used, this seems clearly to be the role Ezekiel envisages for those who were with him in Babylon. Moreover, it explains much of the overwhelming importance he attached to his work as a prophet. Those who would listen to him, and so could learn to think in the terms he brought to them, would be preserved in the skirts of his robe. The metaphor is awkward, but it puts the highest level of significance on the work of the prophet as one whose words would build the nucleus of a new community of Israel.

There is further cause for reflection concerning Ezekiel's repeated message that Jerusalem is to experience a second siege, which will be even more ruinous than the first one. That first disaster forced Ezekiel and his fellow Judeans into exile in Babylon. How does Ezekiel know that a second military campaign will lead to a second siege of Jerusalem, and how can he be so fully informed about the situation in that city when he is in Babylon? We do not know the full answer to this, but it is clear that both the community that stayed in Judah and those who had been taken to Babylon remained in regular communication. The exchange of letters referred to in Jeremiah 29 is sufficient evidence of this. From a human point of view we can see that divided families would have tried to maintain contact, but it is surprising that so much official and semiofficial correspondence was kept up. It clearly suited the Babylonian authorities, who had a most efficient bureaucracy, to allow this.

If this is the case, it indicates that those like Ezekiel who had been taken to Babylon were not exiles or prisoners of war in the ordinary sense. They were more akin to hostages—political prisoners whose fate was to be borne in mind by those in Jerusalem. It is even probable that they were used as a kind of pledge, or social lever, by which the Babylonian authorities hoped to force the hand of King Zedekiah in Judah into compliance with the demands of their stern rule.

On this point the authorities were eventually shown to have miscalculated (we shall see this brought out in Ezekiel 17). Yet, if this was the actual political situation, it shows how relevant was Ezekiel's message that King Zedekiah was not to be trusted to remain submissive to Babylonian rule. Ezekiel knew the political temper and military weakness of the situation in Jerusalem, and, once a further act of rebellion was in the air, it was not difficult to perceive that the city would be besieged a second time by Nebuchadrezzar, the Babylonian ruler. We know in any case, from the book of the prophet Jeremiah, that rebellion was considered, planned, and temporarily decided against before the fatal decisions were eventually made in Jerusalem. The whole period was clearly one of tension and disastrous indecision, with little responsible acceptance of past mistakes. Ezekiel's message both reflects the past experience of Judah's failed political aspirations and builds on his own deep inner foreboding. Judgment upon Judah, expressed through national ruin, formed the central point of his message for the first six years of his work as a prophet. Then, with terrible violence, events brought realization and proof to his grim foretelling.

THE FATE THAT AWAITS JERUSALEM AND JUDAH
Ezekiel 5:5–6:14

5:5 Thus says the Lord GOD: This is Jerusalem; I have set her in the center of the nations, with countries all around her. 6 But she has rebelled against my ordinances and my statutes, becoming more wicked than the nations and the countries all around her, rejecting my ordinances and not following my statutes. 7 Therefore thus says the Lord GOD: Because you are more turbulent than the nations that are all around you, and have not followed my statutes or kept my ordinances, but have acted according to the ordinances of the nations that are all around you; 8 therefore thus says the Lord GOD: I, I myself, am coming against you; I will execute judgments among you in the sight of the nations. 9 And because of all your abominations, I will do to you what I have never yet done, and the like of which I will never do again. 10 Surely, parents shall eat their children in your midst, and children shall eat their parents; I will execute judgments on you, and any of you who survive I will scatter to every wind. 11 Therefore, as I live, says the Lord GOD, surely, because you have defiled my sanctuary with all your detestable things and with all your abominations—therefore I will cut you down; my eye will not spare, and I will have no pity. 12 One third of you shall die of pestilence or be consumed by famine among you; one third shall fall by the sword around you; and one third I will scatter to every wind and will unsheathe the sword after them. . . .

6:8 But I will spare some. Some of you shall escape the sword among the nations and be scattered through the countries. 9 Those of you who escape shall remember me among the nations where they are carried captive, how I was crushed by their wanton heart that turned away from me, and their wanton eyes that turned after their idols. Then they will be loathsome in their own sight for the evils that they have committed, for all their abominations. 10 And they shall know that I am the LORD; I did not threaten in vain to bring this disaster upon them. . . .

Ezekiel 5:5–17 spells out, in the harshest possible terms, Ezekiel's message of doom on Jerusalem. It paints a picture of all the horrors that such a siege will entail (note especially v. 10). Virtually the same message is repeated in 6:1–14, only this time it is expanded to cover the "mountains of Israel," by which the prophet must have intended to include all the ancient homeland of the people.

The two sections reemphasize and try to explain the warning that was portrayed in the dramatic mime actions that precede them. From the modern reader's point of view, the extraordinary aspect of these reiterated declarations is the heavy-handed and uncompromising nature of Ezekiel's insistence on why Jerusalem and Judah must experience such disasters.

The people have been more rebellious (vv. 6–7) and more idolatrous (vv. 9, 11) than any of their neighbors among the surrounding nations. It is a strange reversal of the conventional line of argument to be found in the Old Testament, which warns the people of Israel against behaving like other nations and condemns non-Israelites for their idolatry. Now Ezekiel turns all this around and insists that, after all, the people of Israel and especially the people of Jerusalem have set a worse example of religious and moral behavior than their neighbors. Surely both ways of looking at the situation cannot be right! Yet the seeming difficulty is resolved, once we take account of the way in which the different emphases seek to affirm the same essential point. Nor should we ignore the extent to which the situation in Judah had been adversely affected by earlier cynical rulers (such as Manasseh and Jehoiakim, 609–598 B.C.).

Undoubtedly, too, Ezekiel's message was uncompromising because it was the only way in which he could ensure that his fellow exiles would listen to him. Good and bad behavior, both morally and religiously, is very difficult to quantify in such a way as to enable us to say that one community is consistently worse in its conduct than another. Yet the essential reason for Ezekiel to paint such uncompromising pictures of his fellow Judeans lies in another direction. In the most stark and unrelenting fashion he accuses those who remained in control of affairs in Jerusalem. Yet he rebukes and condemns even more vehemently those like himself, who are now in exile but were once at the very center of religious life in Jerusalem, as equally guilty. His fellow exiles, looking for scapegoats, felt it was those who were responsible for bringing about their own misery who were at fault. Only by insisting that all share the blame can his message bring about genuine national repentance.

So Ezekiel is most careful to avoid the suggestion that he and his fellow exiles in Babylon are innocent, whereas those who are controlling affairs in Judah are guilty. As we shall see, Ezekiel does believe that King Zedekiah and the authorities in Judah were particularly responsible for the disasters that befell Judah a second time. Laying the blame only at the door of those in Judah, however, is too easy a way of looking at the situation. The entire nation of Israel is to blame. The prophet's understanding of wrongdoing and guilt draws all classes and sectors of the community into its net.

Ezekiel had to face the challenge of two prevalent attitudes among those he addressed. The first of these we learned from the book of Jeremiah, where an influential circle in Judah adopted a complacent and over-confident view about Jerusalem and its future, believing that God would look after and protect Jerusalem no matter how its political leaders and people behaved. Having God's temple was taken to be proof that the people had been guaranteed God's unqualified protection (Jer. 7:4)! Now Ezekiel had to expose yet again the fallacy of such complacent nonsense. God does not give this kind of unlimited insurance policy to any human being on earth.

The second attitude was less arrogant and self-congratulatory. It shows between the lines of almost all Ezekiel's early proclamations. It was the widespread belief among those who had become hostages in Babylon that they were paying the price of the mistakes and miscalculations of the royal house and its supporters in Judah. Whether or not they regarded themselves as complicit in the headstrong political folly that had brought humiliation and ruin upon Judah, they nonetheless felt they were being penalized while those who remained in Jerusalem under Babylonian supervision were given a second chance. This feeling brought bitterness and self-pity to the exiles.

Among those in Babylon, Ezekiel had to work hard to dispel this self-pity and to encourage the recognition that those who learned the lesson of penitence in Babylon were the one great hope for the rebirth of the nation. So Ezekiel works persistently to instill a doctrine of repentance, to create a faithful community who will recognize the errors and mistakes of the past, abandon their own self-pity, and work and wait for the nation that would be reborn (see especially 6:8–10). Instead of thinking of themselves as rejects of the past, Ezekiel wants his fellow exiles to regard themselves as the basis and hope for a new future. But this can only be when they take fully into their thinking the widespread and universal nature of sin. Without denying the mistakes of the people left in Jerusalem, Ezekiel's message opens the way to a more positive attitude in the minds of his fellow exiles by showing that all of them share in Judah's sin.

It is in his descriptions and language about sin that Ezekiel has been most heavily subjected to criticism by Christian scholars, and certainly his language here reveals most clearly his priestly roots. His talk of "abominations" (infringements of sacral law, 5:9) and his concern to define all wrongdoing as rebelling against "ordinances" and "statutes" (5:6) indicate a legalistic and rather obsessive kind of reasoning. Yet this is Ezekiel! It is a result of his priestly upbringing, which naturally led him to see all misconduct as infringing upon a sacral order of life.

Clearly this is not a way of looking at life or understanding the nature of sin with which we feel comfortable; we have long since lost any sensitivity to such a worldview. It reflects a world governed by a priestly rule book (in reality a code of holy practice passed on orally by priests from one generation to the next) that has been lost in our modern secular society. Our modern sense of sin arises out of an awareness of the inner personal stresses and motives that distort our sense of what is right and good. So we have to look under the surface very carefully when Ezekiel discusses the nature of human evil. When we do, we find he is speaking sensitively about many of the deepest of all human anxieties and fears. What we must not do is to dismiss his language as superficial and meaningless, as though he thought simply in terms of priestly rules and taboos.

RUIN AND DEVASTATION FOR THE WHOLE LAND OF ISRAEL
Ezekiel 7:1–27

> 7:1 **The word of the LORD came to me:** [2] **You, O mortal, thus says the Lord GOD to the land of Israel:**
>> **An end! The end has come**
>>> **upon the four corners of the land.**
>> [3] **Now the end is upon you.**
>>> **I will let loose my anger upon you;**
>> **I will judge you according to your ways,**
>>> **I will punish you for all your abominations.**
>> [4] **My eye will not spare you, I will have no pity.**
>>> **I will punish you for your ways,**
>>> **while your abominations are among you.**
> **Then you shall know that I am the LORD**
>> [5] **Thus says the Lord GOD:**
>>> **Disaster after disaster! See, it comes. . . .**
>> [10] **See, the day! See, it comes!**

> Your doom has gone out.
> The rod has blossomed, pride has budded. . . .
> [12] The time has come, the day draws near;
>> let not the buyer rejoice, nor the seller mourn,
>> for wrath is upon all their multitude. . . .
> [14] They have blown the horn and made everything ready;
>> but no one goes to battle,
>> for my wrath is upon all their multitude. . . .
> [16] If any survivors escape
>> they shall be found on the mountains
>> like doves of the valleys,
>> all of them moaning over their iniquity. . . .

Their silver and gold cannot save them on the day of the wrath of the LORD. They shall not satisfy their hunger or fill their stomachs with it. For it was the stumbling block of their iniquity. [20] From their beautiful ornament, in which they took pride, they made their abominable images, their detestable things; therefore I will make of it an unclean thing to them.

> [21] I will hand it over to strangers as booty,
>> to the wicked of the earth as plunder;
>> they shall profane it. . . .
> [23] Make a chain!
> For the land is full of bloody crimes;
>> the city is full of violence.
> [24] I will bring the worst of the nations
>> to take possession of their houses. . . .
> [26] Disaster comes upon disaster,
>> rumor follows rumor;
> they shall keep seeking a vision from the prophet;
>> instruction shall perish from the priest,
>> and counsel from the elders.
> [27] The king shall mourn,
>> the prince shall be wrapped in despair,
>> and the hands of the people of the land shall tremble.
> According to their way I will deal with them;
>> according to their own judgments I will judge them.

And they shall know that I am the LORD.

Chapter 7 brings us more powerful word pictures of the ruin and devastation that is shortly to be let loose upon the whole land of Israel. Once again it is made clear that this territory is the subject of the terrifying pictures of the total ruination of the land that Ezekiel foretold. In verse 1, the series of images is emphatically addressed "to the land of Israel." This is the land from which his hearers have come and to which, after five years of exile with no end in sight, they desperately yearn to return. Yet could they but see the ruin and disaster that is soon to befall this land, they would be grateful to God that they will not be there to share its sufferings and misery.

The whole sequence of disaster portraits is set out with systematic care and orderliness:

1. Verses 1–4 build upon the theme of the end that is shortly to be unleashed against the land. It seems very likely that this characterization of utter ruin and devastation as "the end" originated with the prophet Amos, who had, a century and a half earlier, forewarned that God intended to bring an "end" upon the land of Israel (Amos 8:2). Yet in spite of many disasters and political misfortunes, something of the land of Israel survived, even if only in a part of the kingdom of Judah. Now even that is to be swallowed up in ruin.
2. Verses 5–9 spell out the message by speaking of disaster after disaster. Ever since Mesopotamian political ambitions drew Israel and Judah into the web of Assyrian rule during the mid-eighth century B.C., Israel had fared badly. Ezekiel now presents an unbearably gloomy picture as the climax of this tragic experience. Babylon has replaced Assyria as Judah's oppressor and there will be no let up. Complete and utter ruin will come upon the land. God has no pity.
3. Verses 10–13 describe this time of disaster as a day of reckoning. Two images relating to agricultural and commercial life drive home the point. In the springtime, as the first word picture notes, men and women look to the first buds on a tree to see portents of new life. Yet when the blossom has flowered and withered, it is a sign that the springtime has passed (v. 10). In similar fashion, evil and violence have now blossomed and must bring their terrible harvest. Second, both seller and purchaser will have an eye on the day when bills become due, so the day of reckoning for Israel's wrongdoing is now fast approaching (v. 12).

The next picture, in verses 14–19, increases the sense of Judah's utter helplessness in the face of the devastation that awaits. Summoning the people to muster for battle will be useless (v. 14), because none will have the strength or the will to respond. Fugitives will have nowhere safe to hide (v. 16), and silver and gold will be worthless, because no one will be able to buy their personal safety (v. 19).

The mention of silver and gold leads to a number of other ideas and reflections (vv. 20–27), all relevant to the picture of ruin and disaster that will come upon Judah as the result of a second Babylonian attack. Carefully cherished possessions will be stolen as booty of war (v. 21), and unchecked violence will take over throughout the entire land as all governmental justice is abandoned (v. 23).

So Ezekiel reiterates the theme of "disaster . . . upon disaster" in an effort to persuade his hearers that there will shortly be another terrible invasion, siege, and plundering of Jerusalem and the land of Judah. Once again Ezekiel persuades his hearers by generating immensely powerful word pictures. He seeks to take hold of their minds through their eyes, rather than through any process of logical reasoning. If they will not believe the rational warning of the political and religious folly that is taking control of affairs in Judah, maybe they will believe the evidence of their own memories. Like Ezekiel himself, these are people who witnessed and experienced in the recent past the kinds of horrors he describes. His mind, and no doubt theirs also, are full of shocking images of suffering. They must therefore be forewarned that it is all to happen again, and to see the privileged responsibility of their own situation in Babylon.

The extent of the ruin that is to afflict Judah is expressed through a picture that is used by several of the major Old Testament prophets: All fundamental authorities who hold society together will fail (vv. 26–27). In a catalog of leadership roles, the prophet lists prophets, priests, elders, king, and prince; all will be reduced to powerlessness and despair. Society will fall apart because none of the cement of leadership and guidance will any longer exist to hold it together. It may be reading too much into the list Ezekiel gives to note that he puts religious leadership first (prophets and priests), social and family leadership second (elders), and political leadership last (king and prince). It may be a deliberate reversal of the popular estimate of the time, but it may also indicate where the prophet believed the root causes of Israel's downfall were to be found. When religious leadership fails or is misdirected, a fearful vacuum of spiritual values ensues, and no appeals to authority or propping up of institutions can make up for the lack of true spiritual vision.

The concluding summary in 7:27, "And they shall know that I am the LORD," becomes a frequently repeated theme for Ezekiel as a prophet. It reveals how clearly the prophet identifies his words as a manifestation of the active presence of God and touches a sensitive nerve. The formula declares that, whereas in the past the realm of piety and devotion such as Ezekiel and his fellow exiles knew through temple worship (Psalm 46:10) was the approved path of coming to "know" God, now such knowledge will come through the pain of judgment. The familiar story of the Passover service telling how the plagues upon Egypt provided a way to "knowing" God may have influenced the language here (Exod. 7:5, etc.).

This is the deepest—and, in its essential character, most inescapable—path to "knowing" God. It comes about through human pain, suffering, and despair. Ezekiel does not declare this in a self-righteous or gloating fashion (God will make himself known to you one way or the other). Rather, he simply points out a basic human truth. The rules and rhythms of worship are important in giving direction and meaning to life. They teach us how to see God and think of him as part of our daily lives. Yet inevitably, at the point of suffering and human loss, the frailty of human life comes home to us most fully. It is the realization that in the end we have no merits of our own, but are all faced with a creator who is the judge of our affairs, that brings us to the point of truly "knowing" God.

3. The Vision of Jerusalem's Destruction
Ezekiel 8:1–11:25

Undoubtedly Ezekiel was a most uncompromising prophet, and he does not hesitate to paint terrifying pictures of what it means to fall under the judgment of God. It is all a matter of theology in pictures. We might be tempted to think of the prophet as the possessor of a fevered and overexcited imagination, were it not for two important considerations.

First, we must bear in mind the reality of Ezekiel's own experience, one he shared with those who heard him speak his vision to the Babylonian exiles. Like survivors of a terrible ancient holocaust, they witnessed cruel and arbitrary killings such as are described in Ezekiel 9. Although they were themselves spared, in the mystery of God's mercy, even remembering such nightmare experiences would have aroused again all the shocked emotions they were trying to put behind them. From a psychological point of view, Ezekiel—and those fellow exiles who had suffered with him—had to learn to submit these tortured memories to God and find repentance as the path to healing.

The other consideration is less immediately personal but is of the utmost significance for the prophet's book. This hinges upon the prophet's declaration that the temple of Jerusalem is to be destroyed. To grasp the shock and horror that such a threat aroused, we need to remember the deep-seated belief that, far from allowing the destruction of the temple, God would be bound to defend it, even to the point of sending a heavenly army to protect it; this was how Judean tradition had learned to remember the way in which the city of Jerusalem had been spared more than a century earlier, when the Assyrian armies had formed the threat (2 Kings 18:13–19:37; especially 19:34–35). In addition, there was the mistaken assumption that, if the temple were destroyed, God would be denied any place of recognition on earth. To Ezekiel's fellow exiles, as also to those who remained as survivors in Judah, such a destruction appeared tantamount to the death of God. How could it be that God could permit, let alone command, the destruction of the sanctuary called by so holy and divine a name? It did not seem to make sense, for it would amount to God's allowing the very center and source of holiness, glory, and honor to be defiled.

Yet Ezekiel dared to proclaim such an action as imminent and to declare it necessary in order to *protect* the divine honor and glory! God would abandon the temple because it had become a place of idolatry and blasphemy, so there would be no shame or dishonor to the divine name. This is the message that is now spelled out in detail in chapters 8—11. Up to this point, we have heard a message of coming divine judgment upon Judah and Jerusalem. Now this word of judgment is focused sharply on the central catastrophe that will be involved, the ruination of the temple of Jerusalem.

We can see, then, that the vision beginning in 8:1 and ending in 11:25, with the prophet being returned in this trancelike vision to the exiles in Babylon, is a unity. It is a coherent vision drama about the coming siege of Jerusalem, recounting the sins that made this siege an act of religious judgment and presenting an assurance that God will not in any way be hurt or defiled by what happens to the temple. Before human soldiers can defile it with their cruel and wanton killing, God will have left the city, handing it over to human destroyers and preparing other ways to protect and spare a faithful remnant so that a new nation, city, and temple can one day be built. This vision drama is the pivotal center of the entire book of Ezekiel's prophecies, which is a book about judgment, death, and rebirth.

We must inevitably ask some questions about the visionary nature of this remarkable prophetic episode, since nothing else of quite such complexity is to be found in the entire Bible. It is also significant that it has become a kind of pattern and example for further visionary accounts of forthcoming divine acts of judgment, especially in the book of Revelation in the New Testament. We must certainly recognize that at its center lies a genuine psychological vision—probably a series of such experiences that the prophet assembled in written story form. These begin with the prophet being lifted up and transported back to Jerusalem, where secret mysteries are unveiled to him (we should note especially the allusions to these in 8:3). Deeply embedded in these trancelike experiences are memories from the past and nightmare recollections of what happened when he was in Jerusalem before and witnessed its downfall.

No wonder this vision of Ezekiel's has become the pattern and parable of judgment that so many later biblical writers fall back on as a way of picturing the judgment of God in human affairs (we may compare 1 Peter 4:17 for the idea that judgment must "begin with the household of God").

Once such truths were taken on board, as the prophet had sought to do at a personal level, genuine repentance became possible and a very different future could be looked for. Among the glories of this new future would be the building of a new temple and the restoration of a new Israel in its ancient land, cleansed of the reckless follies of its past (Ezekiel 40—48).

Not only does Ezekiel's terrifying vision insist that the destruction of the temple is a real possibility, it does so in such a way as to demonstrate that such a disaster does not mean that any temple, built to honor God, will therefore be meaningless and worthless. On the contrary, when rightly understood and used, a true temple is central to the work of God on earth. So Ezekiel's vision is a remarkable piece of temple theology, explaining the necessity of the old temple's destruction but retaining an awareness that, one day, a new temple can be built where the sins of the past will not be repeated. So the central dramatic vision, in which the destruction of Jerusalem and its temple are portrayed, is prepared for in chapter 8 by showing that this had to come about because of the city's idolatry. The envisioned aftermath then incorporates details, showing God to have already abandoned the temple before its destruction.

THE UNFORGIVABLE SINS
OF JERUSALEM
Ezekiel 8:1–18

> 8:1 In the sixth year, in the sixth month, on the fifth day of the month, as I sat in my house, with the elders of Judah sitting before me, the hand of the Lord GOD fell upon me there. ² I looked, and there was a figure that looked like a human being; below what appeared to be its loins it was fire, and above the loins it was like the appearance of brightness, like gleaming amber. ³ It stretched out the form of a hand, and took me by a lock of my head; and the spirit lifted me up between earth and heaven, and brought me in visions of God to Jerusalem, to the entrance of the gateway of the inner court that faces north, to the seat of the image of jealousy, which provokes to jealousy. ⁴ And the glory of the God of Israel was there, like the vision that I had seen in the valley.
>
> ⁵ Then God said to me, "O mortal, lift up your eyes now in the direction of the north." So I lifted up my eyes toward the north, and there, north of the altar gate, in the entrance, was this image of jealousy. . . .
>
> ⁷ And he brought me to the entrance of the court; I looked, and there was a hole in the wall. ⁸ Then he said to me, "Mortal, dig through the wall"; and when I dug through the wall, there was an entrance. ⁹ He said to me, "Go

in, and see the vile abominations that they are committing here." [10] So I went in and looked; there, portrayed on the wall all around, were all kinds of creeping things, and loathsome animals, and all the idols of the house of Israel. [11] Before them stood seventy of the elders of the house of Israel, with Jaazaniah son of Shaphan standing among them. Each had his censer in his hand, and the fragrant cloud of incense was ascending. . . .

[14] Then he brought me to the entrance of the north gate of the house of the Lord; women were sitting there weeping for Tammuz. . . .

[16] And he brought me into the inner court of the house of the Lord; there, at the entrance of the temple of the Lord, between the porch and the altar, were about twenty-five men, with their backs to the temple of the Lord, and their faces toward the east, prostrating themselves to the sun toward the east. [17] Then he said to me, "Have you seen this, O mortal? Is it not bad enough that the house of Judah commits the abominations done here? Must they fill the land with violence, and provoke my anger still further? See, they are putting the branch to their nose! [18] Therefore I will act in wrath; my eye will not spare, nor will I have pity; and though they cry in my hearing with a loud voice, I will not listen to them."

"One picture is worth a thousand words." But long before the age of news photography and TV reporting made this slogan familiar, the power of visual images to reach and shape the deepest levels of human thought was recognized. As far as we can go in our earliest history, it appears that human beings pictured to themselves the nature of reality before they endeavored to analyze it into its component features. It is not at all surprising, therefore, that so visually sensitive a prophet as Ezekiel should have presented the most important and unwelcome of his prophetic messages pictorially, rather than try to justify it in the formal language of priestly argument. The message is a straightforward and decisive one: Judah has been guilty of idolatry in the very heart of its religious capital, Jerusalem. This truth was a startling, incredible, and difficult one for Ezekiel's fellow exiles to come to terms with. Yet accepting it was vitally important because it led to a second, even more unpalatable truth: The temple of Jerusalem would be destroyed.

For Ezekiel even to breath such words must have seemed an unacceptable betrayal of his training as a priest and a gross act of disloyalty to Israel and to God. The contemporary prophet Jeremiah was actually threatened with death for daring to suggest that the temple could be destroyed (Jer. 26:11). Now Ezekiel employs one truth in order to justify the other. The temple of Jerusalem will be destroyed, but it will not be because the Lord God of Israel is unable to defend it. It will be the divine hand that strikes the blow against the temple because the place has been abused and used as a setting for idolatry. So the charges of idolatry in Ezekiel 8 are preliminary to the sentence of doom that follows in chapters 9—11.

Ezekiel 8 contains a visionary picture of four serious acts of idolatry taking place in the precincts of the temple of Jerusalem. It begins with the prophet reexperiencing the vision of God's presence, this time in the form of a divine messenger, or mediator, whose form is mysterious and only vaguely hinted at—"a figure that looked like a human being" (8:2). This mediating role of a divine messenger is vitally important for the prophet, even though it should probably be understood as an inner vision, on which he only partially focuses. God is bringing him a message about Jerusalem. This then unfolds in a sequence of scenes in which Ezekiel sees idolatrous actions taking place in Jerusalem. These actions occur, either directly inside the temple precincts or in its immediate vicinity. There is, so Ezekiel assures his hearers, idolatry taking place in the courts of the temple of the Lord God of Israel—the one true God who rules all nations and peoples, the God whose command had been that there should be no image or likeness made to represent him (Exod. 20:4–6). Yet the very temple of Jerusalem has witnessed the setting up of various mysterious and strangely conceived images of divine beings that contravene this primary commandment. The proof of this idolatry is presented by four scenes the prophet describes:

1. Verses 5–6. At the entrance to the temple, to the north of the altar gate, stood what Ezekiel describes as "this image of jealousy" (that is, an image—probably a wall carving—that provoked God to a feeling of anger). It is unlikely that it was actually an image of the Lord God of Israel; more probably it was of some mythical creature—a heavenly servant of the deity or perhaps merely a symbol, such as the sun—that Ezekiel regarded as idolatrous. The age of Josiah, when Ezekiel was a child, had been a period in which a major reformation took place and many features of visual symbolism were repudiated (2 Kings 23:4–20), although this occurred largely outside Jerusalem. A century earlier still, the stringent rejection of idolatry had brought significant changes in worship in the capital city during Hezekiah's reign (so especially 2 Kings 18:4, where symbols of Mosaic origin were removed from the temple). It seems that, in spite of the categorical nature of the commandment against images, there was no clear ruling as to what degree of visual symbolism in worship was allowable. Ezekiel's message here shows him to have proclaimed a

very narrow line of interpretation. Others, including some leading officials, had favored a more tolerant line, and in any case some worshipers had clearly retained for private use symbols that had been officially rejected. It may or may not be significant, therefore, that this idolatrous worship took place at the entranceway of the temple. Ezekiel was well aware that even legitimate symbols of worship could be made into idols if a wrong spiritual attitude prevailed.

2. Verses 7–13. In an inner room of the temple, which the prophet shows to have been closed off by a wall that had to be burrowed through (v. 8), the walls were covered with images of strange beasts, almost certainly of mixed form. This secret inner room, which may have been barred from public access, either to prevent its use by the general public because of the special rites performed there or perhaps as a consequence of the half-enforced reformation, was still a place of worship for seventy elders of Israel (v. 11). The mention of Jaazaniah son of Shaphan is especially interesting, because this may have been the same Shaphan who was one of the highest state officials during Josiah's reign (2 Kings 22:3, 8).

3. Verses 14–15. The women weeping for Tammuz at the entrance to the north gate of the temple were probably just outside the temple precincts proper. Weeping for Tammuz was an ancient ritual of Sumerian origin that survived in many forms and was concerned with death and rebirth. It proved to be one of the most deeply persistent forms of religious practice throughout the ancient world, frequently connected with sexual symbolism, which remained popular right up to the Hellenistic age and into the Christian era. It was not unlike some contemporary forms of New Age religion, with its emphasis on the "natural" rhythms of life, death, and rebirth. That it appealed especially to women is no doubt important, since Israelite tradition seems to have allowed women only a very limited degree of participation in public assemblies for worship. In this case, it is tempting to conclude that exclusion from participation in official Israelite worship led women to look elsewhere to express their religious feelings.

4. Verses 16–18. In the inner court of the temple "about twenty-five men" stood with their backs to the central shrine of the temple, facing toward the east and falling down in an act of worship (quite clearly to the rising sun as a symbol of divine light and majesty).

Ezekiel saw each of these actions as an act of idolatry because all were ultimately devoid of proper respect for the Lord God of Israel as the one and only true God. Visual imagery and carefully enacted ritual that hinted, intentionally or not, at disrespect for the Lord as God is thereby forcefully condemned by the prophet. Moreover, they provide, in his great visionary drama, the reason why the temple must be destroyed.

It is not difficult to imagine that Ezekiel's message here must have drawn on memories of things he saw when he was still training as a priest in Jerusalem. These activities would have greatly offended him and may well have been the subject of discussion and argument by members of the priesthood ever since the great reformation of worship in Jerusalem in Josiah's time (2 Kings 22—23). The prophet clearly took a very strict line on the matter of idolatry. For him it was the worst of sins.

Nor is it difficult to understand how, over a period of time, attitudes had hardened over the issue in the religion of Judah. From its very beginnings, the worship practiced in the Jerusalem temple had contained a great deal of visual imagery, some of it employing figures and symbols about which disagreement prevailed over their appropriateness for the worship of the Lord God of Israel. It is not necessary to suppose that there was a sudden lapse into idolatry after Josiah's efforts at reform. It is much more likely that, for as much as a century, many leading priests and government officials in Judah had sought to impose stricter uniformity and interpretation in matters of temple worship but had not always prevailed in their views. During Josiah's reign (639–609 B.C.), this reform movement had enjoyed considerable royal support but had never become wholly dominant. Much of the older popular worship, involving a variety of idolatrous rites, survived. Ezekiel here insists that this failure to assert the strictest religious purity has made the destruction of the temple by God a necessity.

JUDGMENT AT THE HOUSE OF GOD
Ezekiel 9:1–11

9:1 Then he cried in my hearing with a loud voice, saying, "Draw near, you executioners of the city, each with his destroying weapon in his hand." ² And six men came from the direction of the upper gate, which faces north, each with his weapon for slaughter in his hand; among them was a man clothed in linen, with a writing case at his side. They went in and stood beside the bronze altar.

³ Now the glory of the God of Israel had gone up from the cherub on which it rested to the threshold of the house. The LORD called to the man clothed in linen, who had the writing case at his side; ⁴ and said to him, "Go

through the city, through Jerusalem, and put a mark on the foreheads of those who sigh and groan over all the abominations that are committed in it." [5] To the others he said in my hearing, "Pass through the city after him, and kill; your eye shall not spare, and you shall show no pity. [6] Cut down old men, young men and young women, little children and women, but touch no one who has the mark. And begin at my sanctuary." So they began with the elders who were in front of the house. [7] Then he said to them, "Defile the house, and fill the courts with the slain. Go!" So they went out and killed in the city. [8] While they were killing, and I was left alone, I fell prostrate on my face and cried out, "Ah Lord GOD! will you destroy all who remain of Israel as you pour out your wrath upon Jerusalem?" [9] He said to me, "The guilt of the house of Israel and Judah is exceedingly great; the land is full of bloodshed and the city full of perversity; for they say, 'The LORD has forsaken the land, and the LORD does not see.'. . ."

Ezekiel 8 introduced us to an awareness that Israel's sin is centered in the temple of Jerusalem; the very building that was intended to draw people's minds to God was in reality turning them away from true divine knowledge. False images, false ideas, and unworthy desires have made the temple an obstruction to worship and are even encouraging disloyal policies and attitudes of reckless violence. In chapter 9, Ezekiel's vision moves into a more futurist and active mode, as he envisages the forthcoming destruction of both the city of Jerusalem and its temple. He portrays this in the form of six executioners, marching into the city with weapons in their hands and preparing for a terrible slaughter.

Before this can happen, however, two events have to take place. First, the divine presence, embodied in the cherub that conveyed the heavenly throne chariot, must abandon the inner sanctuary of the temple (v. 3). Second, a mysterious figure, wearing official dress and carrying a writing case, is to place a mark on the foreheads of those who genuinely grieve over the wrongs perpetrated in the city (vv. 2–4); these people are to be spared the terrible punishment that is to come. Once this has been accomplished, the terrible work of slaughter is to take place, with the ominous final command to the executioners, "And begin at my sanctuary" (v. 6). The very place to which everyone looks for protection and help is to become the starting point of the dreadful killing, in which not even women and children will be spared.

Clearly these six executioners symbolize the ransacking and rampaging army of soldiers who storm into Jerusalem once the siege is broken. They show no mercy. The whole is a nightmare vision, almost certainly drawing to some extent upon Ezekiel's memories of things he saw during the earlier siege and surrender of Jerusalem. As with a number of Ezekiel's visions, some very precise details are given but the overall picture remains blurred. It is not clear what qualified some victims to receive the mark on their foreheads that guarantees them life. The most we can discern for certain is that some, perhaps only a tiny handful, of Jerusalem's citizens are to be spared. This is a point the prophet has never before declared so plainly, so it may have been necessary to introduce it now.

The executioners, one of whom is clothed in the white (nonmilitary) linen dress of a government official, seem patterned on Babylonian figures. Perhaps the prophet himself had a painful experience that led him to portray the dual aspects of Babylonian authority—military and bureaucratic—as equally cruel and unpredictable. We see here how Ezekiel's visions can take on an almost cinematographic quality, whereas at other times they become quite surreal and fantastic.

The theme of God's abandoning the city and temple of Jerusalem is the third of the major themes of the vision sequence in chapters 8–11. It is expanded on in Ezekiel 10—11 and appears as a slightly confusing subplot that is nevertheless important theologically. Surprisingly, Ezekiel does not name the Babylonian armies as the attackers of Jerusalem, although this is clearly what is meant. For the prophet, it is God who has become Jerusalem's enemy, and the six executioners are serving as agents of divine punishment. The threefold sequence of visionary themes is clear: Jerusalem's idolatry (chapter 8), the judgment of this, and the resulting divine abandonment of Jerusalem that makes the destruction of city and temple possible (chapters 9—11).

Ezekiel's visionary message presents an imaginative and highly stylized portrayal of death and disaster falling upon Jerusalem, and it does so while that event still lies in the future. Probably the worsening political situation in Judah meant it had now become a more credible outcome to present actions. The prophet's sequence of events on the fearful day of Jerusalem's overthrow is terrifying, all the more so because it takes place by divine command. Only two features alleviate the unbroken darkness. First, God has abandoned the temple, so there is no room left for the suggestion that God will suffer a personal defeat by its overthrow. The divine authority is not prejudiced by what happens; on the contrary, it is emphasized by these terrible events. Second, there is to be a remnant of survivors, those who "groan over all the abominations that are committed in it [the city]" (v. 4). How many such survivors there will be and how readily they will identify themselves by their conduct are features that are not spelled out more fully in the prophet's words.

Ezekiel's vision blends the need to drive home to his audience the full awareness of the terrors that are soon to befall Jerusalem with a genuine concern to show that abuse of the temple is bringing about this disaster, not its right and proper use. Even in judgment, God is not unjust or indifferent to the cries of those who are truly penitent. However, the central truth remains highlighted here, more vividly than anywhere else in the Bible, that judgment begins at the house of God. Those who have been most privileged, who have stood closest to the source of light and truth but who have turned their backs upon it (literally, according to 8:16!), will be the first to face the terrible consequences of their actions.

We should never lose sight of the fact that Ezekiel was a priest and therefore viewed religious offenses as the most grievous to God. So it was natural that his prophetic role as a mediator of the divine word should present in visionary-pictorial form the images and symbolism that were familiar from his priestly upbringing. The shock and horror of seeing death and slaughter enacted before one's mental gaze drives home God's message more powerfully than could be achieved by any theorizing about the political mistakes and miscalculations that contributed to Jerusalem's downfall. Undoubtedly, at some level, crass political folly had led Judah to rebel against Babylon for a second time, almost certainly backed up by a measure of reckless presumption in believing that God could, in the end, be relied upon to protect the sanctuary called by the Holy Name.

Yet Ezekiel's message of judgment is surely correct in its diagnosis that such political folly and simplistic religious complacency are the consequences of warped human judgment. Distorted perceptions of reality encouraged the very actions that led Judah to disaster. Idolatry, in all its tantalizing allure, implies leaning on a will-o'-the wisp! It trusts in some thing or power that turns out to have no substantiality when the reckoning has to be made. So the prophetic vision of Jerusalem's terrible judgment stresses the religious roots of Judah's problems and difficulties. This belief was not simply an outgrowth of Ezekiel's priestly upbringing but came out of a deep awareness that only right thinking about God can produce right attitudes and policies in shaping human conduct.

FIRE OVER JERUSALEM
Ezekiel 10:1–22

10:1 **Then I looked, and above the dome that was over the heads of the cherubim there appeared above them something like a sapphire, in form resembling a throne. 2 He said to the man clothed in linen, "Go within the** wheelwork underneath the cherubim; fill your hands with burning coals from among the cherubim, and scatter them over the city." He went in as I looked on. . . .

⁹ I looked, and there were four wheels beside the cherubim, one beside each cherub; and the appearance of the wheels was like gleaming beryl. ¹⁰ And as for their appearance, the four looked alike, something like a wheel within a wheel. . . .

¹⁸ Then the glory of the LORD went out from the threshold of the house and stopped above the cherubim. ¹⁹ The cherubim lifted up their wings and rose up from the earth in my sight as they went out with the wheels beside them. They stopped at the entrance of the east gate of the house of the LORD; and the glory of the God of Israel was above them.

²⁰ These were the living creatures that I saw underneath the God of Israel by the river Chebar; and I knew that they were cherubim. ²¹ Each had four faces, each four wings, and underneath their wings something like human hands. ²² As for what their faces were like, they were the same faces whose appearance I had seen by the river Chebar. Each one moved straight ahead.

The key to understanding this section is to be found in verse 2, which reports how a voice from above the sapphire throne of the heavenly chariot commands the official who is ostentatiously dressed in white linen to go into the inner place of the divine throne—"within the wheelwork underneath the cherubim"—and take up burning coals. These are then to be scattered over the city. This is an act of divine judgment, clearly signifying that after the surrender of Jerusalem to its attackers the city will be set on fire.

The point is an important one since, from a historical perspective, when we compare the fate that befell Jerusalem after its first surrender to the Babylonians in 598 with that which occurred in 587 B.C., there were great differences. When the siege ended in 598 and Jerusalem surrendered, most of the city remained intact. Undoubtedly, there was plundering and violence, but even the Davidic royal house was spared and a royal prince, Zedekiah, allowed to remain on the throne.

It is probable that this relatively lenient treatment in 598 actually contributed to later problems and disasters since it encouraged the fanciful notion that God could always be trusted to look after Jerusalem and protect it. The beliefs of Jeremiah's opponents, as echoed in his prophecies, reveal as much. They show up the kind of arrogant and self-assured policies that increasingly held sway in the kingdom of Judah. It was these beliefs that eventually prompted a second rebellion against Babylon and so incurred a fearful retribution. The Babylonians were not so lenient a

second time. So Ezekiel's visionary picture of God's emissary setting fire
to Jerusalem with coals from the temple altar is a remarkable foretelling
of what actually took place. It serves to reemphasize, if this were still necessary, that judgment will be coming from God. This is the message
Ezekiel was trying to deliver, which his hearers found so hard to accept.
The city would be systematically set to the torch and brought to ruin.

Taken both by itself and as a sequel to what has been described in
Ezekiel 9, the taking of the sacred fire by the striking figure in white linen
points to an action carried out in the temple. The location whence the
coals of fire were taken was either an incense burner in the inner sanctuary or one of the temple's main altars. The act is somehow linked, however, to the description of the heavenly throne chariot that first appeared
to the prophet in Babylon. Very possibly, it was all a jumbled sequence of
images in the prophet's own mind that he could not bring into clear focus. God was both with him, living among the exiles in Babylon, and en-
throned as Lord of the temple in Jerusalem. The paradox is not irrecon-
cilable, although it makes the images of God's presence appear strange.

The repetition of the assertion that the heavenly throne bearers were
the same as those that first appeared to the prophet at his call in Ezekiel
1:15 and 21 is the result of subsequent reflection. It is introduced as a result of the desire to demonstrate that, however mysterious may be the task
of defining God's presence, the divine Being is not confined to one location or even one land. Some scholars have believed that this is one of
Ezekiel's most important theological advances. He emphasized the om-
nipresence of God, insisting that God was present in Babylon when his
fellow exiles felt far away from the place of the divine presence in
Jerusalem. Homesickness became a spiritual sickness. It is noteworthy
that, in the original call vision, the creatures who bear the divine throne
are not named as cherubim, whereas here the name is used repeatedly.

In Babylonian religion, cherubim were intermediary deities, in general
acting as servants of the divine court in heaven. They were responsible for
protecting the divine throne and conveying messages to the deity. With
the stricter monotheism of Israelite faith, their role was reduced until they
were regarded, like the seraphim of Isaiah 6:2, simply as a class of angelic
beings. Their mention here is important both for understanding the character of Ezekiel's visionary reports and for recognizing the immense importance of symbolism to Israelite religion. The prohibition on images of
God did not originally mean that Israel repudiated all visual symbolism in
worship, as the account of the Jerusalem temple building shows extensively (1 Kings 6—8). The importance of this symbolism explains much

about the prophet Ezekiel that appears strange to us. As a priest he had grown up with the temple as the most familiar and impressive of all buildings. He could not think of God without his mind being filled with the symbolism and images that conveyed a sense of the mysterious reality of the divine world. What is now so important as far as the growth of the Bible is concerned is that this prophet has become our major bridge between this older pictorial symbolism of the physical temple (its iconography), in all its ornate splendor, and the inner spiritual vision of the divine heavenly reality. For this reason, later prophets and scribes draw extensively on Ezekiel's book in an effort to fill out a picture of the unseen and unseeable world of heaven.

Once again it seems likely that many features not properly brought into clear focus are symbols that cannot be defined in any normal fashion (for example, the creatures with "four faces" in v. 14 and the movement of the wheels, which proceeded in straight lines "without veering as they moved" in any of four directions, in v. 11). The are intended to show that the divine world is unlike the ordinary world of things seen and experienced. The especially close attention to the wheels is also strange but must certainly recall the deep impression made on the prophet, possibly from his childhood years, by richly decorated wheels he had seen beneath the temple vessels in Jerusalem. For him, their importance was to emphasize the unlimited mobility of God, pointing to the completely unrestricted nature of the divine presence (Prov. 15:3).

BEHIND THE VISION OF JUDGMENT—
THE GUILTY ONES
Ezekiel 11:1-13

> 11:1 The spirit lifted me up and brought me to the east gate of the house of the LORD, which faces east. There, at the entrance of the gateway, were twenty-five men; among them I saw Jaazaniah son of Azzur, and Pelatiah son of Benaiah, officials of the people. ² He said to me, "Mortal, these are the men who devise iniquity and who give wicked counsel in this city; ³ they say, 'The time is not near to build houses; this city is the pot, and we are the meat.' ⁴ Therefore prophesy against them; prophesy, O mortal."
> ⁵ Then the spirit of the LORD fell upon me, and he said to me, "Say, Thus says the LORD: This is what you think, O house of Israel. . . . ⁶ You have killed many in this city, and have filled its streets with the slain. ⁷ Therefore thus says the Lord GOD: The slain whom you have placed within it are the meat, and this city is the pot; but you shall be taken out of it. . . . ¹⁰ You shall fall

by the sword; I will judge you at the border of Israel. And you shall know that I am the LORD. [11] This city shall not be your pot, and you shall not be the meat inside it; I will judge you at the border of Israel. [12] Then you shall know that I am the LORD, whose statutes you have not followed, and whose ordinances you have not kept, but you have acted according to the ordinances of the nations that are around you."

[13] Now, while I was prophesying, Pelatiah son of Benaiah died. Then I fell down on my face, cried with a loud voice, and said, "Ah Lord GOD! will you make a full end of the remnant of Israel?"

We are now brought face-to-face with some of the most deeply personal of Ezekiel's denunciations of the political situation in Jerusalem: He names certain leaders, notably Jaazaniah son of Azzur and Pelatiah son of Benaiah (v. 1), two of twenty-five leading citizens who had counseled badly, and singles them out as especially guilty of bringing disaster upon the nation. The prophet then expands his accusation, laying the same charge against the "house of Israel" (v. 5). The all-inclusive nature of the condemnation appears at first glance to weaken its force but may be intended to show that the whole community in Judah has chosen to follow the bad policies of its hotheaded advisers. Perhaps the king, Zedekiah, was especially on Ezekiel's mind, since the act of judgment "at the border of Israel" (v. 10) describes the circumstances of this ill-fated ruler's capture and arrest, after trying to flee from his doomed city (Jer. 39:4–7 recounts this episode). The broad accusation means there can be no singling out of individual scapegoats in order to exonerate the rest.

What is the charge against these figures? They are men "who devise iniquity and who give wicked counsel in this city" (v. 2). Spelling out the details of this "wicked counsel" seems to bring more shadow than light, with its focus on the city as a cooking pot and its inhabitants as the meat. It seems unlikely that leading citizens in Jerusalem would have pictured their situation in this way to justify their policies. Ezekiel himself then uses this image in order to make the punishment fit the crime in verse 7. There is a further provision that this will not apply to all, since some will be judged and killed "at the border of Israel" (v. 11).

What are we to make of this? What did these bad counselors propose? Guided by our knowledge of the overall situation, that of urging further rebellion against Babylonian control of Judah, we know the policy they advocated was: "Don't settle down to build houses! Take firm action!" But why use the picture of a cooking pot with meat in it (v. 3), which the prophet turns against them (v. 7)? The most straightforward understanding would be to conclude that they intended some reference to their special status that would ensure them of God's favorable protection. Instead of bringing relief and protection to the city, they would instead only fill its streets with the corpses of those killed in battle (v. 6).

The unexpected episode of Pelatiah's death, seen by the prophet in his vision (v. 13), marks a turning point in the dramatic vision sequence, because it raises a cry on Ezekiel's lips concerning the possibility of a remnant. It appears that he saw this sudden death in his imagination, but the event was subsequently confirmed to him, presumably at a much later time. This anguished cry to God, which comes in response to this death, shows Ezekiel to have been deeply shocked. He stood appalled at the severity of the judgment his vision had shown him, which he understood to be an event that was in reality soon to befall Judah. Would there be no remnant left for Israel at all?

After the severity of his earliest warnings of doom, the prophet has given us only a few hints that some will survive (such as those with the special mark on their foreheads, 9:4) who could form a new Israel. From this point on, glimmerings of hope begin to break through, like narrow shafts of light in a dark room. Yet they do not shine with any real brightness until chapter 33, by which time the terrible destruction of Jerusalem that the prophet foretold has been accomplished. The final part of the book is entirely taken up with this hope.

The great vision sequence of Ezekiel 8—11 represents a prophetic way of interpreting events. It may appear one-sided and oversimplified at times, yet it nonetheless makes sense of otherwise seemingly senseless disasters. Military weakness and political miscalculation would all pay a part in Jerusalem's downfall, but in the end such weaknesses and miscalculations rested on a false expectation about God. Headstrong and reckless policies had been pursued, backed up by false hopes about God's protection for city and kingdom. The contemporary prophecies of Jeremiah help to make this plain; he was struggling in Judah to voice a protest against the same political complacency and folly.

The highlighting of the issue of idolatry in this great vision given to the prophet Ezekiel makes it important to reflect upon its place in the Bible as a whole. Idolatry is presented consistently as one of the greatest of sins, second in importance only to that of turning aside to worship a god other than the Lord (see especially Deut. 4:15–31; Isa. 44:9–20). Clearly, idolatry did frequently involve the worship of an alien deity, but sometimes such images could be understood to be symbols of the Lord God. Why then was it wrong?

It is seldom wholly clear what makes such use of images so wrong and so offensive to the true religious spirit. In the New Testament, Paul interprets idolatry as a form of greed (Col. 3:5), but this can only be part of the reason for its wrongfulness and is almost certainly a relatively late interpretation of the issue. Various other considerations have been noted:

1. Idolatry involves the worship of created things rather than the Creator and so is shown to be based on a falsehood. Only the true Creator can be God, who must always be greater than anything that is made.
2. Idolatry implies a human ability to claim access to God, thereby making it a matter of human control in religion. God is made into an object, or power, that human beings can use, when the truth is that God is always the subject who reaches out toward us.
3. We should not overlook the visual aspect of idolatry, especially with regard to a prophet like Ezekiel, who is so full of word pictures of God's reality and activity. Many religious images in ancient times were intentionally shocking and threatening in their nature, in order to instill a sense of fear and mystery in the worshiper. Similarly, the sexual imagery of much pagan religious tradition should be borne in mind. Seldom were the images marked by features of compassion and love. The later resurgence of visual imagery in the Christian tradition with figures of the "Suffering Christ" and "Mary, the Compassionate Mother," sought to replace the threatening character of ancient divine images with more appropriate ones, agreeable to the Christian tradition.
4. Fear of idolatry has frequently led Jewish, Christian, and Muslim traditions into iconoclasm—the rejection and destruction of all visual symbolism in worship, with seriously detrimental results for art and beauty in worship. This rests upon a mistaken interpretation of the wrongfulness of idolatry and ignores the great importance of visual guidance and creativity in a true understanding of God. Ezekiel was on the side of strictness, but he was not an iconoclast, and, as we have sought to emphasize, was most richly aware that we must learn to see God with our inner eye of faith.

THE TURNING POINT OF HOPE
Ezekiel 11:14–25

11:14 **Then the word of the LORD came to me:** [15] **Mortal, your kinsfolk, your own kin, your fellow exiles, the whole house of Israel, all of them, are those of whom the inhabitants of Jerusalem have said, "They have gone far from the LORD; to us this land is given for a possession."** [16] **Therefore say: Thus says the Lord GOD: Though I removed them far away among the nations, and though I scattered them among the countries, yet I have been a sanctuary to them for a little while in the countries where they have gone.** [17] **Therefore say: Thus says the Lord GOD: I will gather you from the peoples, and assemble you out of the countries where you have been scattered, and I will give you the land of Israel. . . .**

[24] **The spirit lifted me up and brought me in a vision by the spirit of God into Chaldea, to the exiles. Then the vision that I had seen left me.** [25] **And I told the exiles all the things that the LORD had shown me.**

We have seen how the vision of judgment on Judah and Jerusalem that began in 8:1 forms the heart and center of the prophet's early message. It concerned people who were far distant geographically from the prophet, which explains why it could only be "seen" in a prophetic vision. However, it was a message the prophet put into a connected story form that he no doubt first told to his fellow exiles. At some point, probably before events actually overtook his forewarnings, he set it down in writing. It was to be his prophetic testimony to explain the divine meaning of such terrifying events. Yet those who heard him speak and who read his words were powerless to do anything to change the course of events in Judah. They were no more than distant bystanders of a tragedy they had not wanted, for which they were not directly responsible. What meaning then could the prophet's words have for them? It is on this score that we can understand why the little section of 11:14–21 is so important to the book and why it marks so key a feature of his message.

Ezekiel addressed despondent and frustrated people. Many had been leading figures of the government and the temple administration in Jerusalem. Now they were hostages to fortune, with no clear assurance that they would ever see Judah again or take up a normal pattern of life. They envied the citizens who had remained behind, and they longed to go back to their homeland. Yet this was not to be, at least for the present; and if Ezekiel's message about the fate that awaited Judah was correct, Jerusalem, with its day of judgment still to come, was no place to return to.

So, when news reached Babylon of the way in which the citizens of Judah had simply written off those who had been taken there, alarm and despair must have reached dire proportions (v. 15 echoes this very clearly).

Quite literally, it seems, those remaining in Judah had simply helped themselves to the properties and lands of those who had been removed. This cynical betrayal of their fellow citizens gains in significance once we accept that those taken to Babylon were being used as hostages in order to exert political pressure on the community in Judah. Ezekiel's picture of the Babylonian end of this situation is amply corroborated from the book of Jeremiah, which reports the Judean side of things. Ezekiel 17 will present further reflections of this cruel betrayal.

4. There Are No Excuses
Ezekiel 12:1–15:8

From 12:1 to the end of chapter 15, Ezekiel's book follows a fairly consistent path. The message of Jerusalem's destruction has been foretold in chapters 4—7 and then spelled out in a dramatic vision sequence in 8:1–11:25. In these follow-up chapters the prophet can be seen knocking away the props by which his hearers sought to resist his message about the coming disaster to Jerusalem. He was, they argued, only a prophet and such things had been said before; he was talking about events a long way off in the future; he wasn't to be trusted because other prophets gave much more comforting and reassuring messages. So ran the catalog of excuses by which Ezekiel's prophecies were to be robbed of their cutting edge. It is no wonder that the prophet appears so often to be uncompromising and fiercely fanatical in his accusations of idolatry.

A visit from the elders who request guidance from God, which is reported in chapter 14, is thus greeted by a sharp refusal on Ezekiel's part and provides the occasion for yet more lectures against idolatry and all its temptations. Yet in this prophetic onslaught we hear words that cannot easily be dismissed as Ezekiel's overzealous enthusiasm to uphold his ancestral faith. We hear from this prophet serious and much-needed warnings against a too-comfortable faith. Faith that has lost its robustness or no longer has a cutting edge ceases to be a real faith. Israel has never lacked false prophets who came along, even in the worst of times, with the comforting and reassuring words, "Don't worry, it may never happen!"

Ezekiel is just one prophet among others, and their words do not agree with his. Moreover, since the hearers were in a miserable and near-desperate situation, there was good reason to think comforting words were in order. In the end, however, if Ezekiel's forewarnings were anywhere near the mark about the critical political situation in Jerusalem and the disastrous events that were certain to befall the city, all such comfort was misguided and false. Its final result could only be to make the popular despair deeper and faith more difficult. So we now find that Ezekiel backs up the harsh warnings he has already given by adding to them a series of sharp rebuffs to all the excuses by which his fellow exiles have sought to shield themselves from the real force of his message.

THE WARNING OF
A SECOND DEPORTATION
Ezekiel 12:1–16

12:1 The word of the LORD came to me: [2] Mortal, you are living in the midst of a rebellious house, who have eyes to see but do not see, who have ears to hear but do not hear; [3] for they are a rebellious house. Therefore, mortal, prepare for yourself an exile's baggage, and go into exile by day in their sight; you shall go like an exile from your place to another place in their sight. Perhaps they will understand, though they are a rebellious house. [4] You shall bring out your baggage by day in their sight, as baggage for exile; and you shall go out yourself at evening in their sight, as those do who go into exile. [5] Dig through the wall in their sight, and carry the baggage through it. [6] In their sight you shall lift the baggage on your shoulder, and carry it out in the dark; you shall cover your face, so that you may not see the land; for I have made you a sign for the house of Israel.

[7] I did just as I was commanded. . . .

[8] In the morning the word of the LORD came to me: [9] Mortal, has not the house of Israel, the rebellious house, said to you, "What are you doing?" [10] Say to them, "Thus says the Lord GOD: This oracle concerns the prince in Jerusalem and all the house of Israel in it." [11] Say, "I am a sign for you: as I have done, so shall it be done to them; they shall go into exile, into captivity." [12] And the prince who is among them shall lift his baggage on his shoulder in the dark, and shall go out; he shall dig through the wall and carry it through; he shall cover his face, so that he may not see the land with his eyes. . . . [15] And they shall know that I am the LORD, when I disperse them among the nations and scatter them through the countries. . . .

There is a recognizable buildup in the sequence with which Ezekiel foretells events that will shortly bring renewed disaster upon Jerusalem: A further siege (Ezekiel 4—7) would be followed by the collapse of the city's resistance and its destruction (chapters 8—9). This would in turn be followed by the death of many of its citizens and the ruination of its beautiful temple (chapters 10—11). Now Ezekiel 12:1–16 continues this pattern by declaring that there will be a renewed act of deportation in which "the rebellious house," the prophet's accusatory title for the people of Israel, will suffer further humiliation. Those who have survived the ravages of famine during the city's time of siege, and the slaughter after its ending, will suffer the cruel prospect of deportation to foreign lands and a lifetime of slavery and humiliation. Ezekiel, together with his fellow exiles in Babylon, is already experiencing the pain and hurt that such a fate entails.

Once again the prophet conveys the message through his preferred medium of street theater, the carefully enacted sign action that will illustrate through silent mime his ominous forewarning. Some unexpected and unclear features here cannot be explained easily. The heart of the difficulty is that the message, as reported, has a twofold application that both distorts and expands its significance. In the opening part, where God's command to enact the dramatic message is given (vv. 2–3), it is made plain that it is the people of Israel as a whole who make up "the rebellious house." Further, the prophet emphatically points out that he is living in the midst of these people (v. 2). (We shall reflect on this point momentarily.)

There is a clear implication that the deportation into exile, which the prophet enacts in his minidrama, is broadly applicable to this people, or at least to some of them. Verses 10 and 12, however, state that the message more specifically "concerns the prince in Jerusalem." It is true that the prince's name is linked with "all the house of Israel" there, but this simply highlights the inconsistent features in the details of what Ezekiel was commanded to enact.

It seems, in fact, that the miming of the departure into exile has been given a twofold reference: first, to the survivors in Jerusalem quite generally and, second, to the fate of King Zedekiah in particular. The inconsistent features are those tying the dramatic scenario to the circumstances in which King Zedekiah sought to escape from his Babylonian enemies by fleeing at night from his stricken city.

It could be that the prophet acted out the drama of leaving Jerusalem to go into exile on more than one occasion and that one of these specifically pointed to the fate of the ruler in the city. The preserved report could then have run together the two accounts. More probably, however, the prophet's original mime related to the fate of ordinary survivors in Jerusalem, who were to be rounded up and deported, just as had happened to Ezekiel and his fellow exiles several years before. This broadly applied warning about the fate of deportation and exile has then been revised and reflected upon in the light of what happened to King Zedekiah. The prophetic mime of Ezekiel has been turned into a reenactment of the terrible fate of the last Davidic king to rule in Jerusalem. It could be Ezekiel who made this connection; more likely it is the work of those scribes and followers who preserved the prophet's words for later generations. The reason for doing this is easy to understand: With the passage of years, the fate that befell the survivors in Jerusalem after the collapse of its second assault by the forces of Babylon began to diminish in significance. The fate of the last of the Davidic kings, however, became a matter of increasing interest, since restoring the kingship to Judah was a prime hope for the future. There is a great deal more about this to be found in the book of Ezekiel, but the issue surfaces here for the first time.

We can best deal with this sign-action report in two separate reflections, since the issues it raises have a considerable bearing in two directions. In the first instance, the prophet's acting out the circumstances of getting ready for exile after being given brief notice, and of doing so "by day" (vv. 4, 7), is clear enough. It indicates the limited time for preparation and the pitifully small bag of personal possessions that those designated for exile could take. The final sight of a beloved city, which was unlikely to be seen again as home, was too painful to contemplate. It is all reasonably self-explanatory and does not pose difficulties in its interpretation. The many film records of the terrible experiences of those deported to death camps during World War II provide the modern reader with ample recent parallels for reflection. No doubt the psychological trauma of such an experience for those who survived lends added force to the opening admonition to the prophet. His compatriots are said to "have eyes to see but do not see" and "ears to hear but do not hear" (v. 2).

Ezekiel's mime points to experiences so traumatic and painful they could not openly be spoken of. Nevertheless, it is surprising that he is said to be living "in the midst of" such a rebellious house, when quite clearly the events referred to are to take place many miles away in Jerusalem. It is one of the passages where the prophet identifies himself and his hearers with those in Jerusalem in a truly remarkable fashion. It seems that, at times, his compassionate nature led him to feel he was "there" when the most painful events took place. To what extent Ezekiel's visionary experiences were the consequence, or the cause, of this sense he had of being transported to his former homeland has been variously estimated. Obviously we cannot now readily answer such questions about the psychology of prophecy. However, it is important to recognize that, alongside the extraordinary trancelike experiences, a deeply felt sense of compassion and belonging shaped the prophet's understanding of what was happening to him.

The application of the sign action to the fate of King Zedekiah becomes clear when we study the report of what happened to him when the siege of Jerusalem was close to its inevitable end. The details are fully reported in Jeremiah 39:1–4. Faced with certain punishment if he surrendered, Zedekiah sought to escape and secretly left the city "at night by way of the king's garden through the gate between the two walls" (Jer. 39:4). It was all in vain, however, since the royal party was overtaken near Jericho and captured. After witnessing the death of his sons, the king was blinded and taken as a prisoner to Babylon, where he almost certainly died soon afterward. The way in which these events are tied to some of the unexpected features of Ezekiel's reported sign action become obvious. The king's loss of his eyes becomes his being unable to see the city (vv. 12–13).

The fate of the last of Judah's reigning Davidic kings was crucial to any hope of rebuilding a new Israel. As so often in the book, details suggesting the prophet reflected morosely and heavily on the themes of judgment and disaster that formed the substance of his early message need to be set in a larger context. These disasters were now history. They could not be forgotten and were not to be ignored, but the essential concern was to accept them as unalterable facts. By doing so, and turning away from them in penitence, it was possible to lay the foundations for a better hope in the future. Only by coming to terms with the past could this new future be taken hold of.

If the fate of the last of Judah's kings was basic to restoring the Davidic kingship to Israel, it is certainly significant that Zedekiah in Judah is referred to as "the prince." This was clearly Ezekiel's way of describing the last of the Davidic dynasty to rule in Jerusalem. Is this also a reflection of the official status of Zedekiah, whom 2 Kings and the book of Jeremiah openly describe as "king"? The situation is not wholly clear but can be more fully considered in regard to Ezekiel's pronouncements in chapters 17 and 19, where the past, present, and future destiny of Israel's kings is made a matter of central concern.

THE PROPHET'S ANGUISH
AND FRUSTRATION
Ezekiel 12:17–28

12:17 **The word of the LORD came to me: ¹⁸ Mortal, eat your bread with quaking, and drink your water with trembling and with fearfulness; ¹⁹ and say to the people of the land, Thus says the Lord GOD concerning the inhabitants of Jerusalem in the land of Israel: They shall eat their bread with fearfulness, and drink their water in dismay, because their land shall be** stripped of all it contains, on account of the violence of all those who live in it. . . .

²¹ The word of the LORD came to me: ²² Mortal, what is this proverb of yours about the land of Israel, which says, "The days are prolonged, and every vision comes to nothing"? ²³ Tell them therefore, "Thus says the Lord GOD: I will put an end to this proverb, and they shall use it no more as a proverb in Israel." But say to them, The days are near, and the fulfillment of every vision. . . . ²⁸ᵇ None of my words will be delayed any longer, but the word that I speak will be fulfilled, says the Lord GOD.

In Ezekiel 12:17–28, we have three short reflections by the prophet in the form of a dialogue between himself and God. In its own fashion, each concerns experiences the prophet had found to be personally hurtful, creating as they did a sense of frustration about his task as a messenger of God. In fact, the entire section 12:1–14:23 is centrally concerned with questions about prophecy and the role of God's prophetic messenger. The various subjects and themes touched upon reflect back on two basic questions: What does it mean that the prophet is God's "sentinel" (3:17)? And what does it mean that he resides "in the midst of a rebellious people" (2:3–8; 12:2–3)?

The reply to the first question must clearly be that it was the prophet's duty to warn people of the dangers that faced them so they could turn away from their headlong plunge to disaster. The answer to the second question lies in recognizing that ingrown attitudes of mind prevented these people from taking the prophet seriously and adopting the appropriate action to avert the danger.

In the first short dialogue (vv. 17–20), God commands Ezekiel to "eat your bread with quaking" and to "drink your water with trembling." This points to the prophet's behavior as another sign action. He was to act so as to display the shock and terror that were shortly to overtake the citizens of Israel as the opposing armies ravaged their lands and cities.

The action and its meaning are straightforward and clear. The question we cannot answer with certainty is whether Ezekiel was deliberately simulating a state of shock or whether this trembling and shaking was an involuntary action to which he gave a historical interpretation. Probably the latter is the case. The nervous trembling occasioned a situation in which Ezekiel was made the object of mockery and ridicule, which in turn provided his hearers with an excuse for not taking his words seriously. His awkward behavior could lead to his looking foolish and his message being ignored.

This nervous and agitated display provides us with one of several indications that Ezekiel's was a very highly strung and easily overwrought personality. His periodic dumbness (3:26) would be a further sign. We see here how completely the prophet has submerged his private feelings and personality in his message. We have to read between the lines to find out more than the most meager of facts about the prophet as a person; his overwhelming concern is to tell us about God and Israel.

The dialogue between the prophet and God that follows in verses 21–25 centers around comments that the prophet must have heard from those around him (v. 22). They laughed at him as a scaremonger and Doomsday Johnny. They said his message simply was not true and, in any case, was similar to warnings from the past that had given needless cause for alarm. The prophet retorts by insisting that his every word is shortly to be fulfilled (v. 25). The people's excuses will soon be swept aside by the actual course of events.

What follows in verses 26–28 continues the same general theme; the prophet brushes aside the spurious reasons his hearers present for not heeding the divine message. When they agree that what he declared as due to happen is true but insist that it will not take place for some considerable time to come, Ezekiel's response is clear and straightforward (v. 23). He insists he is not talking about a distant future time but about events that are very shortly to take place. In this dialogue, we catch a glimpse of hearers who are too cautious to reject the message altogether but are nonetheless anxious to insist that it has no relevance for them.

It is not difficult to find modern counterparts to these various responses. The word of God can be laughed at as ridiculous, rejected as untrue, or, more subtly, respected as true but nonetheless dismissed as only relevant to a more distant time. All such responses are simply excuses for not facing up to reality. Sometimes nothing can be more unwelcome to hear than the truth!

THE FALSE PROPHETS
Ezekiel 13:1–23

13:1 **The word of the LORD came to me: ² Mortal, prophesy against the prophets of Israel who are prophesying; say to those who prophesy out of their own imagination: "Hear the word of the LORD!" ³ Thus says the Lord GOD, Alas for the senseless prophets who follow their own spirit, and have seen nothing! ⁴ Your prophets have been like jackals among ruins, O Israel. ⁵ You have not gone up into the breaches, or repaired a wall for the house of Israel, so that it might stand in battle on the day of the LORD. ⁶ They have envisioned falsehood and lying divination; they say, "Says the LORD," when** the LORD has not sent them, and yet they wait for the fulfillment of their word! . . .

⁸ Therefore thus says the Lord GOD: Because you have uttered falsehood and envisioned lies, I am against you, says the Lord GOD. ⁹ My hand will be against the prophets who see false visions and utter lying divinations; they shall not be in the council of my people, nor be enrolled in the register of the house of Israel, nor shall they enter the land of Israel; and you shall know that I am the Lord GOD. ¹⁰ Because, in truth, because they have misled my people, saying, "Peace," when there is no peace; and because, when the people build a wall, these prophets smear whitewash on it. ¹¹ Say to those who smear whitewash on it that it shall fall. . . .

¹⁷ As for you, mortal, set your face against the daughters of your people, who prophesy out of their own imagination; prophesy against them ¹⁸ and say, Thus says the Lord GOD: Woe to the women who sew bands on all wrists, and make veils for the heads of persons of every height, in the hunt for human lives! Will you hunt down lives among my people, and maintain your own lives? ¹⁹ You have profaned me among my people for handfuls of barley and for pieces of bread, putting to death persons who should not die and keeping alive persons who should not live, by your lies to my people, who listen to lies.

²⁰ Therefore thus says the Lord GOD: I am against your bands with which you hunt lives; I will tear them from your arms, and let the lives go free, the lives that you hunt down like birds. . . .

The theme that has occupied chapter 12—the hindrances to the prophet's word being heard and effectively responded to—continues. This time the issue is not the spurious excuses by which his hearers refuse to acknowledge the force of his words. Instead, it is the problem of false prophets. As soon, and as readily, as Ezekiel declares and enacts a message he has received from God, other prophets come onto the scene in significant numbers and proclaim a message that contradicts his. How are his hearers to distinguish his word from theirs and to know that he alone is speaking the truth?

The prophet Jeremiah experienced similar difficulties, as did Micah at an earlier time. It is likely that ever since prophecy first appeared in Israel, comparable problems had arisen. When prophecy was a widespread spiritual ministry, true and false prophets appeared side by side. How to tell one from the other was always a perplexing problem for the serious-minded observer. Ezekiel finds himself reduced to the only effective weapon he possesses: the power of words. The verbal images he uses to distinguish true prophets from false offer priceless insights into the meaning of a genuinely prophetic understanding of ministry.

The first of his vigorous attacks appears in verses 1–7, where he accuses false prophets of prophesying "out of their own imagination" (v. 2). He proceeds to use two telling metaphors to describe them: They are "like jackals among ruins" (v. 4)—that is, disreputable scavengers and looters who profit from other people's misfortune—and they "have not gone up into the breaches, or repaired a wall" (v. 5). This is a meaningful wartime image of the heroic citizens under siege who crawl out on a city wall damaged by battering rams in order to carry out repairs, at great risk to their lives. So the true prophet sets his own life on the line in putting his message before the people. He has no self-interest, but rather forsakes it to serve his fellow citizens. Not so with false prophets, who seek their own advantage, usually in terms of gifts and money but sometimes simply in the prestige and favor they enjoy for prophesying what people want to hear.

The second attack on false prophets (vv. 8–16) continues along similar lines but introduces some further telling criticisms and word pictures. To "see false visions and utter lying divinations" (v. 9) plainly implies that the false prophets were usually to be heard declaring comforting and reassuring messages. They gave their hearers the words they most wanted to hear. Instead of warning of danger, they turned their faces aside and spoke useless words of reassurance and baseless hope. The picture the prophet uses to describe this empty comfort-giving is that of builders who put up a dangerous and insecure wall, hiding the cracks by smearing a thin coat of whitewashed plaster over it (vv. 10–15). With the next heavy rainstorm, the whitewash comes away, revealing the cracks, and the wall quickly breaks and crumbles. Such are the false prophets, who do not get to the truth. Instead of presenting God's call for repentance and a return to the divine path, they insist that everyone is already all right.

Within this second attack upon false prophets we catch a glimpse of Ezekiel's own soul being laid bare. False prophets will find they have no place in the council, the register, or the land of the people of Israel (v. 9). There can be no share in the renewed and restored Israel of the future for those who have profited so shamefully from the misfortunes of the nation's past. False prophets are not nation builders but nation destroyers.

Brief as is this short admonition directed against false prophets, it points to the hope and expectation in Ezekiel's words. However stark and forbidding the repeated messages of judgment appear to be, his words are not intended to pull down and destroy. Rather, by declaring the truth about Israel's ruin and collapse, they lay a foundation on which a new nation can be established. Even when his charges and accusations appear most uncompromising and shocking, their ultimate aim—achieving genuine repentance and renewal—remains unwavering. Prophecy endeavors to be a message of hope, but in order to fulfill this task it has to be distinguished from the many cheap and empty promises of hope that are no more than spurious attempts to cover up the nation's wounds.

In the third of Ezekiel's sharp tirades against false prophecy, he turns against women prophets (vv. 17–23). There is a special interest in this section, even though it contains some tantalizingly unclear details. We hear little in the Old Testament about women prophets. The few references to be found merely confirm their existence and leave us wanting to find out more. Prophecy was one of the few approved forms of religious ministry conducted by women that we know of in ancient Israel; no legitimate woman priests are mentioned. Isaiah was married to a woman prophet (Isa. 8:3), but in Ezekiel's references here women prophets are heavily condemned. It seems most improbable that he was referring to women who enjoyed any kind of officially approved status. Rather, they were self-appointed figures who indulged in some age-old and popularly accepted forms of spiritual ministry that Ezekiel condemns. What he has to say about their activities points to rites and practices that we usually associate more with magic.

The key features of Ezekiel's charges against women prophets are that they tie bands on people's arms and put veils on their heads, all in pursuit of what he calls their "hunt for human lives" (v. 18). They also see false visions and practice divination (v. 23), although what form this took is not spelled out. We can only guess at the details; clearly wearing headbands and amulets was involved, probably in the hope of procuring healing from disease. Their impotence to achieve this only brought greater disappointment and plunged the victims into despair. This appears to be what is implied by the accusation that they "have disheartened the righteous falsely" (v. 22).

There are ample indications in the Old Testament that health and healing were concerns that especially involved the priesthood rather than any separate medical profession. Very much later, the teacher Ben Sira had to insist categorically that there was a God-given place for the lay medical practitioner and pharmacist (so Ecclus. 38:1–15). Much of the Jewish reluctance to accept this can be traced back to far older times, when matters of health and healing were often inseparably linked to magic and to non-Israelite forms of religion. It seems that the god Baal and the goddess Anat had much to do with giving life (that is, healing). Often this was linked to types of sympathetic magic (that is, constraining demons by tying them with bands and the like), and this certainly appears to be the case here.

To some extent, we can well understand that the situation of being deported into exile in Babylon posed special difficulties for those around Ezekiel. They were cut off from the formal worship of the Jerusalem temple and were certainly not exempt from falling ill. The extent to which they had opportunities for resorting to the normal channels of levitical prayer and guidance in the case of illness was extremely limited. We can hardly be surprised therefore that some of the womenfolk took it upon themselves to revive old customs and remedies in the hope of assisting those in need. Ezekiel saw this as a threat, both to the integrity of Israel's religion and to the right and proper leadership of the priesthood. It was simply one more example of a popular indifference to the demands of faith in a time of crisis, made all the more objectionable to him because it promised help it could not give.

Ezekiel's oracles frequently appear rather harsh and uncompromising in their sharp criticisms of both his fellow exiles in Babylon and those who remained behind in Judah. His proclamation of God's insistence on religious rightness and integrity led him to yield no quarter in his reproofs and attacks upon the idolatrous tendencies of his people. To this extent, his book does not reflect the measure of pain and grief felt by Jeremiah at his warnings of judgment and disaster that were to overtake Jerusalem and its citizens. Ezekiel seems to have been more aloof, more ready to point the finger of blame at those whom he held responsible, than was Jeremiah.

This may be, however, more a consequence of the two men's different writing styles and backgrounds than a valid assessment. They were each human channels of a divine truth. For that truth to be conveyed effectively through them, it was essential that they undergo the full measure and trials of human existence. They could not be lifted out and insulated from the catastrophes their message addressed. Their calling to be prophets of God did not suppress their humanity, and human feelings, but rather required it. So Ezekiel's impatience and hostility toward false men and women prophets can be readily understood. It was no time for cheap remedies and glib assurances when the very existence of Israel as a nation was being threatened.

THE VISIT OF THE ELDERS
Ezekiel 14:1–23

14:1 **Certain elders of Israel came to me and sat down before me. ² And the word of the LORD came to me: ³ Mortal, these men have taken their idols** into their hearts, and placed their iniquity as a stumbling block before them; shall I let myself be consulted by them? [4] Therefore speak to them, and say to them, Thus says the Lord GOD: Any of those of the house of Israel who take their idols into their hearts and place their iniquity as a stumbling block before them, and yet come to the prophet—I the LORD will answer those who come with the multitude of their idols, [5] in order that I may take hold of the hearts of the house of Israel, all of whom are estranged from me through their idols.

[6] Therefore say to the house of Israel, Thus says the Lord GOD: Repent and turn away from your idols; and turn away your faces from all your abominations. . . .

[9] If a prophet is deceived and speaks a word, I, the LORD, have deceived that prophet, and I will stretch out my hand against him, and will destroy him from the midst of my people Israel. [10] And they shall bear their punishment. . . .

[12] The word of the LORD came to me: [13] Mortal, when a land sins against me by acting faithlessly, and I stretch out my hand against it, and break its staff of bread and send famine upon it, and cut off from it human beings and animals, [14] even if Noah, Daniel, and Job, these three, were in it, they would save only their own lives by their righteousness, says the Lord GOD. . . .

[21] For thus says the Lord GOD: How much more when I send upon Jerusalem my four deadly acts of judgment, sword, famine, wild animals, and pestilence, to cut off humans and animals from it! [22] Yet, survivors shall be left in it, sons and daughters who will be brought out; they will come out to you. When you see their ways and their deeds, you will be consoled for the evil that I have brought upon Jerusalem, for all that I have brought upon it. . . . [23b] and you shall know that it was not without cause that I did all that I have done in it, says the Lord GOD.

How often we find ourselves frustrated by the brevity and single-mindedness of a Bible text when simply to have a few verses more about a particular incident would answer our questions! In the case of chapter 14 of Ezekiel, we would dearly love to know what the elders of Israel came to ask the prophet, that he should seek guidance from God on their behalf (v. 1). Clearly it was of considerable importance; it produced a fierce tirade against them, because they "have taken their idols into their hearts" (v. 3).

Having said this, Ezekiel proceeds to expand more fully upon the theme of idolatry, insisting that it acts as a stumbling block, precluding God from answering the prayerful requests for guidance of anyone who has committed idolatry (vv. 4–9). It is a fearful and harshly worded rejoinder and shows Ezekiel's message in its most uncompromising light.

He views his fellow exiles in a sharply unsympathetic manner, accusing them of sharing in the generally pervasive idolatry of Israel's ancestors and categorically asserting that, for this reason, God will not receive their question. Such a retort must have come as a great surprise to the elders, who knew the kind of person Ezekiel was and the issues he felt so keenly about. Obviously they would not have come to him at all if they had supposed they would be greeted with a dressing-down and accused of offensive and irreligious behavior. This is what makes the unknown question so tantalizing.

Although guessing games are fruitless, it has nonetheless been inevitable that scholars should try to find clues as to what the question was for which the elders sought an answer. Suggestions have pursued two paths, both of which are plausible but neither of which allows us any certainty. That the prophet charged his inquirers with idolatry could suggest, first, that something in what they asked was capable of being interpreted as idolatrous. Perhaps they sought to practice some ritual or observe some religious festival that the Israelite priestly tradition forbade outside the consecrated temple area of Jerusalem. Ezekiel would then simply have been upholding the established claims to exclusivity of an approved and properly consecrated place of worship. Since no such place was available in Babylon, it was necessary that they, and all fellow Judean exiles, learn to do without the more formal and external features of traditional worship. To have performed such activities in an unconsecrated foreign location, even with the best of intentions, would have constituted a breach of divine law. It would have been a form of spiritual idolatry, which is presumably what is meant by taking "their idols into their hearts" (v. 4).

The second possibility is suggested by the fact that twice the extended reply refers to the idolatry of those who remained living in the land of Israel (v. 7 refers to "the aliens who reside in Israel" and v. 22 refers to "survivors" who were to be left in Jerusalem after the destruction that was shortly to befall it). The elders' request may then have been concerned with relationships between the exiles in Babylon, who had a good number of priests like Ezekiel among their number, and those city elders who had remained in Jerusalem and who were subsequently brought to Babylon. We already know from Ezekiel 8 that the prophet strongly condemned them because of their tolerance of idolatry. So any yielding of priestly authority to those who had become tolerant of idolatry was bound to be strongly rebuffed by him. In God's eyes they had compromised their true faith in the worst possible way. Since those whom Ezekiel rebuked here were living in Babylon, it would suggest that some of them had spoken openly of their sympathy and support for their brethren in Jerusalem.

We cannot resolve these uncertainties, but it is evident that Ezekiel's stern reply provided him with occasion for no less than four prophetic messages on the theme of the limitations of God's prophetic word. Behind them all lies the hidden question: "Why did God not avert the disaster to Jerusalem as a result of the warnings given by prophets like Jeremiah and Ezekiel?" We know, for instance, that Jeremiah had given such warnings in Jerusalem without being able to effect any change in the national policy, even though his words clearly reached the king on more than one occasion.

The first of Ezekiel's oracles is in verses 6–8, which insist that idolatry in the heart constitutes a stumbling block to hearing the word of God. The second refers to the unsettling and dangerous consequences of false prophets (vv. 9–11). They are to "bear their punishment" (v. 10), indicating that they carried a heavy responsibility for misleading the people.

The third of the prophet's oracles is the longest and is to be found in verses 12–20. It is particularly interesting because it mentions three of the great spiritual ancestors of the nation—Noah, Daniel, and Job—a feature rarely found in the prophetic books. Noah is the well-known survivor of the flood, and the reference to Job points to the fact that, before the present book of Job was composed, its hero was a legendary figure of Israelite tradition. The mention of Daniel is more problematic, since he can hardly be the figure referred to in the present book of that name. However, among Israel's neighbors the Canaanites, evidence survives of the figure of Daniel (or Dan'el) as a legendary hero figure, an intermediary between human beings and the gods. The thrust of Ezekiel's reference, again striking in the sharpness with which it presents the hopelessness of Israel's case, is that even the most righteous and pious of all Israel's spiritual heroes could not have prevailed with God in prayer to save the people. Doom is inevitable.

The last of these four oracles (vv. 21–23) comes as one of the biggest surprises. It refers to those who will survive the catastrophe that is to befall Jerusalem, and who will afterward be brought, as Ezekiel himself was, as exiles to Babylon (v. 22). These would then join the beleaguered and suffering community there. Ezekiel interprets their coming as further evidence of the idolatrous pattern of worship and life that prevails in the city. This certainly suggests that the elders' question arose out of a concern with relationships between exiles in Babylon and those who remained behind in Judah. The arrival of survivors from the doomed city would bring further confirmation of their idolatrous ways, and this must have given additional proof that Jerusalem deserved the judgment that came upon it (v. 23). Altogether it is a severe and uncompromising word, dependent upon Ezekiel's gaining, from the lips of survivors, news of the terrible last days before Jerusalem's collapse and ruin. It adds further strength to the prophet's warnings about the city's inevitable fate and brings out his conviction that the temple has itself been betrayed by the false worship enacted there.

All this harsh rebuke indicates that it is the betrayal of the highest truths and the most worthy ideals that makes Ezekiel's warnings about the temple's destruction so intense. Idolatry was, in the prophet's rebukes, the replacing of the majestic wonder and undefinable greatness of God by a humanly fashioned collection of bits and pieces, aimed at nothing more than using so great a God for selfish human advantage and protection!

It marked a supreme challenge to faith to ask the question: "Why has Jerusalem been destroyed?" Someone who enjoyed the benefits of a priestly upbringing in Jerusalem, as Ezekiel had, could not have found it easy to answer. Yet knowing God's anger against all such idolatry, the prophet argues that, even when there are no outward signs of such spiritual disloyalty, there may nevertheless be an idolatry of the heart. The fact of Jerusalem's destruction was undeniable. The response of the prophet's word draws deeply on his familiarity with the way in which even an outward show of piety can mask an inner feeling of complacent disregard of God. Those who shun the grosser outward symbols of idolatry may nevertheless nurse a secret inner respect and admiration for them.

THE PARABLE OF THE VINE
Ezekiel 15:1–8

15:1 **The word of the LORD came to me:**
    2 **O mortal, how does the wood of the vine surpass all other**
        wood. . . .
    3 **Is wood taken from it to make anything? . . .**
    4 **It is put in the fire for fuel. . . .**
    5 **When it was whole it was used for nothing;**
        how much less—when the fire has consumed it,
        and it is charred—
        can it ever be used for anything!
    6 **Therefore thus says the Lord GOD: Like the wood of the vine among the trees of the forest, which I have given to the fire for fuel, so I will give up the inhabitants of Jerusalem. . . . and you shall know that I am the LORD, when I set my face against them.** 8 **And I will make the land desolate, because they have acted faithlessly, says the Lord GOD.**

As a plant, the grapevine came to symbolize for Israel all that was rich and desirable about life in a settled agricultural land. The fact that a single vine root could support so many branches made it symbolic of prolific growth and fruitfulness. The richness of its sweet-tasting fruit made it desirable, and, most impressive of all, its ability to give wine, when properly harvested and processed, made it a supreme symbol of luxuriant happiness. No wonder that Israel could be likened to a fruitful vine and the land of Israel to a pleasant vineyard (Isa. 5:1–7). It was a natural symbol of well-being and prosperity.

There can be no doubt that Ezekiel and his hearers were fully aware of the conventional usefulness of the metaphor of the vine as a description of Israel. It could even have been the case that those around the prophet were consoling themselves for the weakened and threatened condition of their homeland at the time when the prophet spoke by using the metaphor to portray this. A fragile-looking root can, in spite of appearances, bear much fruit.

Yet now, indicative again of the firmness with which Ezekiel opposed any facile attempt to gloss over the misfortunes of the nation, he turns the metaphor on its head. It becomes a symbol of uselessness and disaster, for a well-known feature of the vine is that it is useless for any kind of wood-work. It cannot be used for construction or for any of the hundred and one uses to which more solid and straight-grained timber can be put. There is only one thing to do with it: Burn it! That is precisely what Ezekiel insists God is about to do to Jerusalem and Judah (v. 7–8). The metaphor of luxury and richness is turned into a metaphor of doom. It is a simple piece of word artistry such as a prophet could employ, and its simplicity and brevity have a most telling effect. Those who look for an easy consolation for their misfortunes in recalling the familiar metaphor that affirms God's love and care for Israel should take note. The vine, when it is no longer producing the fruit for which it is famed, can only be cut down and used as fuel.

5. The Folly of Jerusalem
Ezekiel 16:1–20:49

THE PARABLE OF
THE FOUNDLING GIRL
Ezekiel 16:1–63

16:1 The word of the LORD came to me: 2 Mortal, make known to Jerusalem her abominations, 3 and say, Thus says the Lord GOD to Jerusalem: Your origin and your birth were in the land of the Canaanites; your father was an Amorite, and your mother a Hittite. 4 As for your birth, on the day you were born your navel cord was not cut, nor were you washed with water to cleanse you, nor rubbed with salt, nor wrapped in cloths. 5 No eye pitied you, to do any of these things for you out of compassion for you; but you were thrown out in the open field, for you were abhorred on the day you were born.

6 I passed by you, and saw you flailing about in your blood. As you lay in your blood, I said to you, "Live! 7 and grow up like a plant of the field." You grew up and became tall and arrived at full womanhood; your breasts were formed, and your hair had grown; yet you were naked and bare.

8 I passed by you again and looked on you; you were at the age for love. I spread the edge of my cloak over you, and covered your nakedness: I pledged myself to you and entered into a covenant with you, says the Lord GOD, and you became mine. 9 Then I bathed you with water and washed off the blood from you, and anointed you with oil. 10 I clothed you with embroidered cloth and with sandals of fine leather; I bound you in fine linen and covered you with rich fabric. 11 I adorned you with ornaments. . . . 14 Your fame spread among the nations on account of your beauty, for it was perfect because of my splendor that I had bestowed on you, says the Lord GOD.

15 But you trusted in your beauty, and played the whore because of your fame, and lavished your whorings on any passer-by. 16 You took some of your garments, and made for yourself colorful shrines, and on them played the whore; nothing like this has ever been or ever shall be. 17 You also took

your beautiful jewels of my gold and my silver that I had given you, and made for yourself male images, and with them played the whore.... [21] You slaughtered my children and delivered them up as an offering to them. [22] And in all your abominations and your whorings you did not remember the days of your youth, when you were naked and bare, flailing about in your blood. . . . [26] You played the whore with the Egyptians, your lustful neighbors, multiplying your whoring, to provoke me to anger. [27] Therefore I stretched out my hand against you, reduced your rations, and gave you up to the will of your enemies, the daughters of the Philistines, who were ashamed of your lewd behavior. [28] You played the whore with the Assyrians.... [29] You multiplied your whoring with Chaldea, the land of merchants; and even with this you were not satisfied.

[30] How sick is your heart, says the Lord GOD, that you did all these things, the deeds of a brazen whore. . . . Yet you were not like a whore, because you scorned payment. [32] Adulterous wife, who receives strangers instead of her husband! [33] Gifts are given to all whores; but you gave your gifts to all your lovers, bribing them to come to you from all around for your whorings. [34] So you were different from other women in your whorings: no one solicited you to play the whore; and you gave payment, while no payment was given to you; you were different.

[35] Therefore, O whore, hear the word of the LORD: [36] Thus says the Lord GOD, Because your lust was poured out and your nakedness uncovered in your whoring with your lovers, and because of all your abominable idols, and because of the blood of your children that you gave to them, [37] therefore, I will gather all your lovers, with whom you took pleasure, all those you loved and all those you hated; I will gather them against you from all around, and will uncover your nakedness to them, so that they may see all your nakedness. [38] I will judge you as women who commit adultery and shed blood are judged, and bring blood upon you in wrath and jealousy. [39] I will deliver you into their hands. . . . [43] Because you have not remembered the days of your youth, but have enraged me with all these things; therefore, I have returned your deeds upon your head, says the Lord GOD.

Have you not committed lewdness beyond all your abominations? [44] See, everyone who uses proverbs will use this proverb about you, "Like mother, like daughter." [45] You are the daughter of your mother, who loathed her husband and her children; and you are the sister of your sisters, who loathed their husbands and their children. Your mother was a Hittite and your father an Amorite. [46] Your elder sister is Samaria, who lived with her daughters to the north of you; and your younger sister, who lived to the south of you, is Sodom with her daughters. [47] You not only followed their ways, and acted according to their abominations; within a very little time you were more corrupt than they in all your ways. . . . So be ashamed, you also, and bear your disgrace, for you have made your sisters appear righteous.

53 I will restore their fortunes, the fortunes of Sodom and her daughters and the fortunes of Samaria and her daughters, and I will restore your own fortunes along with theirs, 54 in order that you may bear your disgrace and be ashamed of all that you have done, becoming a consolation to them. 55 As for your sisters, Sodom and her daughters shall return to their former state, Samaria and her daughters shall return to their former state, and you and your daughters shall return to your former state. 56 Was not your sister Sodom a byword in your mouth in the day of your pride, 57 before your wickedness was uncovered? Now you are a mockery to the daughters of Aram and all her neighbors, and to the daughters of the Philistines, those all around who despise you. 58 You must bear the penalty of your lewdness and your abominations, says the LORD.

59 Yes, thus says the Lord GOD: I will deal with you as you have done, you who have despised the oath, breaking the covenant; 60 yet I will remember my covenant with you in the days of your youth, and I will establish with you an everlasting covenant. 61 Then you will remember your ways, and be ashamed. . . . 63b when I forgive you all that you have done, says the Lord GOD.

The reader who already feels that Ezekiel is a hard text to read and makes heavy demands upon the minds and sensitivities of the committed Christian could well be excused for skipping chapter 16. It is a frightening and challenging accusation leveled against Jerusalem, although, for all its harshness, it concludes with a most remarkable assurance of God's love and enduring commitment to the city and its people. The language is strong and sounds coarse to the modern Bible reader. Yet it is worth careful attention as being an Old Testament parable of the prodigal daughter. Quite evidently, it was intended to sound coarse and shocking to those who heard Ezekiel speak in such a manner, and this feature was important to its power to communicate a divine message. So we must look carefully beneath the surface of the text. The address, taken in its entirety, is clearly unsuited for public reading or even public discussion, if all its details are to be closely considered. It is illustrative of the verbal imagery that has given rise to the impression that Ezekiel was a cold and insensitive person, oblivious to those feelings of shame and reticence that are usually expected to guard everyday speech.

Yet for all its violation of the conventional rules of discourse, the chapter is a remarkable illustration of Ezekiel's power to communicate an unwelcome message and of the perspective by which he understood the history of his own beloved city of Jerusalem. It is an allegory, set in the guise of the story of a foundling child—a young girl whose chances at birth for a happy life would have been reckoned at zero. Yet despite this hopeless beginning, she grew up, through the kindness of a stranger, to maturity and marriage. The allegory is frequently compared to that in Ezekiel 23, which deals with the story of two sisters. In Ezekiel 16, the city of Jerusalem is the subject of the allegory, whereas in chapter 23 it is the two kingdoms of Israel and Judah. The message, as now preserved, is a remarkable one in both cases, one of the most penetrating the Old Testament contains, for it is a message of the enduring power of divine love. What makes both allegories painful to read is the harshness of the language. Evidently, this crudity was quite deliberate on the prophet's part, in order to emphasize the baseness of Jerusalem's sinfulness and contrast it with the wonderful beauty and grace of divine love.

Allegories and parables are basically extended forms of metaphor that can appear in many guises. Whereas the simple metaphor usually focuses on one feature of likeness, parables and allegories may explore many similarities and connections. Their purpose is to highlight the features of a thing, or a situation, which may not otherwise be apparent, or even properly understood. The main characteristic of an allegory is that the central actors in the story represent characters in the real world. The story itself may be rather strange and implausible until the identification of who represents whom is worked out. It can have more than one purpose, and this would appear to be the case here. An allegory can give perspective to a situation that everyone knows about but does not at first see for what it is. In this case the allegory, by the associations it makes and the inferences it draws, introduces a way of seeing a situation in a fresh light. By doing so it can make plain what the outcome of the situation is likely to be, especially when such an outcome is what everyone fears will happen but wishes it would not.

As an allegory, the story of the foundling girl employs a form that was clearly popular in storytelling, and earlier prophets were able to use it to good effect. We may compare the parable of the vineyard in Isaiah 5:1–7. The Hebrew word that describes such a speech form covers both short proverbial sayings and allegories of the kind we encounter here. It was later applied to the developed form of the parable. Such a teaching aid was to become of great value both to Jewish rabbis and to the message of Jesus.

So long and intricate is Ezekiel's allegory, with its interwoven themes, it seems almost certainly to have been written from the outset. Ezekiel frequently uses allegory. It suits his aim of creating pictures in the mind of the hearer, in order to affirm a truth and fix it in memory.

Metaphors, when developed, easily become allegories, and word pictures of childhood and marriage are readily expanded to images of faith. Accordingly, it is likely that the image of Jerusalem as a young woman was one that Ezekiel had applied in various ways in his teaching. To expand it into an allegory of Jerusalem's spiritual history was an easy step to take. Here it is shaped into a fully rounded and carefully worded story. It is something to pore over and read, pausing over details, with their hidden implications, rather than a short word picture to hold the hearer's attention.

The story itself is not complex. It is the tale of a foundling girl, left to die by her mother at birth but rescued and nurtured by a loving passerby. This unnamed stranger is God, who takes on the roles of adoptive parent and then husband. In this, as in many points, the allegorical form is rather stretched. However, instead of responding with love, loyalty, and gratitude to her benefactor and husband, the woman becomes persistently and deeply unfaithful.

The girl represents Jerusalem (vv. 2–3), whose long history and mixed ethnic origin—descended from Amorites and Hittites—is briefly alluded to. Woven into accusations of unfaithfulness, with their harshly described images of sexual abandon, are various historical allusions. Jerusalem has harbored false religions, has adapted her ways to those of her non-Israelite neighbors, has engaged in worthless political ties with Egypt and Assyria, and has, to crown her folly, surrendered her own children to be the sacrificial victims of alien lovers. The portrayal is one of unremitting moral corruption of an extreme kind, implying that there is nothing good about Jerusalem's history to report. Understandably, therefore, it goes on to announce that a fearful punishment will be imposed on the city, commensurate with the enormity of the offenses committed (vv. 35–43).

In order to intensify yet more strongly the accusations of Jerusalem's ill-considered and wanton behavior, the allegory expands into a comparison with the behavior of two other cities—Samaria and Sodom—who are portrayed as sisters to Jerusalem (vv. 46–52). Jerusalem is found to have behaved worse than either of them, even though, as Ezekiel well knew, Jerusalem was a very proud city and had grown up to look with deep loathing on the reputed sins of Sodom (vv. 49–50). At this point, the allegory form largely disappears. By his icy blast of accusation and unwelcome comparisons, Ezekiel strips away the last remnants of self-esteem and self-regard with which the citizens of Jerusalem sought to protect themselves.

It comes as all the greater surprise to find that, in its final part, the allegory turns to the future with an assured and unassailable hope (vv. 60–63). God will indeed restore the city and establish afresh his covenant with her. The sins of the past will be forgiven and even the two sisters, who have shown up Jerusalem's shame, will be given to her as daughters (v. 61). As in the story of the prodigal son in the New Testament (Luke 15:17–18), the moment arrives when the woman who grew up as a foundling child comes to her senses and sees her situation for what it really is.

From a purely artistic literary perspective, it is questionable whether Ezekiel's allegory works very well overall. This becomes evident early on, with the awkward adoptive father/husband identification. In several of the details that are recalled later, where different facets of Jerusalem's past misdemeanors are woven into the story, the form is broken in order to fit in the appropriate accusations. Yet, for all this literary awkwardness, it is a remarkably powerful castigation of Jerusalem's sins. The form has clearly been chosen in order to show up Jerusalem's conduct in terms that every normal person would feel to be utterly repulsive and inexcusable. It intends to shock. In consequence, once read, the chapter cannot easily be forgotten. It insists that Jerusalem has had a terrible past of shame, unfaithfulness, and senseless behavior, with which no normal person, with ordinary human feelings, would put up. The happy assurances for the future are therefore all the more unexpected. God's love and forgiveness are truly outstanding. They are the greatest surprise of all!

We may confine our reflections on Ezekiel's allegory to a few main points, partly psychological and partly historical. Clearly, from a psychological perspective, Ezekiel intends to shock his hearers and readers out of their bewilderment and out of the belief that Jerusalem's fate was undeserved. So it is no help whatsoever to suppose that this allegory was the consequence of some perverse power seeking on his part or the consequence of some hidden sexual repression. We can only recognize that he must have seen his hearers in the deepest distress over his message concerning Jerusalem's forthcoming doom. For them, it was the city of their dreams and the most wonderful place on earth. By exposing what the prophet saw as the shadow side of its history, he is seeking to make intelligible the disaster that was about to overtake the place. By stripping away any vestiges of traditional urban pride, he is focusing attention on the need for a rebirth of a more genuine spiritual pride. He wants faith and hope to be centered on God, not based on affection for a beautiful city. The Lord God made Jerusalem great. If this has been true in the past, it can also be true in the future.

The use of sexual images and metaphors appears crude and threatening to us and must certainly have appeared so to the book's first readers. Yet this too is a warning that the desire to hide from openly facing certain issues can be an evasion of real seriousness about personal and family responsibility. Ezekiel pulls skeletons out of every closet! There is, moreover, a further interesting feature to reflect upon. Ezekiel was a priest, by training and by instinct, so it is no surprise that much of his condemnation for his people's wrongdoings is expressed in priestly words and ideas. Idolatry and committing abomination are two of his most frequently used descriptive pictures of evil. Here, he abandons them and resorts instead to descriptions of behavior that no normal person could possibly condone. We could well understand that, at times in the past, his hearers had brushed aside his strictures by accusing him of being a priestly fanatic for whom nothing was ever wholly right.

Here, and again in chapter 23, Ezekiel comes down to the most fundamental of all human perceptions of right and wrong by drawing them from the most intimate personal sphere. It is as if he is determined to say that the sins he has been referring to as wrong are not merely superficial religious offenses, such as the breaking of some taboo or the evasion of some ritual duty. They are the most deeply wounding of all human hurts, all the more hurtful because they result from misguided religious zeal.

It would also be thoughtless to pass from this chapter without noting the light it brings to a number of significant historical issues. The portrayal of Jerusalem's origin from the Hittites and the Amorites is an informative recognition of the ancient and ethnically complex history of the city. Jerusalem indeed had its foundations established on the rise of a very ancient civilization in the Near East. We can put together a story of the city's origins stretching back well into the early second millennium B.C.

In its full range, this account would need to be carried much further back still, since Jerusalem had arisen on the platform of Near Eastern civilization reaching back at least two millennia before this. Yet, when it became the city of David (2 Sam. 5:9), the city was summoned to break with this history in order to make possible a new form of urban spiritual and moral life, based upon the tradition of a covenant with the Lord God. That Ezekiel castigated Jerusalem's failures is not surprising; it was no doubt justified when viewed from his perspective. Yet even these harsh condemnations are a part of his pursuit of the vision of the city of God, and this more positive and hopeful aspect is marvelously brought out in the later parts of his book. In fact, we must recognize that, out of the sense of Jerusalem's past failure and present catastrophe, there emerges, like a phoenix from its ashes, the vision of a new heavenly city. Nowhere else in the Old Testament is the unmerited and persistent love of God more emphatically asserted than here. Only the knowledge of this love makes the possibility of forgiveness credible.

It is important to take note of the extent to which Ezekiel's allegory draws particular attention to the vulnerability of women in ancient Israel. He assumes as widespread the cruel but often regrettably practiced offense of leaving an infant girl to die at birth, because families preferred boys. He takes for granted the degree of women's dependence on the masculine elements of society, fathers and husbands. To pursue this theme further, however, would require a more extensive discussion concerning the patriarchal structure of the biblical social world, a feature that is widely evident in the Old Testament. Ezekiel certainly appears to accept, if not especially to endorse, such attitudes, and it is certainly open to discussion whether his priestly upbringing may have further encouraged them.

AN ALLEGORY CONCERNING
JUDAH'S LAST KINGS
Ezekiel 17:1–24

17:1 **The word of the LORD came to me:** 2 **O mortal, propound a riddle, and speak an allegory to the house of Israel.** 3 **Say: Thus says the Lord GOD:**
    A great eagle . . .
      came to the Lebanon.
    He took the top of the cedar,
  4   **broke off its topmost shoot;**
    He carried it to a land of trade,
      set it in a city of merchants.
  5 **Then he took a seed from the land,**
      placed it in fertile soil. . . .
  6 **It sprouted and became a vine**
      spreading out, but low;
    Its branches turned toward him,
      its roots remained where it stood. . . .

  7 **There was another great eagle,**
      with great wings and much plumage
    And see! This vine stretched out its roots toward him;
    It shot out its branches toward him,
      so that he might water it. . . .
  9 **Say: Thus says the Lord GOD:**
      Will it prosper?

Will he not pull up its roots,
cause its fruit to rot and wither . . . ?
10b When the east wind strikes it,
will it not utterly wither,
wither on the bed where it grew?

11 Then the word of the LORD came to me: 12 Say now to the rebellious house: Do you not know what these things mean? Tell them: The king of Babylon came to Jerusalem, took its king and its officials, and brought them back with him to Babylon. 13 He took one of the royal offspring and made a covenant with him, putting him under oath (he had taken away the chief men of the land), 14 so that the kingdom might be humble and not lift itself up, and that by keeping his covenant it might stand. 15 But he rebelled against him by sending ambassadors to Egypt, in order that they might give him horses and a large army. . . . 16 As I live, says the Lord GOD, surely in the place where the king resides who made him king, whose oath he despised, and whose covenant with him he broke—in Babylon he shall die. 17 Pharaoh with his mighty army and great company will not help him in war, when ramps are cast up and siege-walls built to cut off many lives. 18 Because he despised the oath and broke the covenant, because he gave his hand and yet did all these things, he shall not escape. . . .

22 Thus says the LORD GOD:
I myself will take a sprig
from the lofty top of a cedar;
I will set it out.
I will break off a tender one
from the topmost of its young twigs;
I myself will plant it
on a high and lofty mountain
23 On the mountain height of Israel
I will plant it,
in order that it may produce boughs and bear fruit,
and become a noble cedar. . . .
24c I the LORD have spoken;
I will accomplish it.

Allegories can delay perception of the truth by hiding what is meant until the fictional story is complete; only then does the hearer recognize that the truth is unwelcome. The time taken to work out the implications of a fictional story and its application are sufficient to make the acceptance of its truth all the more startling and clear. This would seem to be the case here. Ezekiel has some political home truths to teach to his fellow exiles that will bring them a great deal of heart-searching and pain. They do not want to listen and so must be made to see that what the prophet is saying is inescapably true!

It is possible that a further influence is at work here, since this allegory reveals Ezekiel speaking out on a controversial political issue. It could have been that to have done so openly would have aroused suspicion and provoked retaliation from opponents in his camp, who would have reported him. The Babylonian authorities clearly kept a watchful eye on what was going on among the Judean exiles "by the river Chebar." By using allegory, Ezekiel could keep his teaching hidden from hostile ears.

The allegory proper concerns the fate of Judah's last kings and is to be found in the poetry of verses 1–10. An interpretation explaining precisely what the allegory means was added later in verses 11–21, much in the manner in which Gospel parables are interpreted (see Matt. 13:36–43). Then, at a stage when the book of the prophet's message was taking its final shape, a reapplication of the allegory was appended in verses 22–24. This reverses the threatening note implicit in the barrage of questions in verses 9–10 with which the original allegory concludes. The tragic end of the last Davidic king in Jerusalem had taken place by this time, and it had become necessary to update the message about the kingship in the light of later prophecies in the book.

"Politics and religion do not mix." We have heard it said many times and have recognized the dangers of too closely identifying spiritual goals with more short-term political ones. Yet it is impossible to separate the two, as the familiar adage might encourage, because political issues enter so directly into everyday living. So it was for Ezekiel's hearers, and it was true even more immediately for those who had stayed behind in Judah. Nowhere else do we hear the prophet touching so directly on issues of the contemporary political scene as we find here.

The allegory concerns the Davidic kingship reigning in Jerusalem and the manner in which this small kingdom has found itself torn between submitting to the imperial control of Babylon, which succeeded Assyria as Judah's imperial ruler, and Egypt. The "great eagle" of verse 3 is the Babylonian power, and the "topmost shoot" of the cedar that is broken off (v. 4) is the figure of Jehoiachin, the youthful king in Jerusalem who was deposed and taken to Babylon (the "land of trade").

Jehoiachin was replaced on the throne in Jerusalem by his uncle, Zedekiah, who is the "vine" of verse 6. For a time the vine fares well, by drawing strength from (that is, being politically compliant with) his Babylonian master (v. 6). However, the centerpiece of the allegory concerns the point that "there was another great eagle" (v. 7), by which the king of

Egypt is meant. In the hope of breaking free from the oppressive rule of Babylon, the vine turns to it hopefully (vv. 7–8). But will it work? The sequence of questions with which the allegory closes forces us to draw our own conclusions. "Will it not utterly wither?" (v. 10): The prophet's tone makes the doom-laden answer unmistakable.

The interpretation in verses 11–21 spells out the meaning of the allegory with no further room for doubt. The Jerusalem king Zedekiah was in a terrible dilemma, vainly trying to keep his oath of loyalty to Babylon, the power that put him on the throne, while secretly engaging in negotiations with Egypt (as well as with other of his neighboring rulers) to break free. The Egyptians were full of proud promises and seemingly had a powerful army with which to bolster up the weak forces of Judah. Yet, more than a century earlier, the representative of the Assyrian king had perceptively called Egypt "that broken reed of a staff" (2 Kings 18:21). Its many promises of assistance to Judah either failed to materialize or proved inadequate. It was not that prophets like Isaiah and Ezekiel—and Jeremiah, who adopted a similar line—were particularly anti-Egyptian or pro-Assyrian (Babylonian). They were simply more openly realistic and willing to learn truths from history, which their rulers apparently never did!

It seems likely, too, if we are to judge by Ezekiel's staunchly spiritual tone and that of all the other prophetic critics of Judah's politics, that they shared a genuine distrust of Judah's false assumptions about God's help. Consistently, these prophets had declared that bad political choices were being hidden behind a cloak of religious complacency. God was being used as Judah's insurance policy against failure, when clearly God had made no such commitment. When there was added to this the general confusion and disinterest in religious loyalty that most people displayed most of the time, the prophets were understandably incensed. The name of God was simply being used to provide a feel-good factor for policies and a way of life that was proving utterly disastrous. The voice of the prophet, even when it had to be veiled in the language of allegory, was the main hope of bringing home the truth about Judah's weak and threatened situation. No doubt many tried to be indifferent to such questions or pretended they no longer cared. Ezekiel's impassioned questions were aimed at forcing even these people to make up their minds. The voice of God would be heard, not in honeyed words of comfort but in bitter words of truth.

The concluding section in verses 22–24 is important for understanding the shape of the book as a whole. It was certainly added to the original allegory later, and its purpose is to affirm that, in the future, God will restore the line of Davidic kings to Jerusalem. This will take place through the figure or descendants of the exiled King Jehoiachin, who is the "sprig from the lofty top of a cedar" referred to, in allegorical guise, in verse 22.

It was clearly necessary, once the tragic events of the downfall of Zedekiah became a part of history (as we noted in respect to chapter 13), to look ahead. Here it is spelled out in the language of the allegory that the kingship will be restored through the youthful ruler who was taken into exile with Ezekiel. We need not pause further over this question. Regrettably, it was a future promise that did not ultimately materialize, but it needed to be thought about in regard to the many basic issues that affected the final collection of Ezekiel's prophecies. The question concerning the future political government of the new Israel was to become central.

Overall, we may learn from this intriguing allegory, with its metaphors of cedar and vine, that even the message of Ezekiel, who has often been thought of as the least political of the prophets, could not be indifferent to the issues that politics raised. Judah's and Jerusalem's fates were ultimately decided, not by a democratic vote of the people but by royal power vested in an individual, aided by a small elite group of advisers. However, it is not this fact but the reckless and foolhardy reasoning behind the king's political blunders that produced Ezekiel's outburst, expressing God's unrestrained anger. Hundreds of lives were lost and a beautiful city ruined, because of a ruler who fumbled the issues and relied on worthless counselors. Jeremiah tells us much the same story from closer to the royal house. The foundation of all policy making is well put in Ezekiel's memorable question: "Will it prosper?" (v. 9).

THE INDIVIDUAL'S FREEDOM
FOR REPENTANCE
Ezekiel 18:1–32

18:1 **The word of the LORD came to me:** [2] **What do you mean by repeating this proverb concerning the land of Israel, "The parents have eaten sour grapes, and the children's teeth are set on edge"?** [3] **As I live, says the Lord GOD, this proverb shall no more be used by you in Israel.** [4] **Know that all lives are mine; the life of the parent as well as the life of the child is mine: it is only the person who sins that shall die.**

[5] **If a man is righteous and does what is lawful and right . . . such a one is righteous; he shall surely live, says the Lord GOD.**

[10] **If he has a son who is violent, a shedder of blood,** [11] **who does any of**

these things (though his father does none of them), who eats upon the mountains, defiles his neighbor's wife. . . . shall he then live? He shall not. He has done all these abominable things. . . .

¹⁴ But if this man has a son who sees all the sins that his father has done, considers, and does not do likewise. . . he shall surely live. ¹⁸ As for his father, because he practiced extortion, robbed his brother, and did what is not good among his people, he dies for his iniquity.

¹⁹ Yet you say, "Why should not the son suffer for the iniquity of the father?" When the son has done what is lawful and right, and has been careful to observe all my statutes, he shall surely live. ²⁰ The person who sins shall die. A child shall not suffer for the iniquity of a parent, nor a parent suffer for the iniquity of a child; the righteousness of the righteous shall be his own, and the wickedness of the wicked shall be his own.

²¹ But if the wicked turn away from all their sins that they have committed and keep all my statutes and do what is lawful and right, they shall surely live; they shall not die. . . . ²³ Have I any pleasure in the death of the wicked, says the Lord GOD, and not rather that they should turn from their ways and live? . . .

²⁵ Yet you say, "The way of the Lord is unfair." Hear now, O house of Israel: Is my way unfair? Is it not your ways that are unfair? . . . Why will you die, O house of Israel? ³² For I have no pleasure in the death of anyone, says the Lord GOD. Turn, then, and live.

"It isn't fair!" How often we have heard that said, and how easily we have slipped into saying it ourselves. Part of the process of growing up is learning to accept the experiences and needs of others around us in family and school situations. We then come to recognize that it is impossible for everything in life to be fair. Learning to cope with this is learning to put up with the real world of varied trials and opportunities. Yet we feel that life should ultimately be fair to each one of us. So to say, "The way of the Lord is unfair" (v. 25) is one of the most serious charges we can place against God. The ways of God, who is perfectly righteous and good, should clearly be fair. We can see, therefore, that for Ezekiel's fellow exiles to come to him with the accusation that God was not being fair was no light matter.

But what did these exiles in Babylon feel was so wrong and so unfair? We do not know all the answers, but the context of this most important address from Ezekiel helps us to understand something of the circumstances. These were people, for the most part drawn from the better educated and wealthier classes of Jerusalem society, who had been taken as hostages to Babylon. Their hope and longing were that one day they would return to their former homes in Judah. But the story of Judah's further rebellion against Babylon, which the allegory in chapter 17 showed us, would clearly make all that impossible. These men and women felt their only chance for a better future had been recklessly thrown away by Zedekiah's disloyalty to Babylon. They were paying the price for the folly of others. Their own survival was now in jeopardy; in any event, there no longer was any proper homeland to which they could hope to return in the near future.

It was all very well for Ezekiel to criticize and pour scorn on the actions of the leaders in Judah, as he had been doing since his call to prophesy. But his audience by the river Chebar in their miserable exile, who were bound to suffer also, at least as much as those whose misfortunes in Judah he anticipated with such horrific detail, felt themselves to be innocent. No wonder they claimed that God was not being fair!

It is vital to recognize this background to Ezekiel's legalistically argued address in chapter 18. The central message is spelled out with passion in its closing words: "For I have no pleasure in the death of anyone, says the Lord GOD. Turn, then, and live" (v. 32). This is a gloriously free and unqualified call to repentance and a new beginning for every single individual. Here is the heart of God's great invitation. Up to this point the prophet has spoken extensively about the fate of whole communities—the city of Jerusalem, the house of Israel, the land of Israel. Yet in reality such communities, whether in the homeland or in exile, are made up of individuals. Is not the fate of such individuals wholly wrapped up in the fate of the groups to which they belong? Ezekiel brings a resounding "No!" to such an idea.

Against it, he uses all his powers of argument, learned by custom and by training as a priest, to show that God is fair and will treat each person on his or her own merits. It is a strongly worded and perhaps overemphasized claim for individual rights and responsibilities, but it makes sense in its context. Those who were with the prophet were driven to near despair because they were no longer in control of their lives. They felt they no longer had any future, through no fault of their own. They believed there could not be a new Israel once the temple they loved (and many had served) lay in ruins, when the land and homes they had owned were reduced to rubble. Against this despair, Ezekiel places God's concern with every single human life: The key to the future lies in the hearts and minds of individuals.

The form of the argument is complex and appears long-winded, since it concerns a hypothetical case of a good man whose son turns to evil but who, in turn, has a righteous son. The prophet argues that, because God is righteous, we are all judged individually on our merits. Yet even this would bring too rigid a judgment to deal with the complexities of real life. So the prophet carries his argument further and in so doing gets to the heart of the matter. Even the wicked can turn away from wrongdoing to begin a new life, following God's ways (vv. 21–22). Then such persons are judged for what they are, not for what they once were.

We could well be forgiven for thinking that this argument breaks up the network of human relationships and the continuities of human life into compartments that are too small and self-contained. Its force, however, is to insist that God provides a genuinely open future for each individual based on what that person really has become. We are neither prisoners of the past nor yet captive to the sins of others. To each, God makes an open appeal: "Turn, then, and live." Each individual life is a separate act of divine creation!

This address by Ezekiel has frequently been compared with the citation of the same popular saying about sour grapes in Jeremiah 31:29–30, with its remarkable sequel in the promise of the "new covenant," in which the law of God will be written on every individual human heart. These two prophets appear to bring to light a new sense of realism about individual life and its spiritual responsibilities. To some degree this is certainly the case, though we must be careful not to overwork the point.

Both prophets stood at the great turning point in Jewish history when the surviving part of the former nation of Israel collapsed and a significant element of the nation found itself living among Gentiles in foreign lands. The age of Jewish dispersion had begun. It was a vitally important development, therefore, to recognize that the Lord God of Israel was not simply a national god. The very title "God of Israel" had to acquire a new significance to take account of the fact that Jews could worship such a deity in foreign lands.

The sense of community, with all its manifold privileges and obligations, is one of the central features of the Bible. The Hebrew Bible is the book of Israel, whereas the New Testament is the book of the church. Yet between these two groups are many links and continuities. The outward shape of a community may change, since it cannot always remain a tribe, a kingdom, or a nation. Communities can have many different forms, since they are composed of individuals. What Ezekiel and Jeremiah were concerned to bring to the fore, in setting the foundations of the New Israel, was the freedom of choice that lies open to each individual. Each can make the decision to repent and find life—a new dimension of life—in which God will remain real and present, even though the familiar landmarks of the old nation of Israel have fallen down.

AN ALLEGORY
CONCERNING TWO LIONS
Ezekiel 19:1–14

19:1 As for you, raise up a lamentation for the princes of Israel, [2] and say:
      What a lioness was your mother among lions! . . .
    [3] She raised up one of her cubs;
      he became a young lion,
    and he learned to catch prey;
      he devoured humans.
    [4] The nations sounded an alarm against him;
      he was caught in their pit;
    and they brought him with hooks
      to the land of Egypt.
    [5] When she saw that she was thwarted,
      that her hope was lost,
    she took another of her cubs and made him a young lion.
    [6] He prowled among the lions;
      he became a young lion,
    and he learned to catch prey;
      he devoured people. . . .
    [8] The nations set upon him from the provinces all around;
    they spread their net over him;
      he was caught in their pit.
    [9] With hooks they put him in a cage,
      and brought him to the king of Babylon. . . .
    [10] Your mother was like a vine in a vineyard transplanted by the
        water,
    fruitful and full of branches from abundant water.
    [11] Its strongest stem became a ruler's scepter. . . .
    [12] But it was plucked up in fury,
      cast down to the ground . . .
    [14b] so that there remains in it no strong stem,
      no scepter for ruling.
  This is a lamentation, and it is used as a lamentation.

It is salutary to reflect that lions were at one time to be found in the Holy Land, especially in the lush terrain of the Jordan Valley. Villages and towns were terrorized by their presence, and pits were dug to trap them. Accordingly, an allegory of two young lions, both fierce and threatening, was meaningful for Ezekiel's contemporaries. The king of beasts provided a suitable symbol of royal power and authority. So the story of two lions, which threatened whole neighborhoods and had to be hunted and trapped, symbolizes the downfall of two powerful kings. Ezekiel's allegory of two lions, cubs of the same lioness, is a pictorial presentation of events concerning two of the last of Judah's royal house. Indirectly, it is also a reflection on their royal mother.

The first of the rulers symbolized in this fashion in Ezekiel 19:2–4 is easily identified by the fact that he was trapped and taken as a prisoner ("with hooks") to Egypt. He is Jehoahaz, who succeeded to the throne in Jerusalem after the death in battle of King Josiah in 609 B.C. He reigned for a mere three months (2 Kings 23:29–33), since he was removed from his throne by the Egyptian pharaoh Neco and replaced by his older brother Jehoiakim.

The second king is less readily identified, since there were two of Judah's last rulers who were taken as prisoners to Babylon (v. 9). The fate of Jehoiachin is reported in 2 Kings 24:15 and that of Zedekiah in 2 Kings 25:6–7; the content of the allegory makes it virtually certain that this latter king is the subject of Ezekiel's funeral dirge. Zedekiah was a brother to the ill-fated Jehoahaz, born from the same royal mother, whose name was Hamutal (2 Kings 24:18). She shows every sign of having exercised a significant role in Judah's political life during these tumultuous years, apparently becoming a dominant figure in palace affairs. The royal court of Jerusalem gave her the title of Queen Mother. Probably she was deeply involved in the intrigues and plots that marked the switches of loyalty between pro-Egyptian and pro-Babylonian policies.

Ezekiel's allegory gives us a brief glimpse into the complexities of palace life in Jerusalem, where the kings had many wives and many children and all the inevitable problems that this entailed regarding royal succession.

The deportation to Egypt of Jehoahaz had long since become history for the prophet, as had the circumstances that placed Zedekiah on the throne in Jerusalem. The significance of his allegory must therefore lie in what it has to say about the future of the second lion, whom we have identified as Zedekiah. At this time, Zedekiah was still on the throne in Jerusalem. The point lies in the assertion that, like his older brother, he too will end up in a foreign "pit," only this time it will be in Babylon.

This adds special meaning to the enigmatic final words of the chapter, which imply that a death has occurred and point out that the entire poem has the form of a funeral dirge. If this were intended as a reference to Zedekiah's death, we should be forced to draw the conclusion that this was a final comment added at a late stage, once this ruler's ignominious decease became a reality. However, it seems far more probable that this note was intended by the prophet to refer to the death of Hamutal. She had herself been taken to Babylon, along with others of the royal household (Jer. 29:2). The poem would then be concerned to demonstrate that this ambitious royal mother's plans had all come to grief. She had had the remarkable and probably unprecedented experience of seeing two of her sons elevated to the royal throne in Jerusalem. Since the poem opens by referring to her august and powerful reputation, we can conclude that Ezekiel's allegory was intended as an obituary for her and a warning to others regarding the dangers of excessive human ambitions.

To this allegory concerning the two lions has been added a further short parable in verses 10–12. Once again, the prophet uses the image of the vine that was applied to the royal house in chapter 17. This time the Queen Mother is the vine and the shoots are her royal princes who succeed to the throne. Again, Zedekiah is clearly the target of the prophet's threat and must be the "strongest stem" of the vine referred to in verse 11. Now the doom-laden final words declare that the vine now can produce "no scepter for ruling." It is a final verdict on the dashed hopes of so eminent a lady. There is no need to see in these words a prophetic refutation of hope for the future of the Davidic kingship. Rather, it declares only that this line cannot continue through Zedekiah, whose sons were soon to be killed before his eyes. We shall consider the larger question, concerning Ezekiel's hope for the future of Judah's kingship, in relation to the promises in chapters 36—37.

It is helpful to pause at the end of this chapter to reflect on the valuable light that shines on political life in Old Testament times. In essence, politics was kingship, since the king was popularly celebrated as a divine gift to the nation and was heralded as ruling by divine authority (Psalm 2, a form of coronation hymn, brings this out very clearly). Yet we find that the Old Testament literature is full of criticism of kings, and of kingship as an institution, as is firmly declared by Samuel (1 Sam. 8:11–18). Kings exceeded their authority by acting unrighteously so the ideal of kingship was never reached, even in such eminent figures as David and Solomon.

Nor can we believe that kings were all-powerful within their own households. When the need arose, palace plots and intrigues played a part in securing the succession of one among many royal princes. In Jerusalem,

Judah's commitment to the royal dynasty of David set narrower limits to royal succession than prevailed in the Northern Kingdom of Israel, where assassinations brought many changes of dynasty. Clearly, powerful families, strong administrators, and, not least, ambitious royal women all carried weight and influence that spread over into royal policy and patronage, as Ezekiel's singling out of the influence of one eminent Queen Mother illustrates. Note that while she herself comes in for no specific criticism, the prophet remarkably shows clearly that her ambitious plans for her sons brought both of them to an untimely death. Personal ambition is all very well, and maternal ambition can be fundamental to the strength of a family, yet, if pressed too far and too ruthlessly, it can lead to great grief.

6. Countdown to Catastrophe
Ezekiel 20:1–24:27

This section, beginning with chapter 20, starts with a date that locates it in the seventh year of exile (591 B.C.). It continues to 24:27, to the eve of the final catastrophe of the downfall of Judah and the destruction of Jerusalem. It is a veritable countdown to disaster. The climactic story of Judah's last days is proclaimed in brief forewarnings, sometimes so brief as scarcely to constitute whole prophecies, declaring how fearsome and terrifying a disaster it will be. What a day of judgment will fall on Judah, its kingly head, and its tormented population! Ezekiel's prophetic forewarnings spare his hearers none of the soul-searing details.

The section opens with a review of the nation's history from its beginning in the land of Egypt when Moses served as the leader who gave them birth as a nation under the rule of God. It concludes with a painful disaster for Ezekiel himself, the death of his wife. Yet even this most personal of tragedies is subsumed under the desire to make clear what God is about to do to the city and its temple, which has been the delight and joy of an entire people.

In between the first address, which lends perspective to the story of judgment that is shortly to unfold by showing that it has become inevitable, and the prophet's personal loss, we have a series of kaleidoscopic images. They commence with a sword song, much as a power-drunk soldier would sing while swinging his blade and boasting of its death-dealing power; they end with women singing songs as they prepare a meal in a giant cooking pot. But it is no meal they are preparing, for the pot is a symbol of Jerusalem, whose citizens are shortly to be handed over to death. The sequence of short scenes enables the prophet to emphasize, and then reemphasize, the message he has already spelled out for his hearers. Now, however, there is little further need to answer the question "Why?" Answers have already been given by the prophet in terms of Israel's long history of idolatry.

Then, as if the message has not already sunk sufficiently deep into the minds of his hearers, the whole story of national unfaithfulness is reasserted in chapter 23 in a parable of two evil sisters. Wrongs and unreasonable behavior, so offensive that it is embarrassing to mention its many forms in normal human society, are described in accusation against Judah and Jerusalem. The prophet shows himself uncompromisingly determined to draw aside the curtain over the shadow side of Israel's past. In pointing his accusing finger at all he now brings into the light of day, he appears to dare his hearers and readers to protest again that God has not been fair in bringing them to judgment!

LEARNING THE LESSONS
OF HISTORY
Ezekiel 20:1–44

20:1 In the seventh year, in the fifth month, on the tenth day of the month, certain elders of Israel came to consult the LORD, and sat down before me. ² And the word of the LORD came to me: ³ Mortal, speak to the elders of Israel, and say to them: Thus says the Lord GOD: Why are you coming? To consult me? As I live, says the Lord GOD, I will not be consulted by you. ⁴ Will you judge them, mortal, will you judge them? Then let them know the abominations of their ancestors. . . . ⁷ And I said to them, Cast away the detestable things your eyes feast on, every one of you, and do not defile yourselves with the idols of Egypt; I am the LORD your God. ⁸ But they rebelled against me and would not listen to me. . . .

Then I thought I would pour out my wrath upon them and spend my anger against them in the midst of the land of Egypt. ⁹ But I acted for the sake of my name, that it should not be profaned in the sight of the nations among whom they lived, in whose sight I made myself known to them in bringing them out of the land of Egypt. ¹⁰ So I led them out of the land of Egypt and brought them into the wilderness. ¹¹ I gave them my statutes and showed them my ordinances, by whose observance everyone shall live. ¹² Moreover I gave them my sabbaths, as a sign between me and them, so that they might know that I the LORD sanctify them. ¹³ But the house of Israel rebelled against me in the wilderness; they did not observe my statutes but rejected my ordinances, by whose observance everyone shall live; and my sabbaths they greatly profaned.

Then I thought I would pour out my wrath upon them in the wilderness, to make an end of them. ¹⁴ But I acted for the sake of my name, so that it should not be profaned in the sight of the nations, in whose sight I had brought them out. . . .

[18] I said to their children in the wilderness, Do not follow the statutes of your parents, nor observe their ordinances, nor defile yourselves with their idols. . . . [21] But the children rebelled against me; they did not follow my statutes, and were not careful to observe my ordinances, by whose observance everyone shall live; they profaned my sabbaths.

Then I thought I would pour out my wrath upon them and spend my anger against them in the wilderness. [22] But I withheld my hand, and acted for the sake of my name, so that it should not be profaned in the sight of the nations. . . . [25] Moreover I gave them statutes that were not good and ordinances by which they could not live. [26] I defiled them through their very gifts, in their offering up all their firstborn, in order that I might horrify them, so that they might know that I am the LORD.

[27] Therefore, mortal, speak to the house of Israel and say to them, Thus says the Lord GOD: In this again your ancestors blasphemed me, by dealing treacherously with me. [28] For when I had brought them into the land that I swore to give them, then wherever they saw any high hill or any leafy tree, there they offered their sacrifices and presented the provocation of their offering. . . .

[32] What is in your mind shall never happen—the thought, "Let us be like the nations, like the tribes of the countries, and worship wood and stone."

[33] As I live, says the Lord GOD, surely with a mighty hand and an outstretched arm, and with wrath poured out, I will be king over you. [34] I will bring you out from the peoples and gather you out of the countries where you are scattered, with a mighty hand and an outstretched arm, and with wrath poured out; [35] and I will bring you into the wilderness of the peoples, and there I will enter into judgment with you face to face. . . . [44] And you shall know that I am the LORD, when I deal with you for my name's sake, not according to your evil ways, or corrupt deeds, O house of Israel, says the Lord GOD.

We can imagine that Ezekiel commanded great respect among his people in their Babylonian exile, but it was a respect combined with fear and more than a hint of distrust. Once again (as earlier, in chapter 14), the elders of Israel in exile come to the prophet asking for guidance from God, and once again he sends them away with a sharp refusal to inquire of God on their behalf and with a stinging rebuff for their idolatry. Clearly, they believe he truly speaks the word of God. At the same time, they must have felt exceedingly uncomfortable with his rebukes. Again, we do not know precisely why the elders seek advice and divine guidance. Nevertheless, it is striking that Ezekiel 20:1 reveals that the prophet kept a precise note of the day and year that the elders came. He has maintained his familiar priestly habit of careful timekeeping even during the privations of exile.

The year is probably significant; it is 591 B.C. We know that by this time King Zedekiah in Judah is deeply embroiled in planning a rebellion against the king of Babylon—a fact already directly referred to in chapter 17. Judah's reckless act of political disloyalty is in the air, and the future of those who were hostages in Babylon is clearly becoming very uncertain. This uncertainty may have been troubling the elders when they came to Ezekiel. Or their visit may be linked to the upsurge of prophets (like those mentioned in Jer. 29:9) who have been giving assurances that the hostages taken to Babylon will shortly be returning to their homeland.

The reply that Ezekiel gives to this request for divine guidance is found in verses 3–31. A sharp and far-reaching rebuke, it starts with the assertion that from its very beginnings Israel has been a nation of idolators and ends (v. 31) with a sharp refusal on God's part to provide any answer to the elders. To this there has been added a further reflection in verses 32–44, which look at the consequences of this verdict in regard to Israel's idolatry. In the light of Israel's punishment, it considers what will be the outcome of the period spent in exile. This certainly answers the question of the elders, which may have been something like "What is to become of us here in Babylon?" A guarded but ultimately hopeful response, it promises that Israel will one day return to its homeland, "the mountain height of Israel" (v. 40, contrasting the land of Judah with the dreary flatness of their exilic abode "by the river Chebar"). Whether it was the prophet himself who made this addition when writing down his prophecies, or whether it was his followers, is hardly important.

The charge that Israel's ancestors were wanton in their disobedience to God focuses on three periods of Israel's past history: the time spent as slaves in Egypt (vv. 5–9), the time spent in the wilderness (vv. 10–26), and the time after the nation had entered and settled in the land of Canaan (vv. 27–31). In each of these periods, the accusation is made that Israel's ancestors disobeyed God's commandments. First, in Egypt, they did not forsake the idols of Egypt (v. 8). Second, in the wilderness, they did not observe the sabbath (vv. 12–13). Third, in the land, they offered false sacrifices, including most horrendously the sacrifice of their own children (v. 31). Bad led to worse and eventually to the worst of all inhuman behavior!

Ezekiel demonstrates a consistent pattern, showing God's beneficent action followed by Israel's response of disloyalty and idolatry. God then determines that punishment is necessary but suspends any action to bring this about. The prophet's implication is clearly that all these times of long-withheld judgment can be prolonged no further and punishment must now come.

Ezekiel is painting a stark and deeply wounding picture of his nation's past, singling out events that undoubtedly happened but making them appear to be the whole story. His message deliberately reverses the popular image of Israel's past that the people have built up for themselves. It is not a story of glorious heroics and achievements but of shame and cruelty beyond measure. Of all the brief summaries of Israel's history—often referred to as a "history of salvation"—this is the starkest and most uncompromisingly replete with accusations of sin. It spiritual theme, although less explicit in its detail, is echoed in Psalm 106.

Why does Ezekiel feel it is important to give so negative a response to the well-meant request from the elders for divine guidance? Why does he retell the story of his nation's past in such a negative manner? It is obvious that he intends to shock and alarm his hearers. Once the initial crisis point has passed, however, the addition of verses 32–44 shows that a more balanced and forward-looking perspective becomes necessary.

We can only answer these questions by rethinking the situation that both the prophet and the elders of Israel were facing. They were, each in their own way, guardians of a great tradition. The elders were instructors in the story of how God had founded the nation of Israel, how the sacred Mount Zion had been chosen as the location for a temple, and how God had providentially watched over the nation's destiny. Yet now most of Jerusalem was in ruins and its surviving features were also soon to be destroyed. Israel was being brought down to point zero. It seemed incredible that God could let this happen. Ezekiel's message, however, seeks to make this event credible by drawing from his knowledge of his people's past all those shameful features they had hidden away. He is opening the door to the secret closet of guilt that the conventions of public life had firmly closed. He is telling a story that is true but that others dare not tell!

Of course, it was not the whole truth, and it was not a way of thinking about the past with which his hearers would be familiar. Yet at this point in Israel's history, it was a necessary basis for thought and reflection. To a people who grew up with the belief that they had been specially chosen and specially favored by God, it came as unwelcome news that they, too, had their guilt and shame. They had to come to terms with the realization that they shared in the sin and evil that was widespread in the world around them. Spiritual pride had made them contemptuous of their Gentile neighbors, but they were not themselves as innocent as they liked to believe. They too had many things to confess, and only by such confession could they find the road to repentance and a new future. Ezekiel's reversal of the conventional triumphalist tone of describing his people's religious past is necessary and even salutary. Israel's history was not all triumph and achievement. It was tarnished with evil, mistakes that needed also to be taken into the national reckoning. It was a sacred story of divine grace, but it was also an all-too-human story of idolatry leading to guilt and cruelty. The past had to be seen as a challenge to repentance, not a call to self-congratulation.

The enlarged perspective, given in verses 32–44, on the meaning of contemporary events for the elders of Israel provides the basis for an answer to their questioning. It clearly takes into its reckoning a knowledge that by this time Jerusalem has fallen and Judah is a nation no more. The present, too, painful as it is with its prospect of a prolonged period of exile, has a part in God's purpose, since it is a time of testing and cleansing. It will be a new wilderness experience (vv. 36–39), which will lead to purging and cleansing; when that is past, there can be a return to the land and a new beginning as a nation (vv. 40–44). The message is clear enough, even though it is clothed in Ezekiel's typical emphasis on the absolute sovereignty of God.

One feature is especially worthy of consideration. It is to be found in the opening challenge of verse 32: Israel can never be "like the nations" and worship wooden and stone images. The prophet appears to read the minds of his hearers, sensing the thoughts of those who retaliated against his somber accusations with the despairing response, "Let us forget about being the people of God." It cannot be, since in God's gracious purpose the power of the divine calling cannot be abandoned as though it were of no consequence. The vision of God, once truly seen, cannot be forgotten.

THE MAKER OF ALLEGORIES
Ezekiel 20:45–49

20:45 **The word of the LORD came to me:** [46] **Mortal, set your face toward the south, preach against the south, and prophesy against the forest land in the Negeb;** [47] **say to the forest of the Negeb, Hear the word of the LORD: Thus says the Lord GOD, I will kindle a fire in you, and it shall devour every green tree in you and every dry tree; the blazing flame shall not be quenched, and all faces from south to north shall be scorched by it.** [48] **All flesh shall see that I the LORD have kindled it; it shall not be quenched.** [49] **Then I said, "Ah Lord GOD! they are saying to me, 'Is he not a maker of allegories?'"**

The short section made up of verses 45–49 provides an interesting insight into Ezekiel's typical preaching and the way in which his hearers reacted to him. In this case, "the south" and "the forest land in the Negeb" must refer to what lay to the south of the place of exile in Babylon, rather than to the region of the Negeb in the south of Judah, which is not forested. The distinction is important because it reflects an awareness of the very flat marshland to which the exiles were taken and the forested mountainous region of Syria that lay between them and their former homeland. The instruction "set your face toward" must indicate that Ezekiel took up a fixed pose when delivering some of his prophecies, a strange mannerism but linked to his intention of projecting his words in the direction of the territory that would be most affected by what he declared. His words were weapons of power.

The message is clear-cut but terrifying. Fire would consume both the dried-out woodland, ready for burning, and the rich, fresh green trees and bushes. This was no ordinary blaze but a major disaster! The metaphor of the burning of both dry and green trees as a picture of God's punitive judgment was to become a familiar one; its use later by Jesus in the New Testament (Luke 23:31) may contain a deliberate echoing of the passage here. The meaning has a sensitive religious side: God's judgment, when it comes, does not make fine distinctions between those who are ready for it and those who are not. This point is picked up in the chapter that immediately follows: The punitive disaster that is to fall upon the people will affect "both righteous and wicked" (21:3).

THE SWORD OVER JERUSALEM
Ezekiel 21:1–32

> 21:1 The word of the LORD came to me: 2 Mortal, set your face toward Jerusalem and preach against the sanctuaries; prophesy against the land of Israel 3 and say to the land of Israel, Thus says the LORD: I am coming against you, and will draw my sword out of its sheath, and will cut off from you both righteous and wicked. . . . 6 Moan therefore, mortal; moan with breaking heart and bitter grief before their eyes. 7 And when they say to you, "Why do you moan?" you shall say, "Because of the news that has come. Every heart will melt and all hands will be feeble, every spirit will faint and all knees will turn to water. See, it comes and it will be fulfilled," says the Lord GOD.
>
> 8 And the word of the LORD came to me: 9 Mortal, prophesy and say: Thus says the Lord; Say:
>
> A sword, a sword is sharpened,
>   it is also polished;
> 10 It is sharpened for slaughter,

honed to flash like lightning! . . .
12 Cry and wail, O mortal,
     for it is against my people;
   it is against all Israel's princes;
       they are thrown to the sword,
       together with my people.
       Ah! Strike the thigh! . . .
14 And you, mortal, prophesy;
     Strike hand to hand,
   Let the sword fall twice, thrice;
       it is a sword for killing.
   A sword for great slaughter—
       it surrounds them. . . .

18 The word of the LORD came to me: 19 Mortal, mark out two roads for the sword of the king of Babylon to come. . . . And . . . 20 mark out the road for the sword to come to Rabbah of the Ammonites or to Judah and to Jerusalem the fortified. 21 For the king of Babylon stands at the parting of the way, at the fork in the two roads, to use divination; he shakes the arrows, he consults the teraphim, he inspects the liver. 22 Into his right hand comes the lot for Jerusalem . . . to set battering rams against the gates, to cast up ramps, to build siege-towers. . . .

25 As for you, vile, wicked prince of Israel,
       you whose day has come,
       the time of final punishment,
26 thus says the Lord GOD:
   Remove the turban, take off the crown;
       things shall not remain as they are. . . .
27b Until he comes whose right it is;
       to him I will give it.

28 As for you, mortal, prophesy, and say, Thus says the Lord GOD concerning the Ammonites, and concerning their reproach; say:
   A sword, a sword! Drawn for slaughter
       Polished to consume, to flash like lightning. . . .
31 I will pour out my indignation upon you,
       with the fire of my wrath
       I will blow upon you. . . .
32b You shall be remembered no more,
       for I the LORD have spoken.

Ezekiel 21 continues the countdown to catastrophe centering on the final defeat of the besieged city of Jerusalem by the attacking Babylonian forces in 587 B.C. The prophet presents a series of short scenes, not unlike those of a movie, indicating the various steps leading up to the siege of Jerusalem and anticipating the fearful carnage that will follow once the city's defenses collapse. The short episodes are aimed at striking a painful chord of fear and alarm in the minds of the prophet's hearers as they are led to imagine the doom awaiting their compatriots. Each one is skillfully chosen, and each, in its own way, manages to draw out some specific feature of the pain and suffering that will be inflicted and that the prophet now sees to be inevitable. No wonder we sense that he was almost choking with rage and recrimination when he reported to his audience the news of King Zedekiah's act of treachery in breaking his oath of allegiance to the king of Babylon (17:7–10).

That act of political recklessness destroyed the remnant of the nation left in Jerusalem; it placed in jeopardy the future of those who had earlier been taken with the prophet to Babylon; not least, it sealed the fate of the king and the royal family. What remains now is the inevitable series of consequences that God foretold through the prophet. What Ezekiel does is to paint word pictures, each of them filled with a measure of grief-laden inescapability. Decisions have been taken that the prophet condemned, and policies have been espoused that he opposed. All that is left for him to do at this stage is to drive home an awareness of the consequences of what has been determined. Once the fuse has been lit, the explosion cannot be avoided.

The first of the prophet's word pictures, in 21:1–7, is of God unsheathing a sword and wielding it menacingly over Jerusalem. This is the bragging action a youthful soldier might take. Pleased and excited with the power of his sword as it sparkles and catches the sunlight, anxious to show it off, he brandishes it to prove his own strength and authority. The pitiable victims of this act of bravado can only moan and grieve in horror at their helplessness (vv. 6–7). It is a terrible image, at first reading a seemingly unsuitable picture of God's action. But it is nevertheless a truly prophetic way of pressing home the awareness that human choices do have real and often terrible consequences. It would be foolish to interpret this to mean that God wills the terrible slaughter that is depicted, since Ezekiel's entire message is focused on a condemnation of the human decisions that led up to it. What these sword songs make plain is that, once the fateful decisions have been made, there will be no sudden divine rescue operation to keep a further and even more disastrous tragedy from befalling Jerusalem and its hapless citizens.

God cannot be expected to intervene and stop the show that these people have planned, as soon as they begin to get hurt. By choosing to take on the might of Babylon yet again, King Zedekiah (who is called "wicked prince" in v. 25) has chosen a policy that from the outset had only the slenderest chance of success. Jeremiah shows us how weak-willed and uncertain the king has been and how easily he has allowed others to make up his mind for him (Jer. 37:1–21). Now he has to pay the price of his folly, and, most tragic for all concerned, many others will be brought down in his fall. They too will be paying the price of this royal foolhardiness.

This point seems to have most got to the prophet's heart to lie at the center of this, the first of his terrifying sword songs. The sword will cut off "both righteous and wicked" (v. 3). There is a realism here that seems inevitably to stand in tension with what the prophet has earlier taught about the way in which God recognizes and respects individual responsibility (chapter 18). Yet this can never be the whole truth, for every human being is caught up in a larger world of events. Here it is openly admitted that those who deserve punishment will suffer, along with the righteous, who clearly do not!

The fact of this unresolvable tension must not lead us into ignoring either aspect of truth. Human individuality is real and creates a genuine measure of freedom, but this does not mean that each person is an island. The prophet himself does not resolve these tensions for us. Rather, he maintains a genuine realism and honesty. Many of those who die in battle are not guilty of having sought it or wanted it. They are innocent victims of other people's ambition and folly.

Once battle commences, no distinction is made between those who deserve to die and those who do not, not even between soldiers and civilians. Ezekiel is certainly realistic in recognizing that the latter are often the major victims of war. Earlier, Ezekiel's imagined picture of judgment falling on Jerusalem had indicated that some would be spared because they had upon their foreheads a special mark placed there by God's messengers (9:4–5). Why they were given this mark is never stated, and since the merciless killing is to affect old and young, women and children, it is clearly not based on any simple calculation of what is deserved. We must accept it as a reflection of the prophet's honest recognition that, once warfare is unleashed, a terrible arbitrariness of life and death comes into play. There is little moral accountability; every attempt to humanize the so-called rules of war has failed miserably.

All we can say is that, by its acceptance of the terrible injustice of war, the prophet's sword song pays full attention to its reality. War may appear to be a great adventure for the brave, but it is inevitably a cruel misfortune for the innocent ones who are also caught up in its horrors. So Ezekiel, who, with Jeremiah, has come down to us as a prophet who most strongly emphasizes individual responsibility, sets this in a realistic context. Communities too are involved in individual choices, and innocent and guilty alike will suffer in the aftermath of bad decisions.

The prophet seems to have a whole catalog of menacing sword songs, for we have two more in 21:8–17. The first, in verses 8–12, appears to be the song of an armorer sharpening a sword for battle. Or perhaps it is simply yet another vivid portrait of a young soldier, anxious to ensure that his weapon is in the utmost readiness. The poor-quality metals of antiquity must have required much attention and careful polishing to keep the swords made from them in fine condition. Nothing can have been more central to a soldier's thinking than his pride in the weapon that could ensure life to him and death to his enemies. So the boastful raising of a sword, flashing in the sunlight like a stroke of lightning, brings a sense of power and reassurance on the eve of battle. But what is one person's boast of strength is the victim's scream of grief and pain as the sword brings death (v. 12). So the prophet's poetic imagination brings home the full terror of war.

Once again Ezekiel has not spared his hearers a sense of pain and hurt in forcing them to consider what must shortly happen to their fellows in Jerusalem, many of whom would have been known personally by name to those in Babylon. It is not for him to hide the truth about war from his hearers by refusing to show the corpses or by suggesting that only nameless enemies will suffer misfortune. He wants people to face the truth, and he does so by taking down the screen of social censorship. He is forcing his hearers and readers to imagine for themselves the events they are talking about, forcing them to remove the cushioning effect of distance. These terrible sword songs, which tax the translator's skill with their brevity and poetic vigor, are nonetheless part of the necessary function of God's word of prophecy. With their poetic skill they bridge the gulf between the theoretical discussion of policies and strategies about war to drive home the human reality of its effects. It is prophets like Jeremiah and Ezekiel who disprove the assumption that the Old Testament should be regarded as a barbarous warmongering work. Israel has suffered too many wars for that to be the case.

Verses 14–17 of chapter 21 proceed to the third of the prophet's sword songs, the presence of which, in a book of prophetic hope, suggests that Ezekiel knew something of the brash military showmanship that has accompanied all armies from early times. He seeks to turn it all around to alert new feelings in his hearers, to highlight the power of the sword from the point of view of its victims. All such mock celebration can only be the artistry of death and suffering. The message the song conveys is all the more terrible because of its stark simplicity. There is no pageantry of battle, only the sad lifting up of the victims of war and the carrying of their corpses into common graves.

If we look ahead to the end of the chapter we have yet another of these terrifying prophecies of doom in the form of a sword song (vv. 28–32), presented with equally great poetic artistry. This time it is not Judah and Jerusalem but the people of Ammon (now chiefly part of Jordan) who are the sword's victims. Here was a people caught up in the same act of rebellion against Babylon that was the fateful policy of King Zedekiah of Judah. The punishment that befalls Judah comes in similar fashion, and only weeks later, to Ammon also. This time, the verdict of destruction is presented with even greater finality, since the very memory of the Ammonite people is threatened with extinction (v. 32).

In between these sword songs, we have a further glimpse into the ancient art of warfare and all its strange accompaniments and pretensions. In 21:18–23, we are given a word picture of the whole military procession of Babylonian power halting in its march to put down the rebellious faction in Jerusalem and Rabbah, the Ammonite capital. In ancient times prophets accompanied all armies, both to encourage the warriors by inspiring them to bold action in the name of their gods and to offer guidance. In this instance the latter situation is envisaged. Ezekiel pictures the king of Babylon leading his forces south to march against Judah and Ammon. On arrival at the fork in the roads where the decision has to be made about which rebel power to tackle first, the king calls on his priests and diviners. They shake arrows out of a quiver to signify a direction; images of deities are asked for guidance (the teraphim of v. 21); even the livers (or clay representations of them) of sacrificed animals are inspected for signs of divine approval and guidance.

Verse 22 then tells us the fateful news: Jerusalem will be dealt with first; on the next day, the armies will set out and march toward Judah's beloved capital city. Ammon must wait till afterward before it too is forced to feel the cruel might of Babylon crushing its rebel will. In a remarkable piece of irony, Ezekiel points out in verse 23 that Judah also was trusting in divine guidance and protection. The gods of Babylon appear as nothing to them. Yet in betraying his solemn oath of loyalty sworn to the king of Babylon, the king of Judah has abandoned his trust in God and cannot now rely on divine support. The very means of divination, which were prohibited in Judah and ridiculed as of no real value, become part of the techniques bringing about their downfall. All the familiar military weapons for the implementation of a siege (v. 22) will then be used against them.

Ezekiel's touches of irony often appear to us cruel and harsh, yet beneath them we can feel his righteous anger and holy indignation. People who have betrayed their oaths, sworn solemnly before God, cannot then pour contempt on the deities and rituals of Babylon that they despise. Had not King Zedekiah despised God by what he had done?

The question of the central figure who stands behind the actions of Judah that brought on the conflict is raised in verses 25–27. It is a short piece, highlighting the fact that the day of judgment is about to come for the ruler in Judah—King Zedekiah, the "wicked prince" of verse 25. There is a note of poignancy in the prophet's cry in verse 26: "Things shall not remain as they are." Sadly, we know all too little of the conflicts of policy and interest that served to shape events in Judah. It becomes clear, both from Ezekiel's prophecies and more fully from Jeremiah's, that opinions were divided over whether to continue in submission to Babylon. Whichever way the decision went, a price had to be paid. Both prophets, however, are convinced that the wrong decision was made and that behind it lay false expectations of God, bolstered by an ill-judged national pride. It is not surprising therefore that here again, set amid prophecies of a rather different kind, the prophet raises an accusing finger to point to the prince (Ezekiel withholds the title of "king" from Zedekiah) on whom the prime responsibility rests.

There is an interesting if easily overlooked note, almost certainly added by an editor, in verse 27: "Until he comes whose right it is; to him I will give it." This is a reference back to the ancient promise of Genesis 49:10 concerning the eminence of the tribe of Judah and the role of the kingship of the Davidic dynasty that it would bring. This short echo of the historic prophetic saying gives assurance that, in spite of Zedekiah's folly and consequent downfall, the divine promise of authority to the house of David will not be forgotten or allowed to fail.

These four passionate prophecies, cast in the form of poems to the power of the sword, serve a unique purpose in the book of Ezekiel. Under the guise of celebrating the power of the sword, they condemn its ruthless, death-dealing effect.

The prophet seems deliberately to have mimicked the boastful songs of soldiers, displaying their skills with bravado and expressing confidence that they will bring death to others, not suffer it themselves. Only literary insensitivity, however, could lead us to suppose that Ezekiel relishes this power or wishes to suggest that God has planned it all. Rather, it is the cries of the victims that sound the loudest and rivet the attention of the reader. Undoubtedly the Old Testament contains a great deal about the warfare of antiquity. Yet to suppose this is done in a crudely militaristic fashion, or to condone war, is wholly mistaken. Only at the very margins of this literature can this be noted. War was part of the tragic and sometimes seemingly inexplicable realities of life. Its hurt, its cruel arbitrariness, and its boasts of power and pageantry are all recognized. Yet, at its heart, there is a terrible pain, and it is the prophet's earnest desire to let this cry of pain be heard. Only by tearing down the screens by which his hearers try to hide their eyes from the truth of what is soon to happen to Judah can Ezekiel make it plain just how serious his message is. There can be no more absurd rebuttal of what he has to say than to dismiss him as a "maker of allegories" (20:49)—an artist with words that have no real purpose other than to entertain.

THE GUILTY CITY
Ezekiel 22:1–31

22:1 The word of the LORD came to me: 2 You, mortal, will you judge, will you judge the bloody city? Then declare to it all its abominable deeds. 3 You shall say, Thus says the Lord GOD: A city! Shedding blood within itself; its time has come; making its idols, defiling itself. 4 You have become guilty by the blood that you have shed, and defiled by the idols that you have made. . . . Therefore I have made you a disgrace before the nations, and a mockery to all the countries. . . .

6 The princes of Israel in you, everyone according to his power, have been bent on shedding blood. 7 Father and mother are treated with contempt in you; the alien residing within you suffers extortion; the orphan and the widow are wronged in you. 8 You have despised my holy things, and profaned my sabbaths. 9 In you are those who slander to shed blood, those in you who eat upon the mountains, who commit lewdness in your midst. 10 In you they uncover their fathers' nakedness; in you they violate women in their menstrual periods. 11 One commits abomination with his neighbor's wife; another lewdly defiles his daughter-in-law; another in you defiles his sister, his father's daughter. 12 In you, they take bribes to shed blood; you take both advance interest and accrued interest, and make gain of your neighbors by extortion; and you have forgotten me, says the Lord GOD. . . . 15 I will scatter you among the nations and disperse you through the countries, and I will purge your filthiness out of you. . . .

17 The word of the LORD came to me: 18 Mortal, the house of Israel has become dross to me; all of them, silver, bronze, tin, iron, and lead. In the smelter they have become dross. . . . 20 As one gathers silver, bronze, iron, lead, and tin into a smelter, to blow the fire upon them in order to melt

them; so I will gather you in my anger and in my wrath, and I will put you in and melt you. . . .

[23] The word of the LORD came to me: [24] Mortal, say to it: You are a land that is not cleansed, not rained upon in the day of indignation. [25] Its princes within it are like a roaring lion tearing the prey; they have devoured human lives; they have taken treasure and precious things; they have made many widows within it. [26] Its priests have done violence to my teaching and have profaned my holy things. . . . [27] Its officials within it are like wolves tearing the prey, shedding blood, destroying lives to get dishonest gain. [28] Its prophets have smeared whitewash on their behalf, seeing false visions and divining lies for them, saying, "Thus says the Lord GOD," when the LORD has not spoken. [29] The people of the land have practiced extortion and committed robbery; they have oppressed the poor and needy, and have extorted from the alien without redress. [30] And I sought for anyone among them who would repair the wall and stand in the breach before me on behalf of the land, so that I would not destroy it; but I found no one. [31] Therefore I have poured out my indignation upon them; I have consumed them with the fire of my wrath; I have returned their conduct upon their heads, says the Lord GOD.

The countdown to the hour when disaster will befall Jerusalem continues in earnest. Ezekiel 22 consists of three separate prophecies with, nevertheless, a central theme: The guilt attaching to Jerusalem has made its punishment inevitable.

The first prophecy, in 22:1–16, sets the general tone. The form is wholly in line with similar prophecies in Isaiah and Jeremiah. Jerusalem is a guilty city, and in order to convince those who find such an accusation to be unwelcome and unbelievable, the prophet presents a catalog of the offenses that have been committed and merit punishment.

The opening lines are fearful enough (vv. 2–5), accusing Jerusalem of being a city full of violence of many kinds (shedding blood is the crime explicitly mentioned, but this can be taken to indicate not simply crimes of murder but a general state of misrule and violent behavior). This social wrong is linked to the making of idols (vv. 3–4), bringing home to us yet again Ezekiel's intense feeling that behind evil behavior lies a deep failure of religious understanding. For him, the making of idols symbolized a way of life in which religious devotion was maintained but was separated from any idea of respect for one's neighbor or for human life generally. Idolatry was pursued as a way of using religious power for one's own benefit and self-preservation, without regard for law and honesty. It was seeking to get things from the gods, without regard for a God-ordered way of life. In short, it was the age-old pursuit of a religion that is "beyond good and evil" and has nothing to do with ideas of right and wrong.

The question of how Jerusalem and Judah appear in the eyes of other nations is seldom far from Ezekiel's reckoning. So we find that the accusation of Jerusalem's violent reputation is raised again when the city is described as "a disgrace before the nations" (v. 4). There is a twofold significance to this: In the first instance the evil reputation of the city brings shame upon it. More especially, however, the prophet insists that God has brought the city into disgrace on account of the ruin that is shortly to overtake it. It cannot offer security, the very thing that cities were designed to bring.

Verses 6–12 provide us with a most revealing list of the offenses that have brought about this need for Jerusalem to be punished. It is extraordinarily concise and comprehensive in the range of conduct that it reveals. It begins, surprisingly enough, with a lack of respect for parents and with the prevalence of the habit of cheating the alien, who lacks supporting family to protect his or her interests. The list that follows is sufficiently self-explanatory: cheating, greed, adultery, bribery, and so on, the kinds of things that have tarnished urban life and growth since early times.

That this seems to be a rather conventional and familiar complaint on the part of the prophet compels us to ask whether all cities have not, for much of their history, been havens for such violence and misrule. However, from the point of view of the social historian, the complaint must be given special attention. It is one of the most informative and challenging of all the prophetic windows on the biblical concern with human conduct and social commitment. The key features are to be found in the facts that it is a city—Jerusalem, Israel's best known and most celebrated city—that stands condemned and that the breakdown of family values heads the list of wrongs (v. 7).

The book of Genesis shows us the earliest phase of social organization of the biblical world, in which the nation's ancestors were grouped into twelve tribes—essentially very large extended families. This family structure affected every feature of life, not only determining relationships between communities but controlling all ideas of justice and shaping the methods of dealing with misconduct. The family heads—the body of clan chieftains—handled all problems and dealt with all complaints and misdemeanors. Patriarchal authority was paramount and was usually effective, even if sometimes arbitrary.

The rise and development of cities gradually eroded this tribal, family-based structure of authority. Cities made possible greater prosperity, better military protection, and security, and they became proud centers of education and culture. Kingship and systems of legal administration grew up within cities. But there was a price to be paid for this new prosperity and security, and it is this price that Ezekiel's catalog of crimes reveals to us. As tribal—that is, patriarchal—authority broke down and largely withered away, the large extended families broke up to live in smaller houses. Neighbors became more important than kin relatives. The book of Deuteronomy shows how attempts were made to keep alive the older feeling of a nation of brothers (Deut. 15:7; 17:15, etc.). Ezekiel's catalog of urban crime shows just how difficult it was to fill the gap left by the collapse of the older world of family values upheld through a society built around feelings of kinship and its attendant responsibilities.

In Old Testament times, the world of the city represented the "modern" world, with all its attendant possibilities and challenges. Yet it becomes very clear from the remarkable insights provided by the great prophets, not least by Ezekiel, that this modern world of the city could become a scene of corruption, violence, and exploitation. Only by pointing every citizen back to a more truly fundamental understanding of justice and morality, based on a knowledge of God, can the word of God address the real needs of the community. There exists a basic challenge in the transition from the old, irrecoverable world of patriarchal tribalism to a vision of the city of God.

We shall see that Ezekiel was in the very forefront of presenting the word of God to meet this challenge. To a remarkable extent, his vision of the true city of God has remained our central focus of hope for a truly spiritual human society. For the prophet, the city of Jerusalem was shortly to lie in ruins. Yet built on the rubble of this ancient and once proud city would be a new Jerusalem, famed not simply for its architecture but for its ability to provide a worthy setting for human achievement and fulfillment. So his condemnation of the old city, harsh and unrelenting as it is, is also a token of his belief in the new city as the proper setting for human advancement.

The conclusion of his far-reaching condemnation of the old city (vv. 13–16) looks ahead to what is to happen to those of its citizens who are lucky enough to survive the coming catastrophe. They will be scattered among the nations, which brings about a period of purging and cleansing before the time of restoration can begin.

The second prophecy about the fate of Jerusalem, in verses 17–22, is in the form of a metaphor, a poetic feature Ezekiel exploited as fully as any other prophet. The image is drawn from metallurgy and is of the smelter. Most of the best-known and most useful metals of antiquity are listed— silver, bronze, tin, iron, and lead (v. 18). Jerusalem is the smelting pot and the raw materials are to be poured into it. Most of these materials turn out to be useless dross. The metaphor is turned in two directions: What was thought to be valuable ore turns out to be useless. To discover this fact, however, requires the heating of the smelter to high temperatures, which becomes a symbol of the fires of the divine anger. Jerusalem's fate is sealed, as far as the prophet now foresees it. This most useful metaphor, taken from the feared and awesome craft of the ancient metalsmith, provides Ezekiel with a suitable picture of warning. It declares what will happen to Jerusalem, but it also contains within itself a hidden reason as to why. Fires of purification and cleansing are needed.

The last of the three prophecies depicting Jerusalem's coming time of judgment (vv. 23–32) repeats and elaborates themes that have appeared in the first. Once again it goes over a catalog of unchecked wrongs that have besmirched the good name of Jerusalem. This time, however, the prophet points more accusingly at those who had the opportunity and power to right many of the wrongs and put an end to the violence—and signally failed to do so. The princes have become like lions—greedy and extortionate, not shrinking from taking the lives of those who stand in their way. They have "made many widows" (v. 25).

One might have expected Ezekiel, brought up in a privileged priestly family in Jerusalem, to have been more conciliatory and warm in his attitude toward priests. Had not they, like him, spoken out against the prevalent abuses? It is not so, for he singles out the priests as equally blameworthy as other leading citizens (v. 26). As he did earlier in chapter 20, he raises the issue of lack of observance of the sabbath day, a feature that clearly remained very difficult to enforce right throughout Old Testament times and even more so amid the complex ethnic population in the Judea of New Testament times. Alongside this, however, he also condemns the failure to maintain a proper distinction between holy and common things, seeing this as a mark of indifference to serious religious regard.

So the catalog of shame continues—officials and even prophets have joined in the prevalent violence and criminal behavior (vv. 27–28). We may be tempted to feel that Ezekiel must have been exaggerating to some extent, but we have little other evidence to indicate how bad the situation was in Jerusalem before its final collapse. The breakdown of trusted and established leadership, made the more keenly felt by the deportation of many eminent and honorable citizens to Babylon, undermined the very foundations on which justice could be built.

The prophet undoubtedly feels deeply and passionately the need to justify the action of God in allowing such a treasured city to succumb to the destructive greed and military power of the Babylonians. At the same time it is likely that, as Judah's political leadership found itself squeezed un-mercifully between the ambitions of Babylon and the useless promises of Egyptian protection, law and order collapsed in this small kingdom. It seems probable that the economy was already in ruins, itself a likely fac-tor in encouraging the king to resort to desperate measures to break free from a near-hopeless situation. In such a setting, the prophet's accusations strongly suggest that others were seeking to grab what they could for themselves in the fevered years of crisis, seizing every opportunity to take advantage of their positions of authority in frantic bids to rescue some-thing for their own and their family's future. In Ezekiel's eyes, they are only hastening the moment of the final collapse.

The reference to God's carrying out of his punishment upon Jerusalem and its citizens in the final verse of this chapter (v. 31), as an event that has already taken place, probably indicates that it was added when the scroll containing Ezekiel's sayings was given its final shape. By this time, Jerusalem had suffered destruction, and the need was to understand the past in order to build for the future. In spite, therefore, of the over-whelmingly somber and threatening tone that pervades Ezekiel 1—24, we must view these chapters against the larger setting of the finished work. The remarkably even division between prophecies of threat (chapters 1—24) and those of promise (chapters 33—48) is held apart by prophecies of a rather different character altogether. These look outside the boundaries of Israel to consider the fate of neighboring nations.

THE TWO EVIL SISTERS
Ezekiel 23:1–49

23:1 **The word of the LORD came to me:** [2] **Mortal, there were two women, the daughters of one mother;** [3] **they played the whore in Egypt. . . .** [4] **Oho-lah was the name of the elder and Oholibah the name of her sister. They be-came mine, and they bore sons and daughters. As for their names, Oholah is Samaria, and Oholibah is Jerusalem.**

[5] **Oholah played the whore while she was mine; she lusted after her lovers the Assyrians, warriors** [6] **clothed in blue, governors and commanders, all of them handsome young men, mounted horsemen. . . .** [9] **Therefore I delivered her into the hands of her lovers, into the hands of the Assyrians, for whom she lusted.** [10] **These uncovered her nakedness; they seized her sons and her daughters; and they killed her with the sword. . . .**

[11] Her sister Oholibah saw this, yet she was more corrupt than she in her lusting and in her whorings, which were worse than those of her sister. [12] She lusted after the Assyrians, governors and commanders, warriors clothed in full armor, mounted horsemen, all of them handsome young men. [13] And I saw that she was defiled; they both took the same way. [14] But she carried her whorings further; she saw male figures carved on the wall, images of Chaldeans portrayed in vermilion, [15] with belts around their waists, with flowing turbans on their heads, all of them looking like officers—a picture of Babylonians whose native land was Chaldea. [16] When she saw them she lusted after them, and sent messengers to them in Chaldea. [17] And the Babylonians came to her into the bed of love, and they defiled her with their lust; and after she defiled herself with them, she turned from them in disgust. . . .

[22] Therefore, O Oholibah, thus says the Lord GOD: I will rouse against you your lovers from whom you turned in disgust, and I will bring them against you from every side: [23] the Babylonians and all the Chaldeans, Pekod and Shoa and Koa, and all the Assyrians with them, handsome young men, governors and commanders all of them, officers and warriors, all of them riding on horses. . . . [28] For thus says the Lord GOD: I will deliver you into the hands of those whom you hate, into the hands of those from whom you turned in disgust; [29] and they shall deal with you in hatred, and take away all the fruit of your labor, and leave you naked and bare, and the nakedness of your whorings shall be exposed. Your lewdness and your whorings [30] have brought this upon you, because you played the whore with the nations, and polluted yourself with their idols. [31] You have gone the way of your sister; therefore I will give her cup into your hand. [32] Thus says the Lord GOD:

> You shall drink your sister's cup,
>> deep and wide;
> you shall be scorned and derided,
>> it holds so much.
> [33] You shall be filled with drunkenness and sorrow.
> A cup of horror and desolation
>> is the cup of your sister Samaria;
> [34] you shall drink it and drain it out,
>> and gnaw its sherds,
>> and tear out your breasts;

for I have spoken, says the Lord GOD. . . ,

[36] The LORD said to me: Mortal, will you judge Oholah and Oholibah? Then declare to them their abominable deeds. [37] For they have committed adultery, and blood is on their hands; with their idols they have committed adultery; and they have even offered up to them for food the children whom they had borne to me. [38] Moreover this they have done to me: they have defiled my sanctuary on the same day and profaned my sabbaths. [39] For when they had slaughtered their children for their idols, on the same day

they came into my sanctuary to profane it. This is what they did in my house. . . .

⁴³ Then I said, Ah, she is worn out with adulteries, but they carry on their sexual acts with her. ⁴⁴ For they have gone in to her, as one goes in to a whore. Thus they went in to Oholah and to Oholibah, wanton women. ⁴⁵ But righteous judges shall declare them guilty of adultery and of bloodshed; because they are adulteresses and blood is on their hands.

⁴⁶ For thus says the Lord GOD: Bring up an assembly against them, and make them an object of terror and of plunder. ⁴⁷ The assembly shall stone them and with their swords they shall cut them down; they shall kill their sons and their daughters, and burn up their houses. ⁴⁸ Thus will I put an end to lewdness in the land, so that all women may take warning and not commit lewdness as you have done. . . .

Chapter 23 provides us with another long allegory used by Ezekiel to drive home this message. It closely parallels that of the foundling child in chapter 16, only this time it concerns two evil sisters, who are given the names Oholah and Oholibah. These represent the cities of Samaria and Jerusalem. The fate of Samaria was determined by its destruction at the hands of the Assyrians more than a century before Ezekiel's time; the fate of Jerusalem is still to be played out but will shortly be accomplished through the terrible defeat and destruction of the city at the hands of the Babylonians. It is Ezekiel's central and familiar message, only now it is explained and justified in terms of Jerusalem's misconduct, expressed in words of the grossest sexual lust and irresponsibility.

Like Ezekiel 16, the prophetic parable does not make for easy reading. It offends the modern reader and must also have shocked its first readers in ancient times. Why then does Ezekiel express his accusations in such crude and disturbing ways, so laboring the point of sexual misconduct as to render the material unsuitable and unusable for public reading in all but the most guarded of settings? Clearly we do not have a ready answer for such a question. There is no reason for supposing, as some have done, that human feelings of shame and reticence were less keenly felt in the biblical world than they are today. Nor need we suppose that Ezekiel suffered from deeply disturbed emotions over human sexuality.

Rather, the explanation for this disturbing parable must rest with Ezekiel's concern to hold together his deepest assurance about the ultimate justice of God and the cruel horror and enormity of Jerusalem's sufferings that were so shortly to happen. A key feature lies in the central concern to portray the political failures of the entire period of the statehood of the two kingdoms of Israel and Judah in terms of sexual infidelity (v. 5, describing Israel's affair with the Assyrians; likewise, Judah's similar affair in v. 12). So the protracted sequence of looking for political arrangements that could procure the identity and security of both kingdoms extended over three centuries. First Assyria and then Egypt and Babylon had been turned to as "lovers" (that is, political saviors) of the two struggling nations. The divine message given to the prophet convinced him that each affair had been doomed to failure as such human liaisons, based only on sexual desire, usually are.

So in spite of the harshness of the language, the political judgment the prophet expresses through his parable is not far off the mark. From the perspective of the modern historian of this ancient world, it is not clear what alternatives there were. Not only Israel and Judah but all the small surrounding nations, which we are to meet more fully in chapters 25—32, were caught up between the two superpowers of Egypt and Mesopotamia. The seesaw policies of looking in one direction or the other, of playing one off against the other, and even of trying to make secret deals with both great powers at the same time were all doomed to failure. Ordinary people suffered in a world that was overwhelmed by the wanton ambitions of powerful kings and their all-too-successful military strength. The prophet's cry of anger is fully understandable, even though we are repelled by the allegorical language in which it is set forth.

The more familiar accusations of the prophet come to the surface in verse 37, where he points once again to extreme actions of cruelty and immorality that have been perpetrated in both Jerusalem and Samaria. These are all the more terrible because they were carried out in the name of religion (vv. 38–39).

Woven into the larger parable is a short "song of the cup" in verses 32–34, which looks like a parody of a drinking song. It develops the idea of the "cup" as a symbol of judgment. In this instance, special emphasis is placed on the point that Jerusalem is to drink the same cup that was drunk by the sister kingdom of Samaria. Hidden behind this is undoubtedly the deep sense of rivalry, based on political divisions, that existed between the two kingdoms.

Samaria became the capital city of Israel when the northern tribes broke their allegiance to the royal dynasty of David. The fact that this city and kingdom had subsequently fallen prey to the imperial expansion of Assyria had led Jerusalem and Judah to a large degree of misplaced complacency. The south had appeared to fare better than its sister kingdom, even though it had been a deliverance won at the cost of unwelcome political subservience. Now the day of reckoning was coming, in which it would become clear, as Ezekiel foresees, that Jerusalem has learned no lessons from her sister's fate and has been given only a temporary reprieve.

In some measure, at least, we are led to feel that Ezekiel weaves such crude language into his parable because his feelings have boiled over. Jerusalem is poised on the brink of destruction and he finds himself set apart as God's chosen announcer of such a terrible catastrophe. He is helpless to prevent it, and yet he has been summoned by God to be the herald of its coming. Like a forlorn messenger bringing news of death to an afflicted relative, he feels the burden of explaining why God had permitted such a tragedy to occur.

Here he summarizes the story of the famed city's conduct in terms commensurate with this fearful judgment. Jerusalem has invited its own destruction by its unjustified complacency and its tolerance of evil. Political misjudgment alone cannot account for such a fate. Accordingly, Ezekiel openly describes Jerusalem's sins in a manner that cannot fail too shock everyone who hears him. This city is guilty of rebelling against the most fundamental of human loyalties and commitments.

Set against the perspective of modern feminist readings of the biblical text, we cannot but feel ill at ease with the harsh way in which guilt and blame for sexual misconduct is presented, in both of Ezekiel's long extended parables, as primarily a female responsibility. It is the foundling girl of Ezekiel 16 and the two evil sisters of Ezekiel 23 who are the guilty figures in both parables; the sins and lust of the male lovers are hinted at in only a marginal way. This undoubtedly reflects the rigid nature of a social and moral code that was heavily patriarchal in its structure and that today poses problems for a more balanced and just concern with sexual equality. The sexual rhetoric of the Old Testament uncovers to us many aspects of the extent to which a patriarchal social structure shaped so much of the biblical social world.

Ezekiel's allegory of the two evil sisters is a part of this ancient biblical worldview that cannot be ignored. To some degree, the unconscious manner in which it appears and is used here as a technique for condemning Israel's political misdeeds increases our sensitivity to the harshness of its language. Nevertheless, it was clearly necessary to Ezekiel to awaken his hearers to an open and honest appraisal of the true character of life in the city from which they had been taken and which they understandably revered.

STRANGE TENSIONS ON
THE EVE OF CATASTROPHE
Ezekiel 24:1–27

24:1 In the ninth year, in the tenth month, on the tenth day of the month, the word of the LORD came to me: [2] Mortal, write down the name of this day, this very day. The king of Babylon has laid siege to Jerusalem this very day. [3] And utter an allegory to the rebellious house and say to them. . .

Set on the pot, set it on,
      pour in water also;
[4] put in it the pieces,
      all the good pieces, the thigh and the shoulder;
   fill it with choice bones. . . .
[5c] boil its pieces,
      seethe also its bones in it.

[6] Therefore thus says the Lord GOD:
Woe to the bloody city,
      the pot whose rust is in it,
      whose rust has not gone out of it!
Empty it piece by piece,
      making no choice at all. . . .
[9] Therefore thus says the Lord GOD:
Woe to the bloody city! . . .
[11] Stand it empty upon the coals,
      so that it may become hot, its copper glow,
      its filth melt in it, its rust be consumed.
[12] In vain I have wearied myself;
      its thick rust does not depart.
      To the fire with its rust!
[13] Yet, when I cleansed you in your filthy lewdness,
      you did not become clean from your filth;
   you shall not again be cleansed
      until I have satisfied my fury upon you. . . .

[15] The word of the LORD came to me: [16] Mortal, with one blow I am about to take away from you the delight of your eyes; yet you shall not mourn or weep, nor shall your tears run down. [17] Sigh, but not aloud; make no mourning for the dead. Bind on your turban, and put your sandals on your feet; do not cover your upper lip or eat the bread of mourners. [18] So I spoke to the people in the morning, and at evening my wife died. . . .

[19] Then the people said to me, "Will you not tell us what these things mean for us, that you are acting this way?" [20] Then I said to them: The word of the LORD came to me: [21] Say to the house of Israel, Thus says the Lord

GOD: I will profane my sanctuary, the pride of your power, the delight of your eyes, and your heart's desire; and your sons and your daughters whom you left behind shall fall by the sword.

[25] And you, mortal, on the day when I take from them their stronghold . . . [26] on that day, one who has escaped will come to you to report to you the news. [27] On that day your mouth shall be opened to the one who has escaped, and you shall speak and no longer be silent. So you shall be a sign to them; and they shall know that I am the LORD.

For five years Ezekiel has preached a consistent message, centered entirely on the fate that is about to befall Jerusalem. To an extent, it is a message about distant events, which his hearers have only limited means of checking or confirming. Yet it is a message with which each one of them is intimately caught up and which is bound to mold and shape their thinking. Their homeland is shortly to be the subject of a further military attack by the armies of Babylon so that Jerusalem, along with its beautiful temple, will be destroyed. The message is simple in its range but devastating in its significance. It seems probable that at first it was greeted with disbelief and indifference, but, as information filters through to the exiles in Babylon about affairs in Judah, the correctness of Ezekiel's reading of the situation becomes ever more convincing. Disbelief gives way to doubt and eventually to deep despondency.

We now reach the turning point of Ezekiel's ministry as a prophet and the central break point in the book that carries his name. The siege of Jerusalem is about to begin. It was destined to last for a year and a half. Its eventual outcome became progressively ever more certain, although there was a brief period of hope when the promised Egyptian support against Babylon appeared but soon collapsed. The siege of Jerusalem was reinstated and its disastrous end became inescapable.

These tragic events, which confirm the rightness of Ezekiel's interpretation of the situation in Judah, are indicated to us in chapter 24 in three separate prophecies. The chapter begins by noting the date when the siege of the city began (vv. 1–2). It could be that the prophet filled in the precise details later, but we should not doubt the prophetic ability to sense, even at a distance, an event of such immense significance. The first of the prophecies then provides a grim parable of this event in the guise of a cooking-pot song (vv. 3–5). It is the kind of harmless work song that would be sung when preparing a meal. The various ingredients of a savory stew are called for and the fire is lit under the pot. But this is no harmless preparation for a meal. The pot is the symbol of Jerusalem!

The theme is developed further in the second of the prophecies, verses 6–14. The pot has a coating of rust, no doubt a common enough occurrence for an iron utensil. This rust needs first to be cleaned away and the pot heated up to ensure that all vestiges of the corrosion are removed. Ezekiel uses the scouring and cleansing of a corroded and unclean pot as a further illustration of the terrible judgment that is beginning to unfold upon Jerusalem. Where the opening song about the cook pot gives us a stern reminder of the fact that Jerusalem is being placed under siege, the second prophecy serves to show why this has to occur.

The third of the prophecies in the chapter is the most extraordinary and, from the point of view of the prophet's personal feelings and attitude, the most complex (vv. 15–27). God warns Ezekiel that his wife is about to die and that he is not to undertake any of the mourning rites and procedures that would be normal for such a sad personal event (vv. 15–17). The reason given is twofold. First, the prophet's grief would be too great to permit expression in the conventional manner. Second, and more significant, his mourning would be no more than one small part of the overwhelming grief that is about to befall the entire nation of Israel, because many sons and daughters will be killed by the sword. Furthermore, the temple of God in Jerusalem—the delight of the eyes of the entire people—will be taken away (v. 21). Against such a disaster, how could Ezekiel's personal tragedy be the subject of acts of mourning when the entire nation is immersed in one great catastrophe?

News of the death of the prophet's wife is foretold one morning, and by evening she is dead (v. 18). The report strongly hints that the death was sudden and was not earlier regarded as likely. Overall, however, it is evident that the prophet, who was clearly the author of the written account of what took place since he records it all in the first person, has drawn together many distinct features. Throughout, it is his conviction that he personally, and everything that happened to him, has become a message from God to the people. His very life has become "a sign to them" (v. 27). He is no longer simply a message bearer but is himself a part of God's message, so completely has the prophet steeped his personality in his calling.

Quite distinct features are wrapped up in this report, of which the most prominent is that Ezekiel feels himself completely unable to perform the normal funerary duties for his wife. He cannot mourn, and he makes no funeral wake to share his grief with others. Instead he dresses as usual (v. 17). Only when asked about this strange and seemingly disrespectful conduct does he explain that it is because his personal grief is only a lesser grief for what is now about to befall all Israel.

There is yet a further brief glimpse into the prophet's shocked and distraught thinking as a whole cluster of misfortunes breaks in on him. Verse 27 refers to the prophet's inability to speak and looks ahead to the ending of this time of dumbness when, some months later, confirmation arrives among the exiles in Babylon in the shape of a survivor from Jerusalem (33:22). It also harks back to the forewarning given Ezekiel shortly after his call that he would, at least for a while, be unable to speak (3:26–27).

This question of Ezekiel's dumbness has remained a puzzle for interpreters. He may have been stricken periodically, and possibly for extended periods, with an inability to speak that had deep psychological causes. At the very least, he had evidently learned to mime actions silently in a form of prophetic dramatic display, which served to intrigue and challenge the minds of those who watched him. He loved street theater as a means of attracting a crowd and reinforcing his message. It is possible that he was even aware that he was not a great orator. All this indicates to scholars, in the difficult quest to understand something of the personality of this prophet, that he experienced traumatic psychological disturbances that may have been related to his unpopular message and the isolation it inflicted on him. Clearly, too, there were factors related to his own unusual personality. God uses weak and unpromising talents to fulfill special purposes (see Paul's reflection in 1 Cor. 1:26–29).

One solution to the problem has been to suggest that the period of dumbness experienced by the prophet was uniquely related to his wife's sudden death. At this time, Ezekiel himself was already in a highly wrought and anxious state of mind as a result of the situation in Jerusalem. The death of his wife, coming, as it apparently did, very suddenly, threw him into a distressing state of shock. One blow coming upon another could have brought him to such a nervous and overwrought condition of mind that he lost all power of speech, regaining it only when news arrives confirming the destruction that has taken place in the beloved home city. It would then simply have been a matter of editorial convenience to have anticipated this unusual experience by mentioning it in advance in connection with the prophet's call. It formed a part of his total bodily and mental absorption in his prophetic calling.

This may be so, but we should in any case relate the prophet's dumbness to the fact that the book of his prophecies bears every indication that its basic core is made up of pieces written by the prophet himself. Earlier prophets were primarily preachers, whose words were recorded by those who followed and listened to them. We have also noted how important it was for Ezekiel to mime his message, firmly indicating that he found this to be a most effective way of attracting the attention of a group of hearers. Nor can we leave out of our reckoning the fact that Ezekiel, as a hostage in a Babylonian settlement camp, may frequently have had difficulty in addressing a large crowd. It is clear from Jeremiah's book (Jer. 29:21–23) that the Babylonian authorities took careful note of what was said by prophets among their Jewish hostages.

7. The Fate of
Other Nations
Ezekiel 25:1–32:32

There is a marked break between the events recounted in chapter 24, which carry us up to the eve of Jerusalem's destruction, and the arrival among the exiles in Babylon of a survivor from the city who is able to confirm what has happened there (33:22). In between, we have a series of prophecies addressed to foreign nations and dealing with their fate against the background of the Babylonian expansionist campaigns in the first half of the sixth century B.C. Judah was not alone in suffering misfortune at this time. The nations dealt with are seven in number, and it is noteworthy that similar collections of foreign-nation prophecies are to be found in all the great prophetic collections of the Old Testament. They are undoubtedly among the more obscure and consequently least read parts of the Old Testament. Yet they open up to us, once something of their background is understood, a much deeper awareness of what prophecy was all about. It was not simply delivering a sharply worded rebuke to Israel and Judah for neglecting God's commandments. It was a serious and wide-ranging look at the world as it was known to ancient Israel and a bold attempt to see the hand of God at work in the complicated and often painful world of international affairs.

The modern reader who seeks to understand the politics of the Old Testament world is amply aided by a comparison with the contemporary international scene in the last half of the twentieth century. This has been dominated by the existence of two superpowers, the U.S.A. and the U.S.S.R., whose policies and differing ideologies have extensively influenced world events and attitudes. Yet behind these two major powers have been whole clusters of smaller nations, which have felt themselves either protected by the shadow of the two dominant nations or threatened by them.

The situation for the world of ancient Israel and Judah was not dissimilar. Not only were these two small kingdoms caught between two great powers, Egypt and Mesopotamia, but a number of other minor kingdoms were similarly involved. These minor kingdoms shared many features of cultural and political development with Israel; sometimes they became rival claimants to territory that had been part of Israel at its largest extent, and they experienced the same threats and difficulties when faced with the great powers.

Israel pursued a strange and tortured relationship with most of them. Some became consistent and implacable enemies of Israel and Judah, with no compromise given. They would take advantage whenever political misfortune beset the biblical community, yet they too found themselves threatened by the same imperial campaigns that brought ruin to Jerusalem. Hastily planned and reluctantly agreed-to arrangements and treaties were accordingly devised in the hope of holding back the tide of Mesopotamian exploitation and control. Deceit and diplomacy went hand in hand!

We have had ample indication that the disastrous acts of rebellion against Babylon that King Zedekiah undertook, which brought about Jerusalem's downfall, were part of a wider plan on the part of Israel's neighbors to coordinate similar action. In the background, Egypt consistently urged such resistance to Babylon, as it had earlier urged resistance to Assyria, since this provided a much-needed buffer to secure its own frontiers. All in all, it would have been impossible to claim that God was guiding the destiny of Israel and Judah while denying that there was any providential meaning in what was happening to the surrounding nations. They were inextricably caught up in the same tangled web of international politics. If God was at work, such work was all encompassing and could not be limited to the supposition that each nation was being looked after by its own national deity. This would only suggest a heavenly competition between rival gods—an absurd view that some ancient observers were actually prepared to contemplate, as is shown by the Assyrian commander's bombastic claim in 2 Kings 18:29–35.

What appear on the surface, therefore, to be remote and difficult prophecies, with little relevance for us, nonetheless point to an important spiritual truth: God is not the God of one nation only. Consequently, when we look to see the divine hand shaping human affairs, we must not interpret this in any self-centered or narrowly blinkered fashion. God is the God of all nations and peoples.

There is a further reason why we should give more than the usual amount of attention to the biblical prophecies addressed to foreign nations. This concerns the fact that nations and nationalism are still very much with us. In fact we can claim that nationalism remains one of the most influential characteristics of modern life. The hope of reaching beyond this to establish justice in international affairs remains a major goal of the modern world. The failure of the League of Nations after World War I and the concern after World War II to establish the United Nations provide us with the most obvious examples of the need to look across the frontiers of nationalism. We are members of a global society.

It is a vital feature of the prophetic writings, therefore, to have lifted human horizons to perceive this truly worldly view. The Bible traces for us a passage from the narrow and selfish ideas of a personal God to a far more credible picture of the Guardian of the universe. It progresses from belief in a deity whose concerns were thought merely to be related to individual families to a recognition that such could only be a foolish parody of the real God, whose very power as Creator made the entire world a single divine kingdom. Peter's comment in Acts 10:35 remains a foundation text for all spiritual understanding: "In every nation anyone who fears him and does what is right is acceptable to him."

FOUR KINGDOMS
OF THE SOUTH
Ezekiel 25:1–27

Ezekiel's foreign-nation series begins with four short prophecies concerning kingdoms that were the immediate neighbors of Judah. Three of them lay to the south and east, while the fourth, Philistia, was located in the southwest, bordering on Egypt. All four prophecies present little more than a passionate call for vengeance on nations that took advantage of Judah's misfortune. They reveal how the redrawing of the political map of the region after the Babylonian campaigns of the early sixth century left a long-term legacy of bitterness and continued fighting. Yet their very presence focuses attention on the deeper problems attendant on the growth of a sense of national identity. All too readily a "national" injustice became a personal grievance, so that long-standing resentments and conflicts emerged. Such was evidently the case throughout Old Testament times; only rarely does the call for a larger world peace rise above them. We find in postexilic literature a continued awareness of the tensions that persisted, long after the original wrongs were perpetrated.

Ammon (Ezekiel 25:1–7)

25:1 **The word of the LORD came to me:** [2] **Mortal, set your face toward the Ammonites and prophesy against them.** [3] **Say to the Ammonites, . . . Because** you said, "Aha!" over my sanctuary when it was profaned, and over the land of Israel when it was made desolate, and over the house of Judah when it went into exile; [4] therefore I am handing you over to the people of the East for a possession. . . . [7b] I will cut you off from the peoples and will make you perish out of the countries; I will destroy you. Then you shall know that I am the LORD.

The first nation addressed is Ammon, covering territory that corresponds roughly to present-day Jordan. Its ancient capital city was Rabbah, the ruins of which lie close to modern Amman. Ezekiel's prophecy is a straightforward threat of judgment that is to befall the Ammonites, inflicted by "the people of the East." This description of the enemy may have been left deliberately vague, although it is certain that the territory of the Ammonites was regularly under threat from marauding bands of tribespeople. No one specific campaign therefore need have been in the prophet's mind.

The reason why the Ammonites are to be punished is more interesting. They had rejoiced, and taken advantage, when Judah and Jerusalem suffered destruction by the Babylonians (vv. 3, 6). This most probably refers to the insidious role played by the people of Ammon in the events that took place in Judah in the short-lived period when the region was placed under the governorship of Gedaliah. Jeremiah 41 tells the whole sad story: how the governor was murdered and how his assassin, a certain Ishmael with royal connections, fled to the Ammonites (Jer. 41:15).

Although we know too little of the part played by the Ammonites, who at first supported Judah's defection from Babylonian control, we can see they were exploiting Judah's troubles to get what territorial advantage they could for themselves. That the Judean governor's murderer could find refuge among them illustrates well the tensions that existed. Presumably he had expected to gain support in Judah, but, seeing that this did not materialize, he had no alternative but to flee to the nearest neighboring kingdom that would offer him protection. The Ammonites may actually have encouraged or even sponsored his act of terrorism.

This prophecy of Ezekiel's serves to illustrate all too clearly the intrigues and enmities that prevailed over the entire region, as they had done for centuries. The cries and reproaches of the prophet against the lack of justice in the dealings of his own people could be magnified many times when applied to the international situation. Nations and the sentiments of nationalism were still in a formative stage of development, since the entire region was only slowly reaching beyond a narrow tribalism. However basic and even one-sided the threats and reproaches of

Ezekiel may now appear, they nonetheless draw attention to a fundamental truth: Justice, if it is to be justice, must be more than a privilege enjoyed within a single tribe or nation; it must be truly universal. No nation can successfully live in isolation for long. Claims to racial or ethnic superiority become offensive precisely because they seek to deny to others the very privileges and virtues that individuals prize so highly for themselves.

The world of the Old Testament clearly lacked the administrative power to establish an effective international basis of peace and good order between nations. Yet it did not lack the insight to recognize its essential importance. It also recognized very clearly that peace between nations could only become a possibility when there existed a foundation of justice between them, whether they were large and powerful or small and weak. The enduring message of the prophecy of Isaiah 2:4 is that there can be no peace between nations without a prior mechanism for the arbitration of justice.

A further consideration is strikingly relevant to an understanding of such prophecies as these. One of the most interesting classes of political documents that archaeologists of the ancient Near East have brought to light are treaty texts, derived both from the ancient Hittite empire of the second millennium B.C. and that of Assyria, closer to Ezekiel's day.

They illustrate a feature of international diplomacy that influenced the entire ancient Near East for at least a thousand years. They show how, by a complex series of negotiated or forcibly imposed agreements, the most strenuous efforts were made by the more successful world powers to create a measure of peace and security between the host of petty nations and cities they endeavored to rule. By a mixture of threats and promises, curses and assurances, they sought to outlaw the factional fighting and endless squabbling that ruined the various regional economies. Certainly, Israel and Judah had been forcibly required to agree to such imposed treaty arrangements by the Assyrians. Yet these attempts at creating a prosperous imperial rule with a superpower at its head did not last for long. Seen in retrospect, they provide little more than a monument to the weakness of human endeavors for a larger peace and the problems attendant upon achieving it.

The foreign-nation prophecies of the Old Testament illustrate yet another aspect of this concern for a truly universal world of peace and justice, originating in an even older setting, one where prophecy offered a glimpse of news and views about the larger world.

Moab (Ezekiel 25:8–11)

25:8 **Thus says the Lord GOD: Because Moab said, The house of Judah is like all the other nations,** [9] **therefore I will lay open the flank of Moab.** . . . [10] **I will give it along with Ammon to the people of the East as a possession.** . . . [11b] **Then they shall know that I am the LORD.**

The second of the foreign-nation prophecies of Ezekiel is addressed to the Moabites, a people whose land lay to the east of the Dead Sea and to the south of the Ammonites. Its message is closely parallel to that uttered against the Ammonites. A long and bitter history had divided the Judeans from the people of Moab since the time of David. The story is not a pleasant or reassuring one. Here were two peoples, striving to establish for themselves a national identity and a secure territory but finding themselves inevitably drawn into cruel competition. There was a long-remembered catalog of atrocities and crimes against Judah and other nations. The prophet Amos reveals the genuinely international sense of horror at the cruelty and vindictiveness that had grown up over the years by recalling an act of desecration carried out by Moabites on the dead body of an Edomite king (Amos 2:1). It is significant as one of the most overtly international crimes against humanity recalled in the Bible where the Israelite people were not the victims.

It seems likely from the sparseness of the information included by Ezekiel in his prophecy against Moab that he has little immediate news concerning this people. He sticks to a general indictment, but clearly he knew all too well the hatred fostered by years of conflict. Against such a background we should remember the story of Ruth, the Moabite woman, whose loyalty to her husband's family and people in Bethlehem singled her out as a worthy ancestor of King David (see Ruth 1:1–22; 2:6; 4:3, 5, 17, 22).

Edom (Ezekiel 25:12–14)

25:12 **Thus says the Lord GOD: Because Edom acted revengefully against the house of Judah and has grievously offended in taking vengeance upon them,** [13] **therefore thus says the Lord GOD, I will stretch out my hand against Edom, and cut off from it humans and animals, and I will make it desolate.** . . . [14b] **and they shall know my vengeance, says the Lord GOD.**

The third of the prophecies from Ezekiel about foreign nations concerns Edom. This was a nation located to the south of Moab whose territory extended to the Dead Sea. Much of the land was semidesert, but Edom maintained control of the valuable trade routes that stretched down the Rift Valley, providing access to Africa. The offense for which the Moabites are to be punished is similar to that of the Ammonites, in that they took advantage of Judah's destruction by the forces of Babylon to move in and claim territory for themselves.

Philistia (Ezekiel 25:15–17)

> 25:15 **Thus says the Lord GOD: Because with unending hostilities the Philistines acted in vengeance, and with malice of heart took revenge in destruction; **[16]** therefore thus says the Lord GOD, I will stretch out my hand against the Philistines, cut off the Cherethites, and destroy the rest of the seacoast. . . .**

Philistia was a very significant, if somewhat enigmatic, neighbor to Israel, occupying the coastal strip down to Egypt. The fact that the Philistines were, from the time of Saul and David, the best known and most celebrated of the rivals to Judah focuses attention upon them. They were ultimately, in the nineteenth century, to give their name to the modern-day Palestinians. The link with the Cherethites (v. 16) has given rise to their possible origin as maritime settlers from Crete. In spite of the biblical portrait of Goliath as a clumsy Philistine giant, it has become clear from archaeological evidence that the Philistines were far from being a primitive or unsophisticated people. It seems likely, however, that from earliest times their distinct culture marked them off from their neighbors in Judah.

There is abundant evidence that the Philistine cities, which formed a kind of loose federation, played a role in the power play between the great powers of Egypt and Mesopotamia, so it comes as no surprise that Ezekiel became incensed, as did some of his fellow Judeans, at the way in which the Philistines exploited Judah's downfall. Intrigue and double-dealing had become a feature of life over the years.

FOUR PROPHECIES AGAINST PHOENICIA
Ezekiel 26:1–21

> 26:1 **In the eleventh year, on the first day of the month, the word of the LORD came to me:** [2] **Mortal, because Tyre said concerning Jerusalem,**
> **"Aha, broken is the gateway of the peoples;**

it has swung open to me;

I shall be replenished, now that it is wasted."

³ Therefore, thus says the Lord GOD:

See, I am against you, O Tyre!

I will hurl many nations against you,

as the sea hurls its waves. . . .

Then they shall know that I am the LORD.

⁷ For thus says the Lord GOD: I will bring against Tyre from the north King Nebuchadrezzar of Babylon, king of kings, together with horses, chariots, cavalry, and a great and powerful army.

⁸ Your daughter-towns in the country

he shall put to the sword.

He shall set up a siege-wall against you,

cast up a ramp against you,

and raise a roof of shields against you. . . .

¹³ I will silence the music of your songs;

the sound of your lyres shall be heard no more.

¹⁴ I will make you a bare rock;

you shall be a place for spreading nets.

You shall never again be rebuilt,

for I the LORD have spoken,

says the Lord GOD.

¹⁵ Thus says the Lord GOD to Tyre: Shall not the coastlands shake at the sound of your fall, when the wounded groan, when slaughter goes on within you? ¹⁶ Then all the princes of the sea shall step down from their thrones; they shall remove their robes and strip off their embroidered garments. They shall clothe themselves with trembling, and shall sit on the ground; they shall tremble every moment, and be appalled at you. ¹⁷ And they shall raise a lamentation over you, and say to you:

How you have vanished from the seas,

O city renowned,

once mighty on the sea,

you and your inhabitants,

who imposed your terror

on all the mainland! . . .

¹⁹ For thus says the Lord GOD: When I make you a city laid waste, like cities that are not inhabited, when I bring up the deep over you, and the great waters cover you, ²⁰ then I will thrust you down with those who descend into the Pit. . . .

We now come to a similar collection of four short prophecies addressed to the Phoenicians and especially directed against their major city and seaport, Tyre. They are followed by a further three prophecies against the same major power but very different in their character and poetic interest. A unique feature relates them all: Their presence in the book of the prophet Ezekiel derives from the thirteen-year-long siege that the Babylonian ruler Nebuchadrezzar waged against Tyre. All of Ezekiel's anti-Tyre prophecies declare a disastrous defeat and destruction of the fortress city. Yet this did not happen; instead, Tyre held out in the siege, no doubt greatly assisted by the possibility of receiving supplies by sea. Although humiliated, the city was not defeated and ransacked. The latest of Ezekiel's prophecies (Ezek. 29:17–20) accepts that the prophesied fall of Tyre has not been realized in an "amending" prophesy, affirming that God has given a victory over Egypt to the Babylonian forces instead of the victory over Tyre, with its rich promise of spoil and plunder.

The Phoenicians were undoubtedly one of the outstanding peoples of Mediterranean antiquity, becoming the foremost seafaring people in the region and pioneering a far-reaching maritime trade. They were a nation of traders, famous throughout the ancient Near East. Ezekiel, along with many others, must have watched with awe as the Phoenician longboats and rounded bargelike trading ships passed close to the coast west of Jerusalem. All modern Western civilization stands in their debt for the invention of the alphabet. This reduced the complicated syllable signs of Mesopotamia to a much more convenient written system, thereby simplifying the task of recording language.

In keeping with their seafaring skills, the Phoenicians became the merchants and intermediaries of the ancient Mediterranean world, enabling the ancient cradles of civilization in the Near East to spread across to the Aegean and Europe. That the Babylonians should have regarded the capture and plundering of Tyre as a unique prize to be won is no surprise. That they failed to do this shows that the techniques of ancient warfare were no match for the natural defense provided by the sea.

The first of the four short prophecies by Ezekiel is found in 26:1–6 and takes the simple form of a threat, using the poetic imagery of waves crashing against the rocks as a picture of attacking forces crashing against, and destroying, Tyre's walls. Apart from the precise date with which it begins (v. 1), which locates it to the time of the beginning of the siege of Jerusalem, nothing specific is said about the occasion of the attack or its justification. That Phoenicia was constantly embroiled in Judean political decisions implies their complicity in the anti-Babylonian alliance. It was sufficient for Ezekiel to express God's anger against this nation for promising much but giving little, when it came to Judah's hour of need.

The second of Ezekiel's prophetic threats against Tyre follows immediately in 26:7–14. It begins with naming Nebuchadrezzar, king of Baby-lon, as the city's opponent and describes the techniques and implements of a siege assault. Ezekiel's message is again a declaration of Tyre's in-evitable downfall, with no clear reason given for it. The prophet follows through his poetic picture as though the attack on Tyre were no different from a normal land assault. Certainly, the sea was Tyre's first and most important line of defense. (Among the most interesting of Assyrian por-trayals on wall reliefs preserved in the British Museum is one of Assyrian assault troops advancing through water, aided by special flotation gear. It is one of the oldest indications of special marine fighting units.)

The third anti-Tyre prophecy is similar (26:15–18), although this time a sharp contrast is drawn between the reputation of the city, which also con-trolled much of the nearby mainland area, and the humiliation of its fall. The fourth prophecy (26:19–21) extends this theme still further by drawing into the poetry a feature familiar to the ancient understanding of the world as set in three stories. The earth lay in the center, and above stretched the upper world of the heavens. Below the inhabited earth, however, lay the dark and forbidding region of the lower earth, or underworld. It was to this nether region that the dead were conveyed, where they were believed to continue a weak, shadowy existence. So Ezekiel declares that the city, which once rose proudly out of the sea, standing in sun-drenched splendor amid the sea mists, will sink into the dark and gloomy underworld. Like a village engulfed by floodwaters, so Tyre will sink into the depths.

These four prophecies, which declare and rejoice in the coming down-fall of Tyre, reveal a depth of hatred and ill-feeling on Ezekiel's part. Such feeling, regrettably, is far from uncharacteristic of foreign-nation prophetic sayings. Some bitterness of feeling can be explained by Ezekiel's sense that Phoenicia had shown itself to be one of several disastrous allies to Judah. Yet beyond this, there appears to be more than a little envy of Tyre's greatness in the ancient world. The advanced civilization and the commercial renown it achieved are seen as a challenge to God's supreme sovereignty.

A PROUD SHIP SINKS
INTO THE DEPTHS
Ezekiel 27:1–36

27:1 **The word of the LORD came to me:** [2] **Now you, mortal, raise a lamen-tation over Tyre,** [3] **and say to Tyre, which sits at the entrance to the sea, mer-chant of the peoples on many coastlands. Thus says the Lord GOD:**

O Tyre, you have said,
"I am perfect in beauty."
[4] Your borders are in the heart of the seas;
your builders made perfect your beauty.
[5] They made all your planks
of fir trees from Senir;
they took a cedar from Lebanon
to make a mast for you. . . .

[12] Tarshish did business with you out of the abundance of your great wealth; silver, iron, tin, and lead they exchanged for your wares. [13] Javan, Tubal, and Meshech traded with you; they exchanged human beings and vessels of bronze for your merchandise. . . . [17] Judah and the land of Israel traded with you; they exchanged for your merchandise wheat from Minneth, millet, honey, oil, and balm. . . .

[25] So you were filled and heavily laden
in the heart of the seas.
[26] Your rowers have brought you
into the high seas.
The east wind has wrecked you
in the heart of the seas. . . .
[28] At the sound of the cry of your pilots
the countryside shakes,
[29] and down from their ships
come all that handle the oar.
The mariners and all the pilots of the sea
stand on the shore
[30] and wail aloud over you,
and cry bitterly. . . .
[32] In their wailing they raise a lamentation for you,
and lament over you:
"Who was ever destroyed like Tyre
in the midst of the sea? . . .
[36] The merchants among the peoples hiss at you;
you have come to a dreadful end
and shall be no more forever.

The last three prophecies of Tyre's downfall are altogether different from the preceding ones and do not contain any clear indication as to the occasions on which they were delivered. Instead of relating directly to the Babylonian campaigns of the early sixth century B.C., they reflect more openly and timelessly than do the first four prophecies an awareness of Tyre's great success as a major civilization. Indeed, they may not have come from the prophet Ezekiel at all but were added later on account of their particular association with Tyre. From a spiritual perspective, their element of rejoicing over the downfall of a great people reads unpleasantly, yet they are magnificent poetry and should certainly not be ignored. Whereas the first four prophecies express a belief in a divine judgment shortly to come upon Tyre because of its role in the rebellion against Babylon, these further prophecies look more deeply into the mystery of evil.

The first of the three, in Ezekiel 27:1–36, is a lamentation of great dignity and poetic vitality. It describes the shipwreck and sinking of a Phoenician merchant trader within sight of land, with the awestruck onlookers on shore standing bewildered and amazed at the tragedy they are witnessing. In presenting such a vivid picture the prophet poet clearly regards the ship, laden with precious merchandise, as symbolic of Tyre itself. It is quite possible that the preceding picture of the city of Tyre sinking down to the underworld occasioned the inclusion of the poem at this point.

The lament is well worth reading for its full knowledge of the range of trading activities that Tyre fostered and largely controlled. Any surviving idea we may have that this was a primitive society is quickly dispelled here. So, also, the portrayal of the ship's sinking carries all the conviction of a report by an observer who has seen such a disaster occur.

We can best set this lament in a larger context of religious thought by recognizing that it draws heavily upon an awareness of the great affluence and wealth of Tyre when compared with the far weaker economic life of Judah. As a rich and affluent first-world trading nation in a predominantly third-world setting, its affluence gave it power and immense prestige.

Almost certainly, Phoenician merchants would have established trading stations in Jerusalem and in such local ports as Joppa. By acting as middlemen for most of the trade in the eastern Mediterranean, the Phoenicians built up for themselves a reputation for greed and exploitation. Whether justified or not, it was clearly how the people of Judah had come to see them. It is not surprising therefore that this lament regards the sinking of a Phoenician trading ship as an act of divine judgment. Whereas those on shore who witness the sinking can cry out in an agony of fellow feeling for the doomed mariners (vv. 29–31), those merchants who had dealt with Tyre could hiss and whistle in derision at the downfall of those who they believed had greatly exploited them (v. 36).

What we have in this lament, therefore, is a third-world reaction when disaster strikes a first-world nation. The sentiments expressed are unpleasant and more than a little shocking, but they are wholly understandable.

JUDGMENT ON THE SIN OF PRIDE
Ezekiel 28:1–10

28:1 The word of the LORD came to me: [2] Mortal, say to the prince of Tyre,
Thus says the Lord GOD:
> Because your heart is proud
> and you have said, "I am a god;
> I sit in the seat of the gods,
> in the heart of the seas,"
> yet you are but a mortal, and no god,
> though you compare your mind
> with the mind of a god. . . .
> [5] By your great wisdom in trade
> you have increased your wealth,
> and your heart has become proud in your wealth.
> [6] Therefore thus says the Lord GOD:
> Because you compare your mind
> with the mind of a god,
> [7] therefore, I will bring strangers against you,
> the most terrible of the nations;
> they shall draw their swords against the beauty of your wisdom
> and defile your splendor. . . .

The second of the longer prophetic poems delivered in expectation of
Tyre's downfall is addressed specifically to one who is called "the prince
of Tyre" (28:1). If this is a poem from Ezekiel's age, this would be the Tyr-
ian king Ittobaal II; however, it could well be of later origin. In any event,
the lament is directed against all human pride and overweening arrogance;
this feature marks the poem as a most remarkable insight into the psychological roots of sin and evil. The picture it offers of the pride of the
prince of Tyre is a widely applicable condemnation of the sin of human
pride in all its many manifestations.

Not surprisingly, the Christian church came to view pride as one of the
most insidious and threatening of all human sins. From the perspective of
a Christian understanding of this prophetic indictment therefore, and the
one that immediately follows it in verses 11–19, its condemnation of human arrogance is most important. Nowhere else in the Bible is the nature
of pride, one of the seven deadly sins, and its roots in the human personality, so dramatically and memorably put. A number of characteristics of
pride are brought out in this section.

First, at the heart of the denunciation, lies the claim expressed in the
boastful saying "I am a god: I sit in the seat of the gods" (v. 2). The

straightforward counterargument is that human mortality proves this is not so. Death, when it comes, will expose the hollowness of such a claim (vv. 9–10).

The second manifestation of human pride is seen to lie in the claim to possess a wisdom superior to that of all other human beings (vv. 3–6). The Daniel who is referred to in 28:3 is the traditional hero of remote antiquity already mentioned in 14:14 and 14:20, who is also known from Canaanite legends. Tyre's great success as a trading nation is ascribed to this great wisdom (v. 5). Defeat will bring an end to such worldly opulence built on mercantile enterprise.

Clearly the reason Tyre was singled out in this prophetic denunciation of pride is that, as a symbol of worldly success, it was regarded as relying too heavily on its outward show of power and too little on its spiritual strength. The error perceived at the root of pride is a failure to recognize the limitations and fragility of all human skills and attainment. The claims to be like God and to possess a wisdom commensurate with the divine wisdom are evident signs of an inability to grasp the true power and wisdom of God. They represent a gross lack of perspective. It is not difficult in the modern world to encounter plenty of examples where human claims to be "like God," or to be the special recipient of godly favor, depend on a serious failure to recognize the true power and range of the divine Being.

THE FALL OF THE MIGHTY ONE
Ezekiel 28:11–19

28:11 Moreover the word of the LORD came to me: 12 Mortal, raise a lamentation over the king of Tyre, and say to him, Thus says the Lord GOD:
> You were the signet of perfection,
>> full of wisdom
>> and perfect in beauty.
> 13 You were in Eden, the garden of God. . . .
> 15 You were blameless in your ways
>> from the day that you were created,
>> until iniquity was found in you.
> 16 In the abundance of your trade
>> you were filled with violence, and you sinned;
>> so I cast you as a profane thing from the mountain of God,
>>> and the guardian cherub drove you out
>>> from among the stones of fire. . . .
> 19 All who know you among the peoples

are appalled at you;
you have come to a dreadful end
and shall be no more forever.

The third of the longer poetic denunciations of the king of Tyre, in 28:11–19, is one of the most memorable passages in the entire book of Ezekiel, and was taken in medieval biblical interpretation to contain a revelation of the fall of Satan from his original place alongside God. Recent interpretation generally agrees that it is a brilliant adaptation of features from a far older myth of the fall of a mighty one, who was originally immortal and who held great power as the agent and servant of God. Variants of the theme point to a belief that, on the heavenly mountain abode of the gods, one of the lesser deities chose to rebel rather than accept a subordinate place in the pantheon. The idea is explored brilliantly in John Milton's poem *Paradise Lost*, which stands among the greatest classics of English poetry. That such a theme of the downfall of the gods who were believed to control the destiny of nations was at one time a feature of Israelite worship is evident from Psalm 82. In this psalm, as here, the theme of the fall from grace on account of pride is a central feature.

We can safely draw the inference from this prophetic passage that many variations existed on the imagery of the fall of the mighty one, sometimes identified as a satan figure. It is a very important insight into the biblical understanding of the nature of sin and evil. Ezekiel's targeting of the sin of pride as the most basic of sins (verse 17) is instructive. It reveals that as early as biblical times an awareness had emerged of the strange results of the acquisition of great power. Reflection on the course of modern history provides ample confirmation of its ruinous effects. Democratic societies have had to learn to develop systems of government in which checks and controls are imposed on those who exercise great power, lest the consequences of its unrestrained use should be unleashed.

We can readily see the importance and necessity in antiquity of such a reflection. The institution of kingship was a strangely ambivalent advance in the development of human society. On the positive side, the rise of civilization itself owes much to the institution, since kings brought greater organization and coordination of resources and effort. The great powers with which Israel was familiar—Egypt, Assyria, Babylon, and Tyre—were civilizations that grew up through the energy and success of the kings who ruled them and who held immense power. The very success of the empires they created was due in no small measure to the ruthless manner in which they used this power. The biblical portrait in Exodus of the pharaoh of

Egypt and his empire is a classical expression of a society built upon coercion. Yet we are admirably shown, in the Exodus presentation, how the ruthless exercise of such unrestrained power could become both barbarously cruel and arbitrarily foolish.

So the prophetic picture of the arrogance of the king of Tyre draws dramatically and brilliantly on several well-known themes. Kingship relied heavily on opulent display and exaggerated propaganda. Power had to be translated into showmanship, a feature that characterizes all ancient kingly rule. The feats and accomplishments of kings, their skill as hunters, and their victories in war were the stock items of ancient historical writing. Palaces were filled with decorations extolling royal achievements, and the ability of kings to bring great prosperity to their citizens was endlessly proclaimed.

The reality, however, was very different; the oppressiveness and destructiveness of royal adventuring were never far away. It is one of the distinguishing characteristics of the Bible that it expresses so much criticism of kingship as an institution, not because the Bible rejects the need for good government but because it recognizes its fragility and the endless temptations that accompany the exercise of power. The aim is not to disown all forms of human government or to decry the need for strong leadership but to set them in perspective. More important still is the need to restrain its excesses. So the king of Tyre is made into the archetypal satan figure.

Almost certainly, this poem makes use of far older legendary imagery about a primordial conflict in heaven and the rebellion of a lesser deity. The fact that it is here given a distinctly human application to the king of Tyre shows the importance of such fundamental imagery about the nature of evil. Perhaps more important still, it reveals the central emphasis placed by the Bible upon human responsibility for evil. Instead of blaming worldly disasters on a heavenly conflict that human beings are powerless to change, it recognizes our direct responsibility for our achievements and failures.

THE DEATH OF THE DRAGON
Ezekiel 29:1–16

29:1 In the tenth year, in the tenth month, on the twelfth day of the month, the word of the LORD came to me: 2 Mortal, set your face against Pharaoh king of Egypt, and prophesy against him and against all Egypt; 3 speak, and say, Thus says the Lord GOD:

> I am against you,
>   Pharaoh king of Egypt,
> the great dragon sprawling
>   in the midst of its channels,
> saying, "My Nile is my own;
>   I made it for myself." . . .
> 5 I will fling you into the wilderness,
>   you and all the fish of your channels;
> you shall fall in the open field,
>   and not be gathered and buried.
> To the animals of the earth and to the birds of the air
>   I have given you as food.
> 6 Then all the inhabitants of Egypt shall know
>   that I am the LORD
> because you were a staff of reed
>   to the house of Israel;
> 7 when they grasped you with the hand, you broke,
>   and tore all their shoulders. . . .

9b Because you said, "The Nile is mine, and I made it," 10 therefore, I am against you, and against your channels, and I will make the land of Egypt an utter waste and desolation. . . . 12b and her cities shall be a desolation forty years among cities that are laid waste. I will scatter the Egyptians among the nations, and disperse them among the countries.

13 Further, thus says the Lord GOD: At the end of forty years I will gather the Egyptians from the peoples among whom they were scattered; 14 and I will restore the fortunes of Egypt, and bring them back to the land of Pathros, the land of their origin; and there they shall be a lowly kingdom. 15 It shall be the most lowly of the kingdoms, and never again exalt itself above the nations; and I will make them so small that they will never again rule over the nations. 16 The Egyptians shall never again be the reliance of the house of Israel; they will recall their iniquity, when they turned to them for aid. Then they shall know that I am the Lord GOD.

There now commences a series of seven prophecies, in Ezekiel 29:1–30:19, directed against Egypt. With the exception of the third one (30:1–19), they are all given precise dates. These dates place them in relation to the events of the siege and downfall of Jerusalem, apart from the short prophecy of 29:17–21, which bears the latest date of any in the book. Chronologically 29:17–21 is out of sequence, both in the book taken as a whole and in the series of prophecies addressed to Egypt. It is nonetheless a most interesting prophecy because of the way in which it reports that Ezekiel's earlier prophecies pronouncing the imminent downfall of Tyre when it was under siege by the king of Babylon were not fulfilled. Consequently a new "amending" prophecy has become necessary. We shall reflect more fully on this intriguing short prophecy in its context.

We should not be surprised that Ezekiel had a message to deliver concerning the fate of Egypt during the Babylonian campaigns that brought such terrible disaster to Judah. Evidently, Egypt was directly involved in the political calculations that encouraged King Zedekiah of Judah to withdraw his allegiance to the Babylonian king in 589–587 B.C. Reliance on Egyptian support proved to be a serious miscalculation, yet it is not difficult to see, even from a cursory glance at a map of the region, that his misreading the situation was understandable. Egypt appeared to be far closer to hand than either of the major powers of Mesopotamia, Assyria or Babylon. Yet for half a millennium, Israel's destiny was shaped more directly by the influences felt from Mesopotamia than by those from Egypt.

Nevertheless, Egypt was one of the great civilizations of antiquity, and the little kingdom of Judah had grown up under its shadow since the very beginning. A reputation for architectural opulence and military strength had given Egypt a name among the major powers, so that promises of military support from this quarter would have been very appealing to a beleaguered king in Jerusalem.

Nor was there any lack of enthusiasm in the Egyptian court for giving all necessary aid to the several minor kingdoms that stood between Egypt's own frontiers and the ambitious rulers of Mesopotamia. Keeping the Mesopotamian wolf from the door was a highly desirable goal in Egypt. But in fact, as historical records show, Egyptian power proved repeatedly to be no match for that of Mesopotamia, and both it and its allies suffered severely as a result. Its military might made a great processional show but proved weak when faced with Assyrian or Babylonian determination.

Ezekiel's prophecies that threaten the defeat of Egypt are therefore fully understandable, not as a reflection of the Judean desire for vengeance on a troublesome neighbor but as a recognition that Egypt was all show and no real friend at all. Egypt repeatedly lived up to its proverbial reputation as a broken reed, which, for all its appearance, was weak and likely to injure anyone who leaned on it. Ezekiel had good reason to see Egypt as the sort of friend Judah could well do without.

It is also worthwhile, in seeking to understand the implications of Ezekiel's prophecies against Egypt, to bear in mind that there was a constant temptation for citizens of Judah to turn to Egypt as a refuge in time of trouble. The story of how Israel's ancestors, the sons of Jacob, fled to

Egypt in a period of drought must have been one that was often repeated in later times. Judean citizens were to be found among the mercenary soldiers enlisted by Egypt, as archaeological evidence of their subsequent permanent settlements there has revealed. When they feared reprisals from Babylon after the murder of Gedaliah, some of Jeremiah's contemporaries fled to Egypt, forcing the prophet Jeremiah to accompany them, apparently against his will and advice (Jeremiah 40—44).

Egypt often presented itself as Judah's friend in time of need, but the reality consistently turned out otherwise. It was appropriate, therefore, that Ezekiel deliver prophecies to warn that Egypt too would be no match for the king of Babylon and would fall prey to Nebuchadrezzar's military power.

The first of Ezekiel's prophecies against Egypt is set out in 29:1–16, using, in its first (poetic) part, the image of Egypt as a great dragon (vv. 1–7). The image is an appropriate one, undoubtedly depending on identification of the crocodile, which was to be found in parts of the Egyptian delta region, as the dragon in question. So the capture and slaying of the dragon has all the ingredients of a crocodile hunt combined with overtones of a great battle with the dragon monster of chaos.

The particular accusation leveled against Egypt is the absurdly exaggerated boast of its king (pharaoh: literally the "great house") to be the maker and lord of the Nile (v. 9). Thereby he was claiming to be a god and so denying the power of the true God. This feature certainly drew something from the complex and heavily symbolic Egyptian mythology concerning the divine status of the Egyptian ruler, who claimed to be self-begotten. Overall, however, we can discern in this vigorous piece of prophetic poetry the conviction that Egypt's downfall is deserved and inevitable. This seems assured to the prophet, even though he clearly has little in the way of direct details to offer concerning the progress of the current military campaign. Its importance, as far as Ezekiel's first hearers were concerned, was to remove from their thinking any expectation that this time Egypt would prove to be the longed-for friend in need who would save King Zedekiah's skin and bring a "miraculous" deliverance to Jerusalem. Such was not to be!

The date at the beginning of the prophecy places it at the time when the Babylonian siege of Jerusalem had just begun and when hope of assistance from Egypt must have been running very high. It was the only line of realistic military rescue left open to Judah. Egyptian support for the rebellion materialized briefly, as we learn from Jeremiah (Jer. 37:3–10; 34:21), resulting in the temporary lifting of the siege of Jerusalem. This appeared at first to be the miraculous salvation that the citizens of Jerusalem had prayed for and relied on. Unfortunately the reprieve was short-lived; the Egyptian forces were quickly crushed, making the reinstatement of the siege all the more terrible in its implications. For the citizens of Jerusalem, it was like the temporary lifting of a death sentence, only to have it reaffirmed a few weeks later.

It comes as something of a surprise to find a hopeful message added to the close of the original prophecy (vv. 13–16), assuring Egypt of a better future after a generation had passed (forty years). This contrasts with the more typical consignment to perpetual oblivion that characterizes several of the foreign-nation prophecies. We can see in this something of the inevitable love-hate relationship with Egypt that the Old Testament reflects.

In the later postexilic period Egypt was to become a major haven for Jewish exiles, and in the Hellenistic period it was a place where a large Jewish population was permanently settled, becoming the largest and most progressive center of Jewish life and learning outside Jerusalem. The great significance of this is readily evident from New Testament times; the Jews of Alexandria were a significant source of Christian converts. A closely comparable and even more favorable portrayal of the role of Egypt in the future life of the people of God is expressed in the prophecy of Isaiah 19:19–25.

LATE PAYMENT FOR
THE BABYLONIAN SOLDIERS
Ezekiel 29:17–21

29:17 **In the twenty-seventh year, in the first month, on the first day of the month, the word of the LORD came to me:** [18] **Mortal, King Nebuchadrezzar of Babylon made his army labor hard against Tyre; every head was made bald and every shoulder was rubbed bare; yet neither he nor his army got anything from Tyre to pay for the labor that he had expended against it.** [19] **Therefore thus says the Lord GOD: I will give the land of Egypt to King Nebuchadrezzar of Babylon; and he shall carry off its wealth and despoil it and plunder it; and it shall be the wages for his army.** [20] **I have given him the land of Egypt as his payment for which he labored, because they worked for me, says the Lord GOD.**

[21] **On that day I will cause a horn to sprout up for the house of Israel, and I will open your lips among them. Then they shall know that I am the LORD.**

This short prophecy, hidden away in the book of Ezekiel and out of chronological order, is unexpectedly interesting because of the light it sheds on the nature of prophecy. It declares, with the typical artistry of Ezekiel in focusing attention on a representative picture of contemporary life, that the Lord God will give victory over Egypt instead of Tyre as payment to Nebuchadrezzar's hard-worked soldiers. The military power of Babylon, as in most ancient nations, was built on mercenary troops for whom the spoils of war they hoped to receive were the chief payment. Clearly, Nebuchadrezzar's forces expected to get rich pickings from the plunder of Tyre, a victory Ezekiel himself forecast for them. Yet this did not happen, even after a thirteen-year-long siege. Such fruitless labor, therefore, would be recompensed, declares this "amending" prophecy from Ezekiel, by the defeat and plunder of Egypt instead.

The open and unabashed way in which the prophet accepts that his earlier threats against Tyre have not materialized in a Babylonian victory—and that some account of this failure needs to be made—is especially interesting. In Ezekiel's view, typical of all biblical prophecy, God alone is sovereign. Prophecy is not a fixed and unalterable judgment but can be supplemented, amended, or even revoked by further prophecies as God's purposes become clearer and events unfold. To believe otherwise would be to deny to God a proper freedom and sovereignty.

In fact we can see that there lies in all prophecy a rightful and very meaningful tension. It may warn, threaten, or promise many things, but it does so with a genuine concern to move and mold the minds of human beings. Such human response is therefore a major factor in subsequent developments. Prophecy is not the declaration of an unalterable fate (the error of historical fatalism). Instead, it warns that present acts and attitudes have consequences. It recalls fundamental assurances and experiences from the past, thereby demonstrating the lines of continuity in all historical events. Yet it keeps open the creative reality of the present moment as a moment of time lived "before God." History itself is a process of creation.

It is a mistake, therefore, to think of world history as though it were simply a dramatic script, already written by God, that is simply being acted out. Instead, the present is a truly creative moment of the divine purpose, and the future is genuinely open. Ezekiel's revised account of God's purpose regarding both Tyre and Egypt fully accepts this openness in the course of events and does not accept that prophecy is worthless or false when new happenings challenge original expectations.

THE DAY OF EGYPT
Ezekiel 30:1–19

30:1 **The word of the LORD came to me:** [2] **Mortal, prophesy, and say, Thus** says the Lord GOD:
> **Wail, "Alas for the day!"**
> [3]   **For a day is near,**
>   **the day of the LORD is near;**
>   **it will be a day of clouds,**
>   **a time of doom for the nations.**
> [4] **A sword shall come upon Egypt,**
>   **and anguish shall be in Ethiopia,**
>   **when the slain fall in Egypt.**
>   **and its wealth is carried away,**
>   **and its foundations are torn down.**
> [5] **Ethiopia, and Put, and Lud, and all Arabia, and Libya, and the people of** the allied land shall fall with them by the sword. . . .
> [10] **Thus says the Lord GOD:**
> **I will put an end to the hordes of Egypt,**
>   **by the hand of King Nebuchadrezzar of Babylon. . . .**
> [19] **Thus I will execute acts of judgment on Egypt.**
>   **Then they shall know that I am the LORD.**

The theme of "the day" was somber and meaningful for Ezekiel, possibly reflecting his priestly upbringing. As one whose education was shaped around carefully calculating the passage of time, so that sabbaths were properly recognized and consecrated and appropriate festivals celebrated, he saw clearly that time was a sacred gift. Time was holy, given by God for the proper performance of human duties and marked at intervals by the right rituals and services. Surely this habit of timekeeping enabled him to maintain a precise record of the dates of his prophecies and of the passage of the years of exile in Babylon. Time measured the stream of life passing through the channel of human history God had set for it. Time had quality as well as length. This holy quality of time had already greatly influenced an earlier prophecy from Ezekiel concerning the impending judgment on Jerusalem (7:10–13). Now a similar prophecy reveals the prophet's sense that the time for Egypt to be judged has drawn near. Such a "day" will not only reveal truths about the present situation but will disclose the significance of a long national history.

It is difficult to see that Ezekiel's prophecy here contains very much more by way of a message than we have already heard in 29:1–16. Everything is concisely summed up in verse 10: "I [God] will put an end to the hordes of Egypt, by the hand of King Nebuchadrezzar of Babylon." However, this is enlarged with extraordinary poetic skill into a broad picture of Egypt's military defeat and ruination. A straightforward assertion that "a sword" will fall upon Egypt is made in verse 4. This is then elaborated by as full a portrayal of the geographical range and diverse features of the land of Egypt as the prophet's skill can command. The intention is quite simply to insist that all Egypt is about to suffer. Yet that might sound too simple and matter-of-fact. So Ezekiel draws a map of judgment in which the several regions of Upper and Lower Egypt are mentioned and the surrounding territories of Ethiopia, Arabia, Lydia, and Libya are all referred to (v. 5). The famous cities of the Nile delta are included. The day of God's judgment is at hand for the Egyptians. There will be no place to hide!

PHARAOH'S BROKEN ARMS
Ezekiel 30:20–26

> 30:20 **In the eleventh year, in the first month, on the seventh day of the month, the word of the LORD came to me:** [21] **Mortal, I have broken the arm of Pharaoh king of Egypt; it has not been bound up for healing or wrapped with a bandage, so that it may become strong to wield the sword.** [22] **Therefore thus says the Lord GOD: I am against Pharaoh king of Egypt, and will break his arms, both the strong arm and the one that was broken; and I will make the sword fall from his hand. . . .** [26] **and I will scatter the Egyptians among the nations and disperse them throughout the countries. Then they shall know that I am the LORD.**

We can never know the many personal tragedies that were played out among the Jewish exiles in Babylon, or the level of freedom that was allowed them; they were nothing more than disposable hostages held in Babylon to serve a larger political purpose. But by the later years of the Babylonian exile, the prophecies contained in Isaiah 40—55, offer many allusions to cruelty and pain, leading to near despair. It seems likely that witnessing these acts of mindless cruelty and vindictiveness suggested this prophecy of the breaking of the Egyptian pharaoh's arms. What Ezekiel declares will happen to the Egyptian ruler is senseless barbarism, repeated out of malice. It makes far from pleasant reading. Clearly, it strengthened the prophet's aim of insisting that there could be no assistance for Jerusalem from Egypt.

This must certainly be regarded as the primary point of the message, which becomes more than a little grotesque if taken as a typical picture of divine activity. As a fellow Jew had to look on, seething with rage but help-less to intervene, when a compatriot was brutally seized and wounded by a Babylonian soldier, so would Judah stand helpless when pharaoh's hour of judgment came. Doom was inevitable.

The picture the prophet draws of mindless cruelty would certainly be inappropriate if taken to show a larger picture of God's character. Clearly, Ezekiel accepts that historical events, with all their seeming arbitrariness, fulfill a divine purpose and so are an expression of God's will. In any case, the message given here is important as a warning to counter the vain hope that Jerusalem will be saved at the last moment by a rescue from Egypt. Pharaoh cannot save himself, let alone Jerusalem!

The aim is to assert the total powerlessness of Judah's promised ally. In this respect it reminds the reader very clearly that, although these foreign-nation prophecies were addressed to distant peoples and lands, their sig-nificance was directly linked to Judah and the fate of the Jews; these were the people who actually heard what the prophet had to say. God was at work among the nations. However difficult it was to discern this larger purpose, the prophet is concerned to insist that Jews are not living on an island. God's purpose is worldwide.

THE PARABLE OF THE CEDAR TREE
Ezekiel 31:1–18

31:1 **In the eleventh year, in the third month, on the first day of the month, the word of the LORD came to me:** 2 **Mortal, say to Pharaoh king of Egypt and to his hordes:**

Whom are you like in your greatness?
3   **Consider Assyria, a cedar of Lebanon.**
with fair branches and forest shade,
        and of great height,
        its top among the clouds. . . .
9 **I made it beautiful**
        with its mass of branches,
        the envy of all the trees of Eden
        that were in the garden of God.
10 **Therefore thus says the Lord GOD: Because it towered high and set its top among the clouds, and its heart was proud of its height,** 11 **I gave it into the hand of the prince of the nations; he has dealt with it as its wickedness deserves. I have cast it out.** 12 **Foreigners from the most terrible of the na-tions have cut it down and left it. . . .**

^{13} On its fallen trunk settle
   all the birds of the air,
 and among its boughs lodge
   all the wild animals
^{14} All this is in order that no trees by the waters may grow to lofty height or set their tops among the clouds, and that no trees that drink water may reach up to them in height.
   For all of them are handed over to death,
     to the world below;
   along with all mortals,
     with those who go down to the Pit.
^{15} Thus says the Lord GOD: On the day it went down to Sheol I closed the deep over it and covered it; I restrained its rivers, and its mighty waters were checked. I clothed Lebanon in gloom for it, and all the trees of the field fainted because of it. ^{16} I made the nations quake at the sound of its fall, when I cast it down to Sheol with those who go down to the Pit; and all the trees of Eden, the choice and best of Lebanon, all that were well watered, were consoled in the world below. ^{17} They also went down to Sheol with it, to those killed by the sword, along with its allies, those who lived in its shade among the nations.

^{18} Which among the trees of Eden was like you in glory and in greatness? Now you shall be brought down with the trees of Eden to the world below; you shall lie among the uncircumcised, with those who are killed by the sword. This is Pharaoh and all his horde, says the Lord GOD.

In this prophecy, which is also a warning that Egypt will fall as prey to the unstoppable power of King Nebuchadrezzar of Babylon, we are reminded of Ezekiel's rich poetic skills. It is once again a parable, a literary artifice in which the favored visual picture-making of the prophet can take full advantage of his poetic gift. The varied features of the imagery of the parable create startling contrasts and so achieve a memorable effect. Egypt is a cedar tree, to the eyes of a countryman of Judah the most impressive and beautiful of trees and a relatively rare sight. The towering cedar of Lebanon had provided essential timber for the temple building of Jerusalem. In its mature form as a living tree it provided a sight that was not easily forgotten, one worthy to adorn the garden of Eden itself (v. 9). So it makes an excellent symbol of the greatness of Egypt, with its remarkable architecture and massive monuments to long-dead pharaohs.

Such a tree, well watered and towering above the lesser fir and plane trees, represented the majesty of Egypt. In this, there comes to the fore the typical Judean love-hate attitude toward the civilization of Egypt, revealing both awe and anger. Israel was a people that had come out of

Egypt, and Moses had been an eminent and influential figure in the pharaonic court. Yet Egypt stood for oppression, for the whip of the slavedriver and the yoke of humiliation. So, for all its beauty, it was a civilization shamed by wickedness (v. 11). It deserved to be punished by God, and now the time had arrived; Nebuchadrezzar can be seen as the agent appointed by God to inflict such judgment (v. 12).

The picture the prophet develops, therefore, is of the felling of this proud and mighty tree. It is to be brought level with the ground and left as a fallen trunk where birds can settle and wild animals can find shelter (v. 13). A judgmental verdict insists that the very height of the cedar has made it an expression of pride—a claim to superiority that is an offense to God (v. 14).

The date given at the beginning (v. 1) places the prophet's parable in the early months of the siege of Jerusalem, when Ezekiel would have been well aware that many of his hearers, like a significant number of the beleaguered Jews in Jerusalem, were still clinging vainly to the hope that Egypt would march forth to deliver the city. We can well understand their need to believe that Judah can yet be saved, since the city's act of rebellion would have relied heavily on Egyptian promises from the outset. Like his contemporary, Jeremiah, Ezekiel is convinced that such hope is worthless and represents a refusal to place real trust in God. In the prophetic message of Ezekiel, as of Jeremiah, all these attempts to put confidence in risky political alliances are looking in the wrong direction—to human beings and not to God—for salvation.

The concluding unit of the poem, in the prose section of verses 15–18, explores more extensively the theme of the descent of the mighty tree to the earth and thence into the dark underworld of Sheol, which was believed to lie beneath it as the realm to which the dead descended. It is added as a basis for broadening and extending the original message of God's judgment upon Egypt at a specific time into a portrayal of a more enduring and ultimate downfall.

Most probably, this was intended to serve as a warning to those many citizens of Judah who sought refuge in Egypt, as did those who fled there after Jerusalem had fallen, taking the prophet Jeremiah with them. After the devastation of Judah, Egypt appeared to offer sanctuary and the possibility of a new beginning. To take such a path, however, was to weaken the basis for renewal in Judah and relapse into a new form of paganism. This is roundly condemned in Jeremiah 44:1–30. Ezekiel, like Jeremiah, views Egypt as a place of false hope. It was so in the past, it was dangerous to think things were different in the present, and it was folly to look to Egypt as a place of hope for the future! The theme was worth emphasizing more than once.

EGYPT'S DOOM IS CERTAIN
Ezekiel 32:1–16

32:1 **In the twelfth year, in the twelfth month, on the first day of the month, the word of the** LORD **came to me:** [2] **Mortal, raise a lamentation over Pharaoh king of Egypt, and say to him:**

> You consider yourself a lion among the nations,
>> but you are like a dragon in the seas;
> you thrash about in your streams,
>> trouble the water with your feet,
>> and foul your streams.

[3] **Thus says the Lord** GOD:
> In an assembly of many peoples
> I will throw my net over you;
> and I will haul you up in my dragnet. . . .

[11] **For thus says the Lord** GOD:
> The sword of the king of Babylon shall come against you.

[12] **I will cause your hordes to fall**
> by the swords of mighty ones,
> all of them most terrible among the nations.
> They shall bring to ruin the pride of Egypt,
> and all its hordes shall perish. . . .

Ezekiel 32:1–16, the lament poem that forms the sixth of the prophecies against Egypt, is again introduced by a precise date (v. 1). This is of interest because it locates the prophecy to the time immediately after Jerusalem fell to the Babylonian armies. Essentially, its message is wholly in accord with earlier prophecies and affirms yet again that Pharaoh king of Egypt will be killed by the sword of the king of Babylon (v. 11). It is not meant literally to be about the personal fate of the Egyptian ruler, but rather expresses the conviction that the Egyptian forces will suffer defeat by the relentless power of Babylon. Once again, poetic imagery gives the prophecy its special power and effect. The "dragon in the seas" to which the Egyptian king is compared in 32:2 is the crocodile, which brought a sense of fear and wonder to any traveler to the swamplands of the lower Nile. Accordingly, Ezekiel pictures the defeat of Egypt as a trapping and slaughtering of one of these fearsome creatures of the region.

There is much color and excitement in Ezekiel's portrayal of coming events. We can only speculate as to why the prophet finds it important to reaffirm his conviction of Egypt's coming downfall after Jerusalem has fallen. Clearly it was a time when a significant community of Jewish refugees was establishing itself in Egypt and beginning to think of this land as offering a hope for the future rebirth of Jewish life. Ezekiel's prophecies declare a firm no to all such expectations. Egypt's judgment is still to come! The importance of this message becomes clearer once we consider chapter 33, in which Ezekiel's own vision of Israel's rebirth is disclosed.

EGYPT'S FINAL HUMILIATION
Ezekiel 32:17–32

32:17 **In the twelfth year, in the first month, on the fifteenth day of the month, the word of the LORD came to me:**
   18 **Mortal, wail over the hordes of Egypt,**
        and send them down,
     with Egypt and the daughters of majestic nations,
        to the world below,
        with those who go down to the Pit.
   19 **"Whom do you surpass in beauty?**
        Go down! Be laid to rest with the uncircumcised!"
20 **They shall fall among those who are killed by the sword. Egypt has been handed over to the sword; carry away both it and its hordes.** 21 **The mighty chiefs shall speak of them, with their helpers, out of the midst of Sheol: "They have come down, they lie still, the uncircumcised, killed by the sword."**

   22 **Assyria is there, and all its company, their graves all around it, all of them killed, fallen by the sword. . . .**

   24 **Elam is there, and all its hordes around its grave; all of them killed, fallen by the sword, who went down uncircumcised into the world below, who spread terror in the land of the living. . . .**

   26 **Meshech and Tubal are there, and all their multitude, their graves all around them, all of them uncircumcised, killed by the sword; for they spread terror in the land of the living. . . .**

   29 **Edom is there, its kings and all its princes, who for all their might are laid with those who are killed by the sword; they lie with the uncircumcised, with those who go down to the Pit.**

   30 **The princes of the north are there, all of them, and all the Sidonians, who have gone down in shame with the slain, for all the terror that they**

caused by their might; they lie uncircumcised with those who are killed by the sword, and bear their shame with those who go down to the Pit. . . .

The final prophecy concerning the downfall of Egypt, found in Ezekiel 32:17–32, offers a kind of cataclysmic finale to Ezekiel's prophecies about Egypt and, more extensively, to his prophecies about the world of nations. It is a dramatic presentation of the twilight of the gods, picturing as it does the death and descent into the underworld of the Egyptian ruler. A recurrent theme throughout the lament concerning the "hordes of Egypt" expresses Ezekiel's feeling, one no doubt shared by most of his fellow exiles, that Egypt was a very large nation but militarily weak.

The picture of the Egyptian pharaoh's downfall is then given dramatic emphasis by a variation on the familiar theme of a descent into the underworld (see Isa. 14:4–21 for a similar treatment of the fall of the ruler of Babylon). This descent into the feared and hidden realm of departed spirits is one in which the once-mighty ruler is pictured as slipping into a dark, lifeless world where only shadowy spirits remain. Here the several nations that at one time looked tremblingly up to Egypt's king at the height of his power now gaze in amazement at his weakness and humiliation. Egypt's glory has departed!

A succession of nations is listed as forming a band of awestruck witnesses to the king of Egypt's end: Assyria, Elam, Meshech, Tubal, Edom, and Phoenicia (Sidon). They occupy the front places to observe the great king's ignominious procession into nothingness. Pharaoh's day is done! Few processions of antiquity can have equaled in magnificence and grandeur the final burial and entombment of an Egyptian pharaoh in his pyramid. Almost an entire lifetime would have been spent in preparation for this moment. Ezekiel now replays such an awesome occasion in reverse. Pharaoh's end is the ultimate proof of his powerlessness. Kingly onlookers stand silent and amazed that this is all that remains of a ruler who was once so strong.

A remarkable feature of this magnificent and heavily ironic poem is the repeated use of the catchphrase killed "by the sword" (vv. 20, 21, 22, 23, 24, 25, 26, 28, 29, 30, 31, 32), which provides a damning indictment of human militarism and military showmanship. Those who have fought and killed so determinedly in life find themselves bitter and shamefaced companions in death!

The list of nations who stand observing Egypt's final downfall makes a fitting close to the whole series of Ezekiel's foreign-nation prophecies. In a significant way, this lament, which singles out one of the great world powers of antiquity, serves to highlight the transitory nature of all human glory. King Nebuchadrezzar has written a remarkable chapter of human history with his long list of triumphs and conquests. When the story is complete it will make a tale that later generations will read with wonder as the list of conquered nations is recited. Yet, strangely, as this account of the martyrdom of nations unfolds, the king of Babylon is the one great actor in the story to whom no word of judgment or lament is addressed.

It is clear that Nebuchadrezzar's acts are assumed throughout each of these great prophecies. He is the agent of God who is to bring judgment upon the nations. Yet Ezekiel never says that his time of judgment will also come. We have to turn instead to Isaiah and Jeremiah for such a message. Why this absence is so marked in the book of Ezekiel can only be speculated on. Probably it was due entirely to the situation in which the prophet found himself. Jeremiah's book provides us with adequate proof that the fate of any prophet among the exiles who presumed to foretell the downfall of the ruler of Babylon was likely to be terrible (Jer. 29:22). There could have been no future for Ezekiel, and no role of leadership for him, had he spoken such a message. It was a truth all could believe but which could only be spoken in silence.

The foreign-nation prophecies of Ezekiel are surprising when taken as a class. The modern reader is likely to find them difficult to understand and respond to with any spiritual warmth. As God's chosen spokesperson, admonishing and rebuking the sins and failings of his own people, Ezekiel gives us a wealth of insight and detail about the problems and tensions of an ancient society. Yet when we look at these foreign-nation prophecies, the picture is less clear. Quite evidently, the prophet's direct personal knowledge and experience of life among the peoples who were the subject of these prophecies were minimal. Accordingly, it was a bold undertaking to declare God's word concerning them. His assertions are built on facts that are broad and general, known for the most part at second hand. His admonishments are focused on such widely known features as the famed seagoing trade of Phoenicia or the geography of Egypt. There is less sense of immediacy and of intimate personal involvement, such as occurs with the rebukes to Israel and Judah. In the case of foreign rulers, the great sin that is condemned par excellence is that of pride—human showmanship and love of power.

Nevertheless, we can admire the great poetic skill with which these prophecies, almost all of them sharply condemnatory in character, present a distinctive challenge of their own. They contain creative imagery and, in Ezekiel's case, more than a few echoes of a remarkably varied world of legend concerning events in a hidden divine world. But we cannot ignore the question of their theological relevance. Obviously, they mark one of the ways in which Ezekiel, as an outstanding figure among the prophets of Israel, delivered a message that made sense of a complex chapter of his nation's history. The conviction that the Lord reigns was fundamental to all worship and adherence to the Lord as the God of Israel. Yet clearly it was not satisfactory to suppose that Israel was caught up in a fierce wrestling match between rival divine beings. Each nation would then have been reduced to the level of helpless onlooker in a struggle fought out among competing gods.

It seems likely that more than a little of such a belief was canvased in the victory inscriptions of the conquering powers of the ancient Near East, boasting of the superiority of one all-powerful god over a host of lesser ones. Proof of superiority was simply the fact of conquest. For Ezekiel, as for all the other prophets from the time of Amos, no such simplistic article of faith was possible. Righteousness demanded faith in a deity who judges all peoples, not just a handful of foreigners. So the prophetic faith that Israel and Judah had been handed over to the judgment of the Lord demanded a larger and more theologically credible understanding of God. God was the God of all nations and peoples, and the divine purposes of history must relate to other peoples besides Israel and Judah. If Jerusalem's sufferings were a judgment from God, so also must the sufferings of neighboring peoples have a similar meaning.

Accordingly, we can see that the foreign-nation prophecies of Ezekiel do serve an important purpose. Probably the closest modern parallel would be to challenge the faith of those who believe that all divine grace and blessing are channeled exclusively through the Christian church. The destiny of the larger world of nations would then be written off as of no concern to God. Obviously, we should find great difficulty with a belief that reduces God to such small dimensions.

However difficult and incomplete the picture, we are driven to believe that, unless all human history is absurd, God is active in and through the world of all peoples. That this should raise a need for careful reflection on what it means to be a special nation, and what it means to belong to a church or synagogue, does not make it unnecessary to think of the larger truth. Discerning the hand of God in human affairs has never been an easy task, but the alternative of dismissing all history as absurd and meaning-less is also unsatisfactory. Ezekiel reminds us that because we live in a sit-uation of grace and privilege does not mean that God is not also genuinely present and active in the wider world, of which we see and know only a very small part. Today, with our vastly enlarged understanding of the uni-verse, Ezekiel raises for us the awareness that other worlds and other be-ings may have an unknown place in the plan of God. The claim that the Lord reigns becomes a remarkably comprehensive truth.

8. The Challenge of Hope
Ezekiel 33:1–37:28

So far, apart from a few editorial comments and supplements, the prophecies we have studied cover the period from the prophet's call in 593 B.C. to Jerusalem's siege and final destruction, which occurred in 587 B.C. This was a period of six-and-a-half years, and there are firm indications that Ezekiel's message remained consistent and sharply focused during that time. If it was the case that Ezekiel lost the power of speech after his wife's death, this would have left his hearers in an uncomfortable "wait and see" state, during which there was ample opportunity for his words to sink into the minds of those who were with him in Babylon as hostages. Their position was now deeply compromised, and their future uncertain. The very reason that once made their presence a useful lever for the imperial plans and politics of Babylon had now largely disappeared.

All this must have been simmering in the minds of Ezekiel's fellow Judeans as they pondered their future. The hope that had kept them going for more than ten years must have appeared increasingly impossible and its abandonment inevitable. There could be no immediate or near return to their old homeland.

Up to the time of the final rebellion of Zedekiah and the campaign to quell the dissident kingdoms of Judah and Ammon, there are positive indications that the Babylonian authorities allowed a fairly continuous and free interchange of correspondence and information between Jerusalem and the encampment in Babylon by the river Chebar where Ezekiel was. Such regular communication is also presupposed by Ezekiel's prophesying, because for much of the time after his call he obviously had reasonably up-to-date information about affairs in Judah. Some of this may be credited to his visionary and imaginative sensitivity, but much was evidently based on a more formal exchange of news and advice. The outrage expressed in Ezekiel 17, for example, seems clearly based on information received about activities in Judah.

This exchange of news, which Ezekiel was able to employ to good effect in his prophesying, dried up after the siege of Jerusalem began; the information blackout lasted several months. For the prophet and his fellow exiles it must have been a period of foreboding, although we can only guess at the gradual way in which the realization prevailed that there was little likelihood that Jerusalem would be able to hold out indefinitely.

It is not hard to imagine how a few well-intentioned former Judeans at first bolstered the flagging hopes of their fellow exiles by recalling stories of the marvelous deliverance Jerusalem experienced more than a century earlier when the Assyrian forces of Sennacherib failed to take the city (Isaiah 36—37). Yet to hope for this to be repeated was clinging to an illusion. The rightness of Ezekiel's long forewarned message of disaster must have looked increasingly assured. Hope was fast fading; only the final dreaded word of confirmation that Jerusalem had fallen was lacking. This came, as might be expected, in the person of a survivor who was brought as a prisoner to Babylon (Ezek. 33:21–22; the NRSV's "fugitive" is misleading, because no right-minded survivor would have sought refuge in the enemy homeland). Quite certainly, he was the first of many; the Babylonian authorities implemented a further round of deportations after Jerusalem was captured in 587. No further proof of Ezekiel's prophetic interpretation of events was needed. Jerusalem was ruined and Judah's cause was lost! Ezekiel had been proved right, and all hope of a last-minute reprieve for the beloved city was gone.

We can picture the mixture of awe, alarm, and despair that now gripped the Judean exiles in Babylon, their numbers daily swelling as new survivors from Jerusalem joined them. It was the point zero of Israel's existence, a catastrophe that was made all the more fearful because there now appeared to be no reasonable avenue of hope left. Yet this is the moment when Ezekiel's whole prophetic message takes on a new direction and a new vitality: The word of the Lord is the source of all hope. It is the moment when the most basic of all human feelings and instincts has to face reality. God has given Israel its existence in the beginning. If that existence is a genuine expression of the divine will, Israel can be born again and a new nation can be given life. It was, in the whole of Old Testament history, the most challenging and triumphant moment for the prophetic experience. It was the point at which, when other helpers failed and other comforts were exhausted, the fundamental promise of God was all that was left.

This message of hope is what Ezekiel now offers to his compatriots, and it is recorded, in all its rich poetry, in chapters 33—37 of the prophet's book. It is given a concluding triumphant expression in parable form in Ezekiel 37, with the portrayal of an ancient battlefield graveyard suddenly and miraculously stirring with a new life. It is the message of resurrection! The language is that of a parable, not of a foretelling about life after death. Nevertheless, it promises the resurrection of the nation of Israel, as the word of God is to give new life to dead bones.

From the perspective of giving insight into the human condition and opening a vista on a dimension of spiritual truth, it is a remarkable achievement. Hope is one of the three primary virtues, according to Paul (1 Cor. 13:13). When set in a particular historical and national context, as it is with Ezekiel, we can sense the reason for this high valuation. Only hope can counter depression. Only hope can revitalize shattered and exhausted bodies. Only hope can penetrate the darkness and uncertainty of the future to provide a beacon of light. And when hope can no longer be found in the intrinsic possibilities of a situation, one must look beyond that situation to find a more enduring basis. One must look to the word of God for an undeniable affirmation that the divine promises, implicit in creation and in past historical experience, remain valid. God wills a future for his people!

In setting out his message of hope, Ezekiel remains tied to a few central features drawn from the knowledge of God's history with Israel in the past. These are simple and basic:

1. The divine sovereign power will not be thwarted by human willfulness and unbelief.
2. God's promise to the house of David—the king who ruled according to God's purpose—is more important than the practical mistakes and failures of subsequent kings.
3. The sacredness of the land of Israel that was once given to the nation's ancestors takes priority over the defiling of that territory by Israel's sins and the land-hungry greed of neighboring peoples.

Over and against these basic truths are undoubted and formidable objections: Israel has sullied the name of God in the past by its conduct; the kings who succeeded David have not matched the founder's vision and boldness; foreigners (Edomites) now occupy much of the Holy Land that once was part of Israel. In asserting the power and possibility of hope, Ezekiel points to the objections that appear to preclude the realization of that hope. One by one, he rebuts them and asserts that, if human sin is great, yet are the grace and power of God greater!

Seen in context, it is clear that Ezekiel's prophetic message of hope was addressed at a particular point of time to a particular group of people who had been plunged into the deepest despair. However, because the prophecies were recorded in writing and the unfolding years witnessed major changes in the political and social scene, the message acquired a larger and more enduring quality: It came to be regarded as a fundamental vision of hope that could be revised and reapplied to later generations as new challenges emerged. Although this message lacks something of the lyrical quality of the biblical expressions of hope in the Psalms and in Isaiah 40—55, it nonetheless became an established charter for later Judaism.

From a Christian viewpoint, it is in the book of Revelation in the New Testament that the message of hope proclaimed and recorded by Ezekiel is given its fullest Christian expression. Its combination of practical, this-worldly features with a richly spiritual and heavenly awareness of the ultimate purposes of God for humankind makes it a wonderfully influential feature of the Bible. A message of hope couched in vague words and ideas, no matter how true, lacks the gripping power of a great vision of a new society and a new quality of life. It is that dressing of hope in the clothes of visionary pictures that makes Ezekiel's message such a lasting and memorable one.

THE GREAT TURNING POINT
Ezekiel 33:1–33

33:1 The word of the LORD came to me: 2 O Mortal, speak to your people and say to them, If I bring the sword upon a land, and the people of the land take one of their number as their sentinel; 3 and if the sentinel sees the sword coming upon the land and blows the trumpet and warns the people; 4 then if any who hear the sound of the trumpet do not take warning, and the sword comes and takes them away, their blood shall be upon their own heads. 5 They heard the sound of the trumpet and did not take warning; their blood shall be upon themselves. But if they had taken warning, they would have saved their lives. 6 But if the sentinel sees the sword coming and does not blow the trumpet, so that the people are not warned, and the sword comes and takes any of them, they are taken away in their iniquity, but their blood I will require at the sentinel's hand.
    7 So you, mortal, I have made a sentinel for the house of Israel; whenever you hear a word from my mouth, you shall given them warning from me. 8 If I say to the wicked, "O wicked ones, you shall surely die," and you do not speak to warn the wicked to turn from their ways, the wicked shall die

in their iniquity, but their blood I will require at your hand. [9] But if you warn the wicked to turn from their ways, and they do not turn from their ways, the wicked shall die in their iniquity, but you will have saved your life.

[10] Now you, mortal, say to the house of Israel, Thus you have said: "Our transgressions and our sins weigh upon us, and we waste away because of them; how then can we live?" [11] Say to them, As I live, says the Lord GOD, I have no pleasure in the death of the wicked, but that the wicked turn from their ways and live; turn back, turn back from your evil ways; for why will you die, O house of Israel? . . .

[17] Yet your people say, "The way of the Lord is not just," when it is their own way that is not just. [18] When the righteous turn from their righteousness, and commit iniquity, they shall die for it. [19] And when the wicked turn from their wickedness, and do what is lawful and right, they shall live by it. [20] Yet you say, "The way of the Lord is not just." O house of Israel, I will judge all of you according to your ways!

[21] In the twelfth year of our exile, in the tenth month, on the fifth day of the month, someone who had escaped from Jerusalem came to me and said, "The city has fallen." [22] Now the hand of the LORD had been upon me the evening before the fugitive came; but he had opened my mouth by the time the fugitive came to me in the morning; so my mouth was opened, and I was no longer unable to speak.

[23] The word of the LORD came to me: [24] Mortal, the inhabitants of these waste places in the land of Israel keep saying, "Abraham was only one man, yet he got possession of the land; but we are many; the land is surely given us to possess." [25] Therefore say to them, Thus says the Lord GOD: You eat flesh with the blood, and lift up your eyes to your idols, and shed blood; shall you then possess the land? [26] You depend on your swords, you commit abominations, and each of you defiles his neighbor's wife; shall you then possess the land? . . .

[30] As for you, mortal, your people who talk together about you by the walls, and at the doors of the houses, say to one another, each to a neighbor, "Come and hear what the word is that comes from the LORD." . . . [32] To them you are like a singer of love songs, one who has a beautiful voice and plays well on an instrument; they hear what you say, but they will not do it. [33] When this comes—and come it will!——then they shall know that a prophet has been among them.

From the point of view of the literary structure of the book, chapter 33 carries the reader back to the events recorded in Ezekiel 24. The chapters that intervene, dealing as they do with the destiny of non-Israelite peoples, establish a kind of pause. Several of the prophecies do in fact relate directly to the period of a year and a half in which Jerusalem was under siege by the armies of Babylon. It is as though the reader is given time to reflect deeply about the import and its meaning for the nations of all that has been said and written up to the time when Jerusalem faces its most severe threat. Chapter 33 resumes the story. Most pertinently, verses 21–22 report an incident that resolves two significant issues. The arrival of a survivor from Jerusalem among the exiles in Babylon, bringing confirmation of the disaster that has overtaken the city and its temple, resolves the question of the truth of Ezekiel's earlier message. Just before this event, and indicative of the changing situation it heralds, Ezekiel recovers his power of speech. So now this great prophet has both a new message to proclaim and a new voice with which to proclaim it.

It is noteworthy that the chapter begins in verses 1–9 with a restatement of the prophet's role as a guard, or watchman, for the community. It repeats, with similar wording, the commissioning speech of God to the prophet that first occurs in Ezekiel 3:16–21. It seems pointless to ask whether such an address is more authentically placed at the outset of his ministry or at this major turning point. In a sense, both must be true. The awareness that his concern must now be to proclaim a message of hope to a despondent and unbelieving people marked a new beginning for Ezekiel. Most probably, the entire comparison of the role of a prophet to that of a city watchman was a result of Ezekiel's reflection on his ministry and its meaning for the people. In particular, it challenged him to reflect on his apparent initial failure to awaken a widespread response—a feature that is well brought out by his awareness of facing a rebellious and hostile audience (2:1–7). Significantly also, the task of the sentinel becomes divisive, since some heed his warnings, and respond, while others fail to do so.

Will Ezekiel's task be any more successful now that he has a positive and hope-filled message to give? Initially, we might have expected this to be so. Good news is more welcome and acceptable than bad news! All the more intriguing, therefore, is the unexpected conclusion to chapter 33, which speaks about the kind of response from his audience that he is now experiencing. The prophet's reception is compared to that accorded to a popular singer, "a singer of love songs" (v. 32). His words are well received and even openly applauded, but will they achieve the life-transforming result he seeks? It may well be the case that the very inclusion of such a comment from the prophet is intended as a kind of ironic challenge to his hearers and readers. It is not enough to listen and applaud, admiring the brilliant images and the fine poetry. Only a changed way of life will be a proper response to his prophesying.

So we find in chapter 33 three separate passages about Ezekiel's work as a prophet. He is a sentinel for the house of Israel (33:1–9), so those who hear his message bear the responsibility for what they hear and how they respond. He is now a vindicated prophet, because all his earlier warnings have been amply confirmed by what has occurred in Jerusalem (33:21–22). And the reputation and awe this brings him have undoubtedly drawn a larger audience and a new admiration (33:30–33). But will this newly won reputation win for his words any deeper effect?

Between these three passages, we have two very deeply thought-through declarations concerning the shape Ezekiel's message is to take from this point on.

The first is found in verses 10–20 and has very close echoes of the message that was spelled out more extensively in chapter 18. It concerns the removal of the burden of the past. Sinners are sinners, and they can hardly complain when they are compelled to live with the consequences of their sin! Yet individuals do not live isolated lives, set apart from those of their families and neighbors. Everything Ezekiel has endeavored to explain about the destruction of Jerusalem was built on the contention that it was a punishment for the past sins of the nation of Israel. What hope then can there be for those who turn away from this past with a deep feeling of shame and a desire for repentance?

Certainly, we are entitled to feel that Ezekiel's heavy emphasis on the sins of Israel from its very beginnings in Egypt leave little room for any within the nation to repudiate this past and turn with hope toward a better future. It is not surprising, therefore, that Ezekiel's book here repeats the argument, already set out in chapter 18, that repentance is both possible and necessary. An additional factor comes into play with the knowledge that Ezekiel's warnings of the doom awaiting Jerusalem and Judah have proved terribly true to events. Jerusalem and its temple lie in ruins, and the community in Judah, who so clearly regarded themselves as the surviving remnant from which would spring forth the new Israel, find this hope is shattered. The eye of faith has now turned unhesitatingly to those who were taken with Ezekiel into exile in Babylon. They are the hope for the rebirth of Israel, but they can only become a genuine part of this hope by heeding the call to the radical repentance the prophet demands. Half measures and halfheartedness are not enough. Nor is it enough simply to admire and applaud Ezekiel's words. Only changed lives can take hold of the hope that the situation now calls for.

A clear structure binds the prophet's reflections on the nature and meaning of his work with the message that is now central to his future proclamation. There is hope and there is to be a rebirth of Israel. The first issue to be settled is defining who will form the remnant from whom this national rebirth will be achieved. It previously seemed obvious, both to those who remained in Jerusalem and to those who were brought with Ezekiel to Babylon, that the future lay with those who remained in the beloved city, Jerusalem. The precious land, the holy city, and especially its unique temple were all self-evident guarantees that God would give new life to Israel from within the land itself.

Now all that has happened in a decade of tragedy makes clear that this can no longer be considered. More important than any of these external symbols of hope and assurance is the fact that priority must be accorded to the preaching and hearing of the word of God. Only those who hear and respond to the call of God can have a place in the new Israel. So repentance and a repudiation of Israel's idolatrous past are the foremost requirements for entry into the new arena of promise. Only when these requirements are met can the external signs of Israel's divinely chosen privilege be accorded a place. Only when a penitent remnant turns to God can the more formal gifts of land, kingship, and prosperity be returned to them.

So we find in 33:23–29 the second fundamental declaration of Ezekiel's prophetic priorities. Its message will change the entire shape of Israel for many generations to come! The old order has passed and a new order is about to be born. The message is simple enough: The survivors who remained in the land of Israel (for a time the prophet Jeremiah was among them) forfeited their privileged position to be the faithful remnant of Israel. Instead, this privilege and opportunity now lies at the feet of those who were in Babylon and whose faithfulness to God was ministered to by the prophet Ezekiel. Evidence of this radical shift of focus is provided by the shameless lives and indifference to all that represents the order of holiness demonstrated by those who survived in Jerusalem (v. 25). Much as they may seek to bolster their reputation and opportunity by recalling the primary call of God to their ancestor Abraham (v. 24), all such self-serving theologizing of the tradition is useless. God is not deceived!

With such a radical shift of spiritual priorities, Ezekiel establishes his claim that the remnant through whom God will work to give birth to a new Israel is the remnant of scattered exiles whose only proof of acceptance with God was their penitent trust in the divine word. It is not surprising that such a major message as this, which marks the spiritual turning point for the exiles in Babylon, requires a solemn warning to bring it to a conclusion (vv. 30–33). It is not the outward hearing and applauding of the word of God, however well intended, but only transformed lives that will show that the message of God has truly been heard.

THE GOOD AND BAD SHEPHERDS
Ezekiel 34:1–31

34:1 The word of the LORD came to me: [2] Mortal, prophesy against the shepherds of Israel: prophesy, and say to them—to the shepherds: Thus says the Lord GOD: Ah, you shepherds of Israel who have been feeding yourselves! Should not shepherds feed the sheep? [3] You eat the fat, you clothe yourselves with the wool, you slaughter the fatlings; but you do not feed the sheep. [4] You have not strengthened the weak, you have not healed the sick, you have not bound up the injured, you have not brought back the strayed, you have not sought the lost, but with force and harshness you have ruled them. [5] So they were scattered, because there was no shepherd; and scattered, they became food for all the wild animals. . . . [7] Therefore, you shepherds, hear the word of the LORD: . . . [10] Thus says the Lord GOD, I am against the shepherds; and I will demand my sheep at their hand, and put a stop to their feeding the sheep; no longer shall the shepherds feed themselves. I will rescue my sheep from their mouths, so that they may not be food for them.

[11] For thus says the Lord GOD: I myself will search for my sheep, and will seek them out. [12] As shepherds seek out their flocks when they are among their scattered sheep, so I will seek out my sheep. I will rescue them from all the places to which they have been scattered on a day of clouds and thick darkness. . . . [15] I myself will be the shepherd of my sheep, and I will make them lie down, says the Lord GOD. [16] I will seek the lost, and I will bring back the strayed, and I will bind up the injured, and I will strengthen the weak, but the fat and the strong I will destroy, I will feed them with justice. . . .

[20] Therefore, thus says the Lord GOD to them: I myself will judge between the fat sheep and the lean sheep. [21] Because you pushed with flank and shoulder, and butted at all the weak animals with your horns until you scattered them far and wide, [22] I will save my flock, and they shall no longer be ravaged; and I will judge between sheep and sheep.

[23] I will set up over them one shepherd, my servant David, and he shall feed them: he shall feed them and be their shepherd. [24] And I, the LORD, will be their God, and my servant David shall be prince among them; I, the LORD, have spoken.

[25] I will make with them a covenant of peace and banish wild animals from the land, so that they may live in the wild and sleep in the woods securely. [26] I will make them and the region around my hill a blessing; and I will send down the showers in their season; they shall be showers of blessing. . . . [29] I will provide for them a splendid vegetation so that they shall no more be consumed with hunger in the land, and no longer suffer the insults of the nations. [30] They shall know that I, the LORD their God, am with them, and that they, the house of Israel, are my people, says the Lord GOD. [31] You

are my sheep, the sheep of my pasture and I am your God, says the Lord
GOD.

From this point on, three themes dominate the understanding of rebirth
and renewal as Ezekiel interprets it: kingship, land, and holiness. It is
wholly in order that this should be so, since Ezekiel's insistence that the
new Israel will be born from those who were so pitiably taken as hostages
to Babylon, and forced into near slavery there, was an unexpected doctrine. Kingship, in particular the unique kingship associated with the dynasty of David, lies at the heart of Israel's sense of being chosen. That God
chose David and his sons to rule over Israel was a way of asserting that
God was blessing and protecting Israel as his people. But by Ezekiel's day
the image of the house of David had become a sadly tarnished one. The
later kings of so famous a line had proved far from popular with their own
people and displayed little of the greatness that tradition accords their illustrious ancestor and founder, as the later chapters of 2 Kings make clear.
Zedekiah, the last of the Davidic line to sit on the throne in Jerusalem, finished his days in shame and defeat and died a tragic and miserable death.
Yet no metaphor of kingship was more entrenched in the popular vocab-
ulary of Israel than that of the shepherd with his flock. Its origins can be
traced in Mesopotamia back to the early years of the second millennium
B.C., when Babylonian kings justified their right to rule. Its use in the celebrated twenty-third psalm may owe something to this earlier use of the
image of shepherd by ancient early kings.

Yet if "shepherd" is an appropriate symbolic title for a king, Ezekiel
rightly judges that Israel has suffered an ample share of bad shepherds.
Kings have played no small part in the nation's downfall, a point that is
amply reinforced by the story of that collapse recorded in the biblical narrative history. So we have in 34:1–10 a remarkable and far-reaching condemnation of the abuse of power by Israel's kings. They have failed miserably to do their job. Instead of feeding the sheep, they ate them (v. 10)!

Ezekiel asserts that in the future the shepherds who rule over Israel will
be faithful to their task (vv. 11–16). All the familiar pictures of a consci-
entious shepherd doing his work are employed to show the qualities of
good government that bring blessing and prosperity to a nation. It is noteworthy that, for all his recognition of the damage done by bad kings,
Ezekiel does not reject the institution itself. Probably such a political possibility could not readily have been envisaged; a popular democracy was
not then a recognized ideal in Israel. Instead, the full weight of responsibility is placed by Israel's prophets on the institution of kingship—and by

implication on all related offices of public leadership—as a form of commitment and service for the benefit of others.

The obligation that will fall on the future rulers of Israel is clear, and it is further spelled out by Ezekiel in other passages. The decisive affirmation is given in verses 23–24, which merit close attention. There is no reason to doubt their authenticity, and Ezekiel's striking emphasis on the divine right of "my servant David" is worth noting carefully. The Davidic dynasty had, by an act of God's providence, survived the disasters of 598 and 587 B.C. through the deportation to Babylon of Jehoiachin and his family. There is no reason to doubt that, after 587 and possibly from the time of the original deportation, Ezekiel regarded this young prince as the legitimate heir of the royal line of David. The historian who concluded his story of Judah's downfall in 2 Kings 25:27–30 with a note about Jehoiachin's release from imprisonment in Babylon in the year 561 B.C. must have come to share this view that Jehoiachin had been providentially set aside to ensure the continuance of the Davidic line.

In Ezekiel's significant promise in Ezekiel 34:23–24, it is noteworthy that the future king is designated "my servant David," strongly hinting that the greatness and spirit of David himself will come alive again in the new ruler. Yet he is denied the title "king," the prophet preferring simply to call him "prince." Whether the motive for this was primarily political (that is, not to offend the Babylonian authorities) or theological (that is, only God could properly be "king" over Israel) is not clear. Possibly both points carry some weight.

Two further parts of the chapter command attention. First, in verses 17–22, the prophet addresses the flock, quite clearly stressing the point that kings do not rule alone but are heads over a people. The flock may behave badly, thereby making the shepherd's task impossible. Jeremiah hints strongly that Zedekiah, the last of the Davidic line to rule in Jerusalem, was harried and pushed by a powerful party of advisers. By turning to say something to the community who are to be ruled, Ezekiel exploits the possibilities of the metaphor of the kingly shepherd to draw attention to the responsibilities of the flock.

Finally, the chapter concludes (vv. 25–31) with a wider promise concerning the state of the world in the future age of Israel's renewal. This time, it promises, there will be peace and orderliness throughout all creation. The promise closely parallels the similar passage in Isaiah 11:6–9 concerning the removal of all violence from the natural world. It has most probably been added to Ezekiel's prophecy at a later time and looks outward to see a perfect and peaceful world order. Very probably it echoes widely known myths concerning a primeval "age of innocence," from which the whole of creation has lapsed but which will be restored at a future time.

Even though we must judge these simplistic images of a nonviolent vegetarian world to be strangely unrelated to our knowledge of the violent historical origins of the natural world, the promise nevertheless brings home some vital truths. Paul reflects these early Jewish ideas in hinting that the violence of the natural world was imposed as a result of human disobedience to God (Rom. 8:20). All violence is seen as offensive to God. A deep-seated belief in the providential concern for a healthy and beneficial order for all living things becomes a vital feature of the biblical commitment to concern for the natural world. The environment itself, the adequate provision of food, and the removal of all shame and humiliation (v. 29) are seen to belong to the fulfillment of life as God intends it to be.

Several recent shifts of spiritual perception have served to emphasize more forcefully than hitherto the obligation on the human race for an appropriate commitment to the world of animals and plants. The drastic threat to the survival of several major species of wild animals, the dwindling stock of the world's wild places as a consequence of deforestation and overintensive farming, and not least the pollution of much of the natural world as a consequence of industrial exploitation have all contributed to a deepened sense that the world order is threatened. At one time, it was widely believed that this order had within itself a self-correcting and self-adjusting mechanism. Sadly, recent history shows this is not so; it belongs properly to the spiritual lordship (Gen. 1:28) of the human species to take active steps to care for the natural world.

RETRIBUTION UPON THE LAND OF EDOM
Ezekiel 35:1–15

> 35:1 **The word of the LORD came to me:** [2] **Mortal, set your face against Mount Seir, and prophesy against it,** [3] **and say to it, Thus says the Lord GOD:**
> **. . .** [5] **Because you cherished an ancient enmity, and gave over the people of Israel to the power of the sword at the time of their calamity, at the time of their final punishment;** [6] **therefore, as I live, says the Lord GOD, I will prepare you for blood, and blood shall pursue you; since you did not hate bloodshed; bloodshed shall pursue you.** [7] **I will make Mount Seir a waste and a desolation; and I will cut off from it all who come and go. . . .**
> [10] **Because you said, "These two nations and these two countries shall be**

mine, and we will take possession of them,"—although the LORD was there—[11] therefore, as I live, says the Lord GOD, I will deal with you according to the anger and envy that you showed because of your hatred against them; and I will make myself known among you, when I judge you. . . .

At first glance this chapter, which threatens God's judgment on the land of Edom, appears to be misplaced and to belong among the prophecies against foreign nations that are to be found in chapters 25—32. This is not so, however; this denunciation of the people of Edom and the harshly worded threat against them is set here for a reason. After the catastrophe of 587 B.C. the land of Judah lay in ruins, with no strong, effective governmental center to maintain law and to protect villages and towns. This situation was grievously exploited by the people of Edom, who took advantage of Judah's weakness to cross from their territory east of the river Jordan to take possession of land in Judah (this is reemphasized in 36:5). Naturally, such opportunism was deeply resented and added to the long-standing sense of bitterness a new dimension of hatred and desire for revenge. We find this yearning for redress and for God to exact a proper punishment upon Edom here.

In considerable measure, the land-grabbing excesses of the Edomites are typical of the kind of practical objection that could be raised against Ezekiel's message of hope. First among his concerns is the matter of kingship. This appears carefully and designedly taken care of by the survival among the exiles in Babylon of a Judean royal household with several princes (as is shown by the list of their names and descendants in 1 Chronicles 3:16–23). In turning next to the question of land, Ezekiel faces the fact that the territory of Israel and Judah has not remained unoccupied and empty since it was devastated by the armies of Babylon. Eager land hunters have moved in from across the border in Edom and are obviously not going to give back land they stole without a fight. Ezekiel's conviction is that God himself will take care of this situation and punish Edom for its opportunistic seizure of land and villages that previously belonged to Judah.

One unusual and highly significant feature in the prophecy could easily be overlooked. Ezekiel, like all the major prophets of Israel, essentially considers the chosen people to be one people, usually called Israel but sometimes divided between Ephraim and Judah or Israel and Judah. In practical terms, ever since the death of Solomon more than three centuries before, the people were effectively divided in two when the tribes of the northern part refused to recognize the special rights of the Davidic dynasty to rule over the united nation (see Isaiah's "both houses of Israel,"

Isa. 8:14). In the eyes of the world, then, they appear as two nations. Yet the prophets shunned such a term, as did the historian of 1 and 2 Kings, who wrote his history with difficulty in order to uphold this sense of the nation's oneness; to speak of Israel as "two nations" is consistently avoided. It is rather a surprise therefore to find placed on the lips of the people of Edom in Ezekiel 35:10 the assertion that Israel is two nations and two countries. Almost certainly, it reflects the way in which the Edomite people did look upon Judah and Israel (or Ephraim). Yet the point is worth noting that it was not Ezekiel's natural way of thinking or writing.

In his parables of the foundling girl (Ezekiel 16) and the two evil sisters (Ezekiel 23), the historical fact of Israel's past political divisions weighs heavily upon Ezekiel's thinking about the failures of the past. It is a point that will be taken up even more forcefully by him in a piece of dramatic street theater in 37:15–28. Division means weakness and eventual disaster; unity means faithfulness, loyalty, and strength. However hard unity is to establish and maintain, it is a virtue worth striving for. There may therefore be a conscious touch of rebuke in setting in the mouths of the Edomites the very consciousness of Israel's division and weakness that the prophet felt to be wrong. To see Israel as two divided peoples was how the Edomites viewed things, not how God saw them!

THE PROMISE OF
THE LAND OF ISRAEL
Ezekiel 36:1–15

36:1 **And you, mortal, prophesy to the mountains of Israel, and say: O mountains of Israel, hear the word of the LORD. [2] Thus says the Lord GOD: Because the enemy said of you, "Aha!" and, "The ancient heights have become our possession," [3] therefore prophesy, and say: Thus says the Lord GOD: Because they made you desolate indeed, and crushed you from all sides, so that you became the possession of the rest of the nations, and you became an object of gossip and slander among the people. . . . [6] Therefore prophesy concerning the land of Israel, and say to the mountains and hills, to the watercourses and valleys, Thus says the Lord GOD: I am speaking in my jealous wrath, because you have suffered the insults of the nations; [7] therefore thus says the Lord GOD: I swear that the nations that are all around you shall themselves suffer insults.**

[8] But you, O mountains of Israel, shall shoot out your branches, and yield your fruit to my people Israel; for they shall soon come home. [9] See now, I

am for you; I will turn to you, and you shall be tilled and sown; [10] **and I will multiply your population, the whole house of Israel, all of it; the towns shall be inhabited and the waste places rebuilt;** [11] **and I will multiply human beings and animals upon you. They shall increase and be fruitful; and I will cause you to be inhabited as in your former times, and will do more good to you than ever before. Then you shall know that I am the LORD. . . .**

Ezekiel's message now develops more fully its central theology of hope and renewal. The land of Israel was the pride and delight of the nation. It was regarded in the priestly thinking with which Ezekiel has been familiar since childhood as the special possession and gift of God; we find this openly spelled out in Leviticus 25:23, and Leviticus 25 in its entirety explains the deep spiritual significance of the land of Israel and why it came to be thought of as a uniquely holy land. For one who thought in such a manner, and for the fellow Judeans who shared with Ezekiel a miserable existence in Babylon, the land was home in the fullest possible sense. Nothing in Ezekiel's challenging doctrine that God has appointed the repentant exiles in Babylon to form the nucleus of the reborn Israel can replace the sense of failure and hopelessness that surrounds the loss of the land.

Accordingly, Ezekiel clings firmly to the belief that the land will be restored to the nation and will once again be the blessed homeland of Israel—sacred, fertile, a gift to ensure prosperity. Ringing in his words we hear the taunts and jibes he has heard expressed by the Babylonians and probably by some of his own people. "The Lord must be a complete failure as a god, otherwise Israel would not have been driven out from its land. If the Lord were really God, you would not be here!" Against such insults and taunts, Ezekiel sets up his firmest promise of faith: The land of Israel will once again be settled by God's people, and its towns and villages will be rebuilt (especially vv. 9–11). The land will once again be Israel's land, resplendent in all its bounty and goodness. Instead of Israel suffering insults and taunts, it will be the nations roundabout who hear such words (v. 7).

The message is very important because it retains the significance of the land as a central part of Israel's faith. Exile in Babylon and dispersion among the nations do not mean that God has forsaken the land of Israel; nor does it mean the land is no longer important for the future existence and spiritual well-being of the people. Far from it! The land remains as important as ever, but there has to be a time of waiting and cleansing before Israel can go back home. That this was so, and that Ezekiel's hearers took a good deal of convincing that such a promise was a realistic one, is shown by the further development of the point that follows in the prophecy.

WHY THE LAND WAS LOST
Ezekiel 36:16–21

36:16 **The word of the LORD came to me:** [17] **Mortal, when the house of Israel lived on their own soil, they defiled it with their ways and their deeds.** . . . [18] **So I poured out my wrath upon them for the blood that they had shed upon the land, and for the idols with which they had defiled it.** [19] **I scattered them among the nations.** . . . [20] **But when they came to the nations, wherever they came, they profaned my holy name, in that it was said of them, "These are the people of the LORD, and yet they had to go out of his land."** [21] **But I had concern for my holy name, which the house of Israel had profaned among the nations to which they came.**

In order to give credence to the contention that Israel is suffering a temporary state of exile, which had a clear beginning and will have a definite end, Ezekiel saw the necessity of explaining why this should have become inevitable. Past failures and disasters were the consequences of Israel's sins, but why should this require the people to be driven out of the land? It appears to stand in sharp contradiction to the very idea that this was in a real sense God's land. Verses 16–21 develop Ezekiel's priestly theology of the land in a unique and interesting manner. Not only did the people dishonor themselves and their religious calling when they sinned, they defiled the land on which they were settled (v. 18). In this, Ezekiel's spiritual reckoning gives full weight to the ancient and deep-rooted doctrine that violence and the shedding of blood render the land unclean. Blood, shed violently in criminal behavior, can cry out to God for the wrongdoer to be punished, as in the case of the murder of Abel by Cain (Gen. 4:10: "your brother's blood is crying out to me from the ground!"). Unsolved murders, in which the corpse of a victim is found with no clear indication of how and by whom the crime was committed, still need careful investigation so that innocent citizens may be absolved from responsibility (this is shown in the requirements given in Deut. 21:1–9 for a special ritual to absolve the community from bloodguilt in such cases).

So Ezekiel is able to turn around the objection raised by his doubting hearers that if Israel's land was God's land they would not have been driven from it. On the contrary, he insists, it is precisely because it *is* God's land that they had to be turned out so the land could be cleansed and purged (vv. 19–20). However, such a doctrine, if pushed to its full extent, would suggest that there is little chance of Israel's going back to the homeland, if their present state is a punishment from God. With all the passionate conviction drawn from his faith in God's sovereignty, Ezekiel insists that the supreme holiness of God's name is more important than the holiness of God's land and God's people. Such a name can never be defiled, so God will act for the sake of the divine reputation among the nations to bring Israel back to its former homeland.

An especially interesting feature here is the way in which the concept of holiness fashions Ezekiel's argument. As a priest he grew up with a deep-rooted conviction that the life of the temple and its properly performed rituals and services ensures the holiness of the land and people of Israel. For a while, that ministry of sanctification was clearly set in abeyance by what happened to the Jerusalem temple. It must have seemed to many that the entire work of holiness had been frustrated. Yet Ezekiel falls back on the most basic of his spiritual armory of thought: The most holy reality of all is the reality of God's name. That holiness can never be besmirched or nullified by human beings. So, ultimately, God will defend the holiness of the divine name by restoring Israel to the land.

THE SOVEREIGNTY OF GOD
AND THE POWER OF THE NAME
Ezekiel 36:22–37

> 36:22 Therefore say to the house of Israel, Thus says the Lord GOD: It is not for your sake, O house of Israel, that I am about to act, but for the sake of my holy name, which you have profaned among the nations to which you came. [23] I will sanctify my great name, which has been profaned among the nations, and which you have profaned among them. . . . [24] I will take you from the nations, and gather you from all the countries, and bring you into your own land. [25] I will sprinkle clean water upon you, and you shall be clean from all your uncleannesses, and from all your idols I will cleanse you. [26] A new heart I will give you, and a new spirit I will put within you; and I will remove from your body the heart of stone and give you a heart of flesh. [27] I will put my spirit within you, and make you follow my statutes and be careful to observe my ordinances. [28] Then you shall live in the land that I gave to your ancestors; and you shall be my people, and I will be your God.

29 I will save you from all you uncleannesses, and I will summon the grain and make it abundant and lay no famine upon you. . . .

33 Thus says the Lord GOD: On the day that I cleanse you from all your iniquities, I will cause the towns to be inhabited, and the waste places shall be rebuilt. . . . 36 Then the nations that are left all around you shall know that I, the LORD, have rebuilt the ruined places, and replanted that which was desolate; I, the LORD, have spoken, and I will do it. . . .

An intriguing path of logic and reasoning is shaping the development of Ezekiel's argument that the modern reader may find difficult to follow. For most citizens in secularized Western society, the concept of holiness does not convey the power and awesomeness that it carried in the ancient world. In fact it would appear from the wording of the command of Jesus to his followers that they should seek to be "perfect," rather than to be "holy" (Matt. 5:48), that even by New Testament times the idea of holiness had become mixed and confused. Yet Ezekiel's doctrine here of the holiness of God leads him to set out a passionately evangelical argument concerning God's saving power, producing a passage that anticipates the Pauline doctrine of the sovereignty of divine grace in a most remarkable fashion. God himself will act to ensure the future restoration and renewal of Israel. It will not be an action dependent on the good behavior and good intentions of the people but, rather, will be based on the sovereign power of God's holiness to act to uphold the honor and reputation of so great a name (especially vv. 22–23).

Such an initiative on the part of God might, it could be argued, be greeted with coldness and indifference by Israel as a people—especially those who were on the edge of despair in their painful Babylonian exile! Ezekiel counters this dispiriting rejoinder by arguing that, just as God cleansed and renewed Israel as a people through the temple services, so will a future act of spiritual sprinkling and cleansing take place to make a new people fit for the new Israel (v. 25). More startling still, this doctrine of a new inner spiritual renewal is summed up with a truly evangelical assurance: "A new heart I will give you, and a new spirit I will put within you" (v. 26). Nowhere else in the Old Testament, except in a closely parallel passage in Jeremiah 31:33–34, does the message of the power of the divine spirit to energize and renew the minds and hearts of people come so completely to the fore. Renewal and hope are gifts of grace, not of human achievement! What is needed is a sense of human emptiness, rather than of human potential, since that emptiness can be filled by the grace and power of God.

Of course, such a doctrine can become unbalanced and overdrawn, as it has in some aspects of Christian tradition, yet it may be seen in all its majesty in its proper setting. It is the true antidote to despair, perhaps the only such antidote, when addressing a community that feels it has been pushed down into a well of hopelessness. God alone possesses the power and the will to lift them free. God is indeed the "help of the helpless"!

Ezekiel develops the theme further by saying that all life-giving properties of holiness will be restored to Israel (vv. 29–30), showing how he shares his contemporaries' semiphysical understanding of holiness as a form of divine energy. Very movingly also, he deals with the problem of the painful memories of the past that Israel can never expect to shake off (v. 31). Such memories can have an accusing and destructive force, frustrating and nullifying the full effect of God's intention to create a new and joyful people. Yet it is not necessary that memories of the past raise such a finger of negative accusation. They can be turned to good effect by reinforcing the awareness that Israel's renewal is a gift of grace and that grace remains constant.

The final section of the chapter (vv. 33–38) serves as a summary of the hope that Ezekiel seeks to give the people. It repeats the basic features that have already been set out: The land will be repopulated, towns and cities will be rebuilt, and the fields will once again be farmed. A final touch returns to the theme of the shepherd and his flock, by means of which Ezekiel dealt with the question of the future government of the nation. As flocks increase with the season of lambing, so will Israel increase in numbers again. A personal note is struck by the recollection of the crowded festival days that marked the Jerusalem that Ezekiel remembers from his youth (v. 38). It is a dream worth keeping alive!

THE VISION OF
A RESURRECTED NATION
Ezekiel 37:1–14

37:1 **The hand of the LORD came upon me, and he brought me out by the spirit of the LORD and set me down in the middle of a valley; it was full of bones. ² He led me all around them; there were very many lying in the valley, and they were very dry. ³ He said to me, "Mortal, can these bones live?" I answered, "O Lord GOD, you know." ⁴ Then he said to me, "Prophesy to these bones, and say to them: O dry bones, hear the word of the LORD. ⁵ Thus says the Lord GOD to these bones: I will cause breath to enter you, and you shall live. ⁶ I will lay sinews on you, and will cause flesh to come** upon you, and cover you with skin, and put breath in you, and you shall live; and you shall know that I am the LORD."

⁷ So I prophesied as I had been commanded; and as I prophesied, suddenly there was a noise, a rattling, and the bones came together, bone to its bone. ⁸ I looked, and there were sinews on them, and flesh had come upon them, and skin had covered them; but there was no breath in them. ⁹ Then he said to me, "Prophesy to the breath, prophesy, mortal, and say to the breath: Thus says the Lord GOD: Come from the four winds, O breath, and breathe upon these slain, that they may live." ¹⁰ I prophesied as he commanded me, and the breath came into them, and they lived, and stood on their feet, a vast multitude.

¹¹ Then he said to me, "Mortal, these bones are the whole house of Israel. They say, 'Our bones are dried up, and our hope is lost; we are cut off completely.' ¹² Therefore prophesy, and say to them, Thus says the Lord GOD: I am going to open your graves, and bring you up from your graves, O my people; and I will bring you back to the land of Israel. ¹³ And you shall know that I am the LORD, when I open your graves, and bring you up from your graves, O my people. ¹⁴ I will put my spirit within you, and you shall live, and I will place you on your own soil; then you shall know that I, the LORD, have spoken and will act," says the LORD.

Great ideas and themes carry the greatest weight and endure the longest when they are given a visionary form. Such images are essential to a prophet like Ezekiel, for whom seeing with the eye of faith is a fundamental feature of believing. Word pictures possess the ability to clothe ideas with color and shape. That which he sets out in 37:1–14 has understandably become just such a picture; it has defied the limitations of historical time and setting to become an enduring vision of hope. It is a description of an act of resurrection, although we must recognize that it is not about personal resurrection and life after death but about the resurrection of a nation. Israel will be reborn. To this extent, the envisioned picture says nothing that Ezekiel has not already said in his description of national renewal in chapter 36. However, the magnificent image of long-dead soldiers resurrected from an ancient battlefield gives this word picture its power to stay in the mind as a timeless expression of spiritual hope.

Many concerned persons, mindful of national history, will spend time looking out over a landscape that once thundered with the noise and din of battle. Whether from a more distant past or a recent one, visitors seldom leave the scene where such a clash of arms occurred without feeling awestruck by its memories. Some have even felt themselves to have been invisibly touched by the hands of the victims of such ancient battles.

Ezekiel, with his highly emotional temperament, must certainly have experienced such feelings, must have thought back on places in the land of Israel that were the killing fields of past conflicts. Very probably, the conviction that the Holy Land had been polluted by the violent shedding of blood (36:18) awakened a concerned awareness of the blood shed on Israel's battlefields. The vision that he here unfolds is of such a battlefield coming noisily and startlingly to new life. Bone is joined to bone and flesh appears on the whitened skeletons of long-dead warriors to create new persons. A new Israel is to be born from the lifeless corpses of the dead.

What adds to this picture, but would appear grotesque if it were deprived of its spiritual content, is the emphasis on the power of the prophetic word to summon the breath (that is, spirit) of God (vv. 9–10). It is hard to find any more sharply defined and exalted word picture of the power of human speech than that given here. A calling to the four winds might seem a gesture of futility, were it not that the winds contain the life-giving power of God to bring renewal. The visionary picture that Ezekiel presents reveals his consciousness of the responsibility he carries as a prophet. So far as detail is concerned, even though nothing is added to the portrayal of the new Israel that has not already been given, there is a new sense of its certainty. It is now clothed with a symbolism that emphasizes its total dependence on the power of God. Human weakness and emptiness and divine power and fullness are here set out as two complementary realities that will ensure that Israel has a future.

The reader sensitive to the vitality of speech and to the relationship between word and picture will find that Ezekiel is here able to turn a popular saying into a memorable vision. The sort of comment of despair that Ezekiel was hearing every day is reported in verse 11. "Our bones are dried up" expresses the sense of physical weakness and hopelessness that was an understandable reaction to the situation. It is the saying of men and women at the end of their tether. Yet standing against this hopelessness is the ability of the prophet to awaken a belief in hope, established on an awareness of God's reality and power. What seems impossible in human terms is possible to God.

ONE NATION, ONE RULER
Ezekiel 37:15–28

37:15 **The word of the LORD came to me:** [16] **Mortal, take a stick and write on it, "For Judah, and the Israelites associated with it"; then take another stick and write on it, "For Joseph (the stick of Ephraim) and all the house of**

Israel associated with it"; [17] and join them together into one stick, so that they may become one in your hand. [18] And when your people say to you, "Will you not show us what you mean by these?" [19] say to them, Thus says the Lord GOD: I am about to take the stick of Joseph (which is in the hand of Ephraim) and the tribes of Israel associated with it; and I will put the stick of Judah upon it, and make them one stick, in order that they may be one in my hand. [20] When the sticks on which you write are in your hand before their eyes, [21] then say to them, Thus says the Lord GOD: I will take the people of Israel from the nations among which they have gone, and will gather them from every quarter, and bring them to their own land. [22] I will make them one nation in the land, on the mountains of Israel; and one king shall be king over them all. . . .

[24] My servant David shall be king over them; and they shall all have one shepherd. They shall follow my ordinances and be careful to observe my statutes. . . . [26] I will make a covenant of peace with them; it shall be an everlasting covenant with them; and I will bless them and multiply them, and will set my sanctuary among them forevermore. [27] My dwelling place shall be with them; and I will be their God, and they shall be my people. . . .

The short visionary outline of the new Israel that is to be born is brought to a conclusion with two themes. The first concerns the unity of Israel as God's people (vv. 15–23), and the second reaffirms the unity of the nation under a single Davidic ruler (vv. 24–28). The message about the unity of Israel is given expression by a dramatic gesture in which Ezekiel joins two sticks in his hand, one bearing the name Joseph and the other bearing the name Judah (v. 19). It appears to be a roundabout and complicated way of making an obvious point. Yet the point cannot have been all that obvious to the prophet's hearers. Something special was needed in order to make the message remain in the minds of those who saw the prophet's action.

From close study of the historical and political development of ancient Israel, opinion among scholars remains significantly divided over the question: Was Israel an original unity that simply broke apart under the strains brought about by Solomon's oppressive reign (1 Kings 12)? The opposing view is that in the earliest period the group of southern clans that made up the tribe of Judah and the group of northern clans that constituted Israel (Joseph) were really quite separate. Only the shared worship of the Lord as God and the success and leadership of David brought them briefly together to form a united people of Israel. The breakup after Solomon's death was thus a reversion to an earlier division.

Whatever their origins may have been, the idea of Israel as a unity was clearly very important to the prophets of the Old Testament and to none more so than Ezekiel. We have already seen that he felt the division of the two entities of Israel and Judah to have been part of the rebelliousness that brought ruin upon the people. For the future, therefore, the reunification of Israel was essential. In reality, we can see from a historical perspective that Israel was destined to remain divided for a very long time to come. But it was not the old tribal divisions that came to dominate the political scene, it was the split between an Israel that continued as a multiplicity of small communities scattered among the nations and a small, more nationally oriented community in Judah. Restored nationhood in the fullest sense was a dream that was to elude Israel for many centuries after Ezekiel's day.

From the vantage point of time, Ezekiel's vision for the future of Israel can be seen to have a strangely contradictory effect. By his assertion of the divine purpose and protection for Israel to remain scattered among the nations, however much this was regarded as a temporary necessity, the age of dispersion acquired acceptance and spiritual meaning. Yet in Ezekiel's eyes it was only thought to be a short-term emergency in God's plan. Its ending was to be real and definitive. In historical fact, the experience of a temporary exile was to pass, almost imperceptibly, into a new interpretation of Israel as a scattered leaven of witness bearers among many nations. In such scattered form, Judaism survived. Not until the formation of the modern state of Israel in 1947 did the tension reemerge between Israel as a nation and Judaism as a dispersed leaven of Jewish communities settled among the nations. It is possible to argue that, both for Jews and Christians, the biblical legacy of the idea of a "people of God" left a fruitful if unresolved tension between religious individualism and a consciousness of national corporate responsibility.

A final summary in verses 24–28 concludes Ezekiel's great series of prophecies of hope. It contains two basic assurances. The first assertion is that an heir of the dynasty of David will once again be king over Israel. This reaffirms the promise of 34:23–24, only this time the meaningful title of *king* is employed for the new ruler. Whether or not this is by the hand of Ezekiel, who would now be abandoning his earlier restraint about using the title, is not clear. More probably it is the work of an editor who recapitulated the promise from the earlier Ezekiel saying and was less cautious about employing the traditional title. The fact that various titles are employed for the new civil ruler at different points throughout the book—prince, shepherd, king—should be taken as indicative of the changing political scene in which the prophetic book took shape. The important point was to assert God's order and rule, whatever political restraints influenced the use of titles.

The second assertion is that God will once again dwell among the people, clearly implying that a new temple sanctuary is to be built. Both themes bear a relationship to the understanding of Israel's unity. The oneness of God is to be reflected in the oneness of the people, and the reemergence of a renewed Davidic kingship will put an end to the divisiveness that contributed to the downfall of the old Israel.

9. Interlude:
A Final Viewpoint
Ezekiel 38:1–39:24

Chapters 38 and 39 have proved to be one of the most mysterious and most contested parts of the book of Ezekiel. The section forms a sequel to the message of hope and deals with a threat to Israel from a prince called Gog, of the land of Magog. The threat is a major one and comes "out of the remotest parts of the north" (38:15). God arises to defend Israel against this Gog and swiftly brings terrible destruction upon him. After he is defeated, the weapons and armor of his warriors are destroyed in a huge conflagration, and the corpses of his dead soldiers are left as a sacrificial feast for birds of prey. It is all an unexpected and in most respects unwelcome aftermath to the bold and confident message of hope expressed in chapters 33–37.

Scholarly opinion remains divided about the origin and purpose of this text, which adds a rather ominous postscript to the ringing tones of the earlier message of assured hope. In some parts of the section, notably in 38:17–23, there is a marked awareness that the time of the great prophets of Israel already lies in a distant past ("I spoke in former days by my servants the prophets of Israel," 38:17). This suggests that what we are presented with here is no longer a report of Ezekiel's message given during the early years of the Babylonian exile; it is a much later message, added at a time when Ezekiel's grand assurances still seemed unfulfilled and the prosperity they promised needed to be looked at afresh.

Various suggestions have been put forward as to who this Gog of the land of Magog could have been. In Genesis 10:2, the name Magog refers to a Japhethite nation, and this may have offered some clue to ancient readers. Either Alexander the Great (fourth century B.C.), or Antiochus Eupator (a second-century Hellenistic Syrian ruler) have been considered as possibilities. The name may have been left deliberately obscure to indicate a line of rulers or even an as yet unidentified foreign power. Defining who Gog actually was is not such an important question. More interesting is the vital contribution these two chapters make toward understanding Ezekiel's book as a whole.

Clearly, Ezekiel's message was given at a time when Israel's national fortunes were at their lowest ebb and hope seemed all but impossible. He painted a picture of a return to the land and a national renewal culminating in the rebuilding of the temple of Jerusalem and Israel's return to full independent nationhood. In the event, such a hope was only partly realized by the end of the sixth century B.C. Undoubtedly, all grand visions are inevitably compromised by the untidy and incomplete nature of historical reality. So Israel's return and restoration were less than ideal. The story is revealed to us by the prophecies of Haggai and Zechariah, and later problems and controversies concerning Israel's restoration are reported to us by Ezra and Nehemiah. Ezekiel's enthusiastic portrayal of a blessed and resplendent new Israel is more richly colored than proved possible in actual events.

This is not to say that Ezekiel's vision was in any sense false, only that its fulfillment was incomplete. National strife continued within Israel, new conflicts arose with neighboring powers, and, most significantly, the dispersion of Jews among the nations did not come to an end. So the fulfillment that took place a half century or so after Ezekiel's grand vision needed, in the course of time, to be updated and set in a new perspective. In a sense, Ezekiel's picture of a new Israel and a new Jerusalem became the foundation of a greater vision, transcending the possibilities of earthbound reality.

This is exactly how it is taken and developed in the New Testament book of Revelation, especially Revelation 21, which shows Ezekiel's historically circumscribed hope enlarged to a worldwide supernatural hope for the future of all humanity. The prophet's vision, seen in a time of crisis, comes to be regarded as a signpost to a larger vision of the complete purpose of God. The chapters about Gog of Magog were probably introduced at least two centuries after Ezekiel's time to show that the full range of the prophet's vision of hope had still not been fulfilled. They mark a significant stage in the development of the larger prophetic hope.

They are nevertheless vital to the book, since without them the prophecies of Ezekiel would be simply a matter of past history, telling us only about the sufferings and hopes of a people at a crisis period in their national fortunes. The inclusion of these two chapters about later threats and conflicts places the original prophecies in the larger setting of Israel's ongoing history. They show how the prophetic message of hope offers a window on a much larger hope about the purpose of God for Israel and the world. They break out from the confines of the period of Ezekiel's original prophecies to show us his vision's timeless meaning.

ENTER GOG, A NEW CHALLENGER
Ezekiel 38:1–9

38:1 **The word of the LORD came to me:** [2] **Mortal, set your face toward Gog, of the land of Magog, the chief prince of Meschech and Tubal. Prophesy against him** [3] **and say: Thus says the Lord GOD: I am against you, O Gog, chief prince of Meshech and Tubal. . . .**

[7] **Be ready and keep ready, you and all the companies that are assembled around you, and hold yourselves in reserve for them.** [8] **After many days you shall be mustered; in the latter years you shall go against a land restored from war, a land where people were gathered from many nations on the mountains of Israel. . . .**

The prophecies about Gog of the land of Magog extend from 38:1 to 39:24. The opening unit, 38:1–9, introduces the enemy army and lists its allied forces (v. 5). We might have hoped for some historical clues as to the identity of the enemy, but the information is inconclusive. It is not even certain whether the nations described form a coalition or merely provide mercenary units for the army of Gog. Verse 8 gives a strong hint that the prophecy originated long after the time of Ezekiel's words of hope concerning the restoration of a new settlement in the land of Israel.

THE EVIL PLANS OF GOG
Ezekiel 38:10–16

38:10. . . . **Therefore, mortal, prophesy, and say to Gog: Thus says the Lord GOD: On that day when my people Israel are living securely, you will rouse yourself** [15] **and come from your place out of the remotest parts of the north, you and many peoples with you, all of them riding on horses, a great horde, a mighty army;** [16] **you will come up against my people Israel, like a cloud covering the earth. In the latter days I will bring you against my land, so that the nations may know me, when through you, O Gog, I display my holiness before their eyes.**

The warlike intentions of Gog are spelled out in all their cruelty and starkness in 38:10–16. They convey a sense of ultimacy; this is to be a final showdown of hostile and idol-worshiping powers against God and the people of God. So the message is given that this is not just one more war but a massive conflict, a war to end all wars. At issue is the holiness and sovereignty of God (v. 16). A consciousness that the promised restoration of Israel has not brought a complete end to the problems and conflicts of Jews reverberates through the prophecy. A more decisive victory is needed.

GOG AND THE FINAL BATTLE BETWEEN GOOD AND EVIL
Ezekiel 38:17–23

38:17 **Thus says the Lord GOD: . . . ¹⁸ On that day, when Gog comes against the land of Israel, says the Lord GOD, my wrath shall be aroused. . . . ²¹ I will summon the sword against Gog in all my mountains, says the Lord GOD; the swords of all will be against their comrades. ²² With pestilence and bloodshed I will enter into judgment with him; and I will pour down torrential rains and hailstones, fire and sulfur, upon him and his troops and the many peoples that are with him. ²³ So I will display my greatness and my holiness and make myself known in the eyes of many nations. Then they shall know that I am the LORD.**

The sense of a final conflict between God and a vast massed array of human forces of evil is given even clearer expression in 38:17–23. We have already pointed out that this is best taken as a further addition to the original prophecies, which gives them an exceptionally forceful character. No longer does it appear that what is described is a conflict between human powers at all. God is directly waging war, using weapons that belong exclusively to the Sovereign of the universe—pestilence, torrential rains, hailstones, fire, and sulfur (v. 22). The careful reader is likely to be reminded of the account of the defeat of the Assyrian king Sennacherib's army outside Jerusalem by "the angel of the Lord" (2 Kings 19:35).

In keeping with the overall character of the Gog prophecies, but enlarging this still further in a supraworldly manner, what is described is a final conflict between the forces of good and evil, a theme that is brought out in its starkest form in the books of Daniel and Revelation. In a great many features its development represents one of the enduring ways in which the message of prophecy has exercised a lasting influence upon Christian church history. It reveals a picture of conflict between good and evil continuing right until the final endpoint of human history. Appropriately, it places God on the side of righteousness and goodness, but it is significant in the way in which it accords a sense of realism about the forces of evil. It challenges any belief in the inevitability of progress in human government and world order. Evil cannot easily and readily be wrung from the fabric of human folly. There can be no gradual squeezing out of the sin-soaked garments of history.

At the same time, this text in no way condones any surrender to lethargy and despair. Commitment for what is right and godly belongs to the very heart of human existence. There can be no indifference to the challenge of evil, and so it is appropriate that, in this remarkable short prophetic section, the power of Gog becomes virtually synonymous with the power of all satanic forces. There is a challenge of godlessness against the holiness and creative purpose of God. The conflict is real, life-threatening, and must ultimately lead to the triumph of God and the overthrow of evil. It is a remarkable picture—perhaps best described as a kind of mythic drama—in which the reality of the force of evil is set within particular limits. God is sovereign over all creation, but this sovereignty is not yet fully realized and will only be accomplished in a great final battle. This message of conflict and suffering brings us close to recognizing that a cross lies at the heart of all human history.

THE DEFEAT OF THE INVADERS
Ezekiel 39:1–16

> 39:1 And you, mortal, prophesy against Gog, and say: Thus says the Lord GOD: I am against you, O Gog, chief prince of Meshech and Tubal! . . . 5 You shall fall in the open field; for I have spoken, says the Lord GOD. 6 I will send fire on Magog and on those who live securely in the coastlands; and they shall know that I am the LORD. . . .
>
> 11 On that day I will give to Gog a place for burial in Israel, the Valley of the Travelers east of the sea; it shall block the path of the travelers, for there Gog and all his horde will be buried; it shall be called the Valley of Hamon-gog. 12 Seven months the house of Israel shall spend burying them, in order to cleanse the land. . . . 15 As the searchers pass through the land, anyone who sees a human bone shall set up a sign by it, until the buriers have buried it in the Valley of Hamon-gog. 16 (A city Hamonah is there also.) Thus they shall cleanse the land.

The attack upon the restored Israel by Gog, chief prince of Meshech and Tubal, is clearly a great shock to the Jewish community. This real fear and alarm point to the conclusion that some actual historical experience lies behind the Gog prophecies. For the rest, the lack of clear detail and the exaggerated dramatic elements would seem to imply some form of mythical "last battle." A genuine experience has probably been dressed up in traditional clothes. At all events, the important feature here is the insistence that all that is happening to the Jewish people, which appears to threaten their very survival, is restrained by the controlling hand of God. Gog's attack is allowed to take place under the hand of God, who is secretly controlling the battle and its outcome. So the prophecy has a reassuring tone.

10. The New Israel
Ezekiel 40:1–48:35

The book of the prophecies of Ezekiel is brought to a conclusion in 40:1–48:35 with a long and detailed vision of what the restored Israel will be like, precisely dated to the twenty-fifth year of Ezekiel's exile in Babylon (573 B.C.). This places it at a significant point in the prophet's and his fellow sufferers' time of waiting and hoping. Apart from the exception of the prophecy regarding Egypt that revises the threat against Tyre (29:17–21), this is the latest prophecy in the book. A grand conclusion of this kind is what we should expect, and the vision of the new temple and the renewed Israel provides a memorable climax to the prophecies of hope that dominate chapters 33—39. Hope, if couched in ideas and grandiose schemes, can be tentative and vague, but hope focused in a clear-cut vision has a magnetic power. Viewed from the perspective of the book as a whole, these nine chapters establish that the book, in its overall plan and shape, is about renewal and hope. Its two great themes are (1) God's immeasurable power to bring about Israel's restoration and (2) the holiness that will bring grace and power to the new Israel.

The vision can confidently be taken as a genuine work from Ezekiel. In company with the other major visions of the book, it shows abundant signs of careful planning and construction. No longer are there blurred or confusing edges to the pictures. The vision is presented in the form of a report in which the prophet is lifted up by "the hand of the Lord" (40:1) and set down on a high mountain in the land of Israel. There he is met by an unnamed man who acts as a tour guide to show the prophet around.

The vision makes it clear that the primary feature of the restored Israel is to be a new temple, and this is described in some considerable detail. Ezekiel must often have pictured to himself in his painful exile the old temple of Jerusalem and remembered the upbringing he enjoyed there. A triumphant feature of the report is found in 43:1–5, which tells of the return of the divine glory to the sanctuary. This reverses and counters the departure of the divine glory that Ezekiel witnessed taking place in his terrifying vision of judgment in chapters 8—11. Taken together, the two visions—of God's abandonment of the temple and of the glorious return—show the significance and profundity of Ezekiel's thinking about the meaning of the temple. Its destruction did not signify the powerlessness of God, because the glory departed before this occurred. By the same token it will not be the new building, simply as a human construction, that matters, but the presence of God's glory there. Such thinking was important to counter the views of those despairing skeptics who viewed the ruination of the temple as a sign of the death of God!

That Israel was compelled to survive temporarily with no proper sanctuary was not because a sanctuary was not necessary but, rather, because of Israel's past sins of idolatry. A time of waiting and cleansing was necessary in order to make a new temple for God's glory to reside within and Israel a holy nation once again. A pictorial theologizing of this appears movingly in 47:1–12.

A description of Ezekiel's tour around the new sanctuary forms the heart of the prophet's vision. Added to this report and elaborating on it extensively are a long series of rules and prescriptions governing several major features of life and worship in the restored Israel. It is doubtful that these formed a part of the original vision experience. Instead, they were probably grafted onto it in order to define the administration and order of the new community. The vision calls for practical arrangements, and it is highly improbable that the prophet himself was responsible for them. Rather, these regulations would have been added after the prophet's death. Nevertheless, they stick closely to concerns and convictions that Ezekiel's prophecies embrace. They breathe the air of people who thought in priestly categories. It could be that a prolonged process of growth and expansion to the original vision took place as the prophet's disciples gave their mind to specific problems and details. Much more likely, however, is the conclusion that the vision was elaborated at a significant time when the moment arrived to turn its promises into practice.

This would carry us forward to the period between the years 520–516 B.C., when the task of rebuilding the destroyed Jerusalem sanctuary was undertaken. The story is revealed more fully through the prophecies of Haggai (1:7–11; 2:1–9) and of Zechariah (4:1–10) and is reported in Ezra (3:1–13; 6:13–15). The vision, Ezekiel's great legacy for Israel's rebirth, requires practical working out of its many implications and details. Especially was this so in the wake of the period of more than half a century in which the remnants of Israel were divided between survivors in Judah and others who had become dispersed throughout various parts of the now-collapsed Babylonian empire. It was inevitable that religious divisions and rivalries that require resolution should have sprung up during this period. We need particularly to bear in mind that Ezekiel and those who shared his Babylonian exile were from the leading priestly families of Jerusalem. It seems probable that the rebuilding of the temple, which was certainly subjected to heavy criticism (see Hag. 1:2), was undertaken in an effort to provide a practical symbol of unity for the increasingly divided and separated communities of Jews. The temple, rather than the political leadership, became the badge of Jewish loyalty and unity, a situation that is everywhere evident in the New Testament writings. It is small wonder then that Ezekiel's vision of the new temple became a foundation text for the Judaism that arose after the Babylonian exile.

We have already seen how Ezekiel's prophecies disclose the contentious and deeply resented seizure of land and property in Judah by foreigners, which left a major problem for later generations of claimants to sort out. When we add to this the fact that the new Persian administration, which had taken over from Babylon, imposed demands and restrictions of its own in setting up a wholly new pattern of imperial government, we can understand that practical decisions of a far-reaching kind had to be made. It is no surprise therefore to find issues concerning civil government and land distribution included in the program for Israel's rebirth.

Appropriately, Ezekiel 40—48 is not just a vision of a new and restored Israel but a practical "renewal program" for national reorganization. Understandably, these chapters display a markedly priestly character, indicating that their final form was made by spiritual heirs of the prophet Ezekiel who, like him, traced their family roots to the Jerusalem priesthood. Primarily, they cover religious matters relating to the temple and those who were to administer its services. Yet alongside this, other issues are dealt with in an authoritative manner. These concern government under the headship of one who is called "the prince" (44:3). No mention is made of the fact that he is to be a descendant of the dynasty of David, although this is not ruled out (Zerubbabel, who took a leading role in rebuilding the temple in the years 520–516, was of royal Davidic parentage). We are also struck by the fact that the title "king" appears to have been deliberately avoided.

This accommodates Persian constraints and demands, rather than Judean political theology. Yet in this area too there must have been a good deal of divided opinion among the leaders in Jerusalem. By the time the temple was rebuilt, the royal family had been in exile for three quarters of a century. They now represented a dynasty of those who would, in modern speech, be described as pretenders to the throne of Jerusalem. Even if the imperial Persian administration had been willing to support their return to royal office, many in Judah would have been alarmed by such a move. In any event, it was not until several centuries later (the middle of the second century B.C.) that a new line of Judean kings was established (the Hasmonean dynasty). This later resumption of the royal title brought further conflict and trouble. So the title "prince" in Ezekiel's renewal program tells us something meaningful about the setting up of a new political order under the umbrella of Persian rule.

To the modern reader, the vision of Ezekiel 40—48 touches on many issues that appear historically antique and complex. Yet they were important to the rebirth of Judaism after the calamity that occurred in 587 B.C., and they touch on important spiritual issues. To say the least, the section reveals how prophecy (vision) needs to be complemented and given practicality by rules and regulations (law). The Bible is a handbook of both, and often they have stood in some degree of tension with each other. Prophets have not always, and perhaps not often, been well-organized and practical figures. Pragmatists and organizers have often found themselves frustrated and irked by the unrealistic demands of visionaries. In the history of later biblical thinking, it is noteworthy that Ezekiel's vision acquired twofold meaning and significance.

First, it was quite evidently an immediate and well-directed summons to build a temple in Jerusalem on the site where the ruins of the old building lay, torn down and burned by Babylonian enemies. This was achieved in the years 520–516 B.C., and this event marks a great turning point for the renewal of Jewish life and faith. Yet, second, Ezekiel's vision is suffused with the promise of a yet greater and grander New Jerusalem—a heavenly city resplendent with a temple far more glorious than any earthbound site could contain (as in Revelation 21). One vision has become the pattern and stimulus for the other.

Both features of Ezekiel's vision are important as portrayals of the meaning of the divine society. The building of the kingdom of God is a task for here and now and requires bricks and mortar, money, and self-denial. Yet it is also an impossible dream, a kingdom that cannot be built with human skills and effort. The vision is of the full realization of the meaning of human society in a heavenly kingdom in which God is the light and sanctifying presence. It is Ezekiel's vision that sets this twofold pattern in motion.

Another feature of Ezekiel's renewal program is worthy of close examination. This concerns the extent to which it presents a shortened and summarized program for the new Israel that mirrors in its main outlines, the original constitution for Israel given through Moses (Exodus–Deuteronomy). Ezekiel is a new Moses figure. Like his illustrious predecessor, he does not live to see his vision—also seen from afar, from an unnamed mountaintop (Deut. 34:1–6)—turned into reality.

THE VISION AND
THE HEAVENLY GUIDE
Ezekiel 40:1–16

40:1 **In the twenty-fifth year of our exile, at the beginning of the year, on the tenth day of the month, in the fourteenth year after the city was struck down, on that very day, the hand of the LORD was upon me, and he brought me there.** 2 **He brought me, in visions of God, to the land of Israel, and set me down upon a very high mountain, on which was a structure like a city to the south.** 3 **When he brought me there, a man was there, whose appearance shone like bronze, with a linen cord and measuring reed in his hand; and he was standing in the gateway.** 4 **The man said to me, "Mortal, look closely and listen attentively, and set your mind upon all that I shall show you, for you were brought here in order that I might show it to you; declare all that you see to the house of Israel."**
    5 **Now there was a wall all around the outside of the temple area. The length of the measuring reed in the man's hand was six long cubits, each being a cubit and a handbreadth in length; so he measured the thickness of the wall, one reed; and the height, one reed.** 6 **Then he went into the gateway facing east, going up its steps, and measured the threshold of the gate, one reed deep. . . .** 8 **Then he measured the inner vestibule of the gateway, one cubit.** 9 **Then he measured the vestibule of the gateway, eight cubits; and its pilasters, two cubits; and the vestibule of the gate was at the inner end.** 10 **There were three recesses on either side of the east gate; the three were of the same size; and the pilasters on either side were of the same size.** 11 **Then he measured the width of the opening of the gateway, ten cubits; and the width of the gateway, thirteen cubits. . . .** 13 **Then he measured the gate from the back of the one recess to the back of the other, a width of twenty-five cubits, from wall to wall.** 14 **He measured also the vestibule, twenty cubits; and the gate next to the pilaster on every side of the court. . . .**

We cannot know what opportunities Ezekiel had, as an exile in Babylon, to witness the remarkable and imposing buildings in the city of Babylon itself. When relics of these ancient buildings were recovered in the nineteenth century, their size and magnificence amazed European archaeologists. Ezekiel and his fellow Judeans must have been similarly impressed. Yet no building possessed the beauty and appeal of the old temple in Jerusalem, even as the memory of its appearance faded with the passing of time.

Ezekiel is taken in his vision to see the new temple, and we are able to sense his excitement and enthusiasm as his heavenly guide shows him the various buildings and passages of its re-creation. The role of the heavenly guide is significant because, from this time onward, a vision in which a heavenly interpreter explains and points out features of the heavenly world becomes a basic feature of Jewish literature. How can human beings understand heavenly realities? Clearly they cannot, since we have no basis for comparison with which to work. Yet God can provide a guide for fumbling human minds who will explain the pattern and meaning of heavenly things in terms mere human beings can grasp—a doctrine that has remained important to every Christian understanding of the meaning and possibility of revelation.

A further feature of the description of the new temple strikes our attention. It is a building whose plan was made in heaven and can only be copied on earth. As a holy and divine structure, all temples were meeting places between earth and heaven. So Moses was given the plan of the tabernacle by God (Exod. 24:1–32:16). The measurements of the new temple, therefore, which at first appear overly meticulous, are important as expressing a divine symmetry and balance. Although this concept of a divine proportion and shapeliness has largely disappeared from modern secular architecture, it is important to recall how deeply it shaped and served the architectural achievements of antiquity and the medieval world. That a building should be "something beautiful for God" was a proper response to recognizing that God was the supreme author and architect of beauty.

THE OUTER COURT
Ezekiel 40:17–37

40:17 **Then he brought me into the outer court; there were chambers there, and a pavement, all around the court. . . .** [19] **Then he measured the distance from the inner front of the lower gate to the outer front of the inner court, one hundred cubits.**

[20] **Then he measured the gate of the outer court that faced north—its depth and width. . . .** [23] **Opposite the gate on the north, as on the east, was**

a gate to the inner court; he measured from gate to gate, one hundred cubits.

[24] Then he led me toward the south. . . . [27] There was a gate on the south of the inner court; and he measured from gate to gate toward the south, one hundred cubits.

[28] Then he brought me to the inner court by the south gate, and he measured the south gate; it was of the same dimensions as the others. . . .

[32] Then he brought me to the inner court on the east side, and he measured the gate; it was of the same size as the others. . . .

[35] Then he brought me to the north gate, and he measured it; it had the same dimensions as the others. . . .

The progress through the visionary temple continues with Ezekiel's movement into the outer court. This contained many of the ancillary rooms and lesser buildings that were essential to the temple's effective functioning. Once again, there is great concern for proportion and symmetry in all measurements. Form and function go together, and a deep conviction that proper proportion and balance can convey a sense of the design and orderliness of the Creator's mind is evident. The mathematical numbers are of interest—twenty-five, fifty, and one hundred reveal a system in which careful geometric divisions and subdivisions were observed. So, too, the heavenly guide acts as a skillful architect and engineer, carrying with him a measuring rod as his essential aid. We are reminded of the mysterious figure with the writing case in 9:2. Undoubtedly Ezekiel had watched and been impressed by the many officials who ran the Babylonian state!

The decoration of the pilasters with palm trees (vv. 16, 26, etc.) reflects a widely evidenced feature of ancient holy buildings. The palm tree, both in its impressive height and beauty and its mysterious sexuality, made it appropriate as a symbol of vitality and identified it as a "tree of life." The original Solomonic temple had even more varied symbolism, including flowers, pomegranates, and cherubim (1 Kings 6:29, 32; 7:36, 42); Ezekiel's portrayal displays a certain degree of restraint.

Ezekiel must have walked through the original buildings of the temple in Jerusalem many times, so that to dwell imaginatively on its details provided him with a welcome assurance of the reality of God. However imposing and even awe-inspiring the sacred buildings of Babylon were that gave the city its name (*babilu* is gate of God), there could be for Ezekiel only one true gateway to the divine presence. To his inner sight, that spiritual reality never disappeared but remained with him in Babylon as a kind of mystical presence (see Ezek. 11:16).

FURTHER BUILDINGS AND
FURNISHINGS OF THE TEMPLE
Ezekiel 40:38–41:26

40:38 There was a chamber with its door in the vestibule of the gate, where the burnt offering was to be washed. [39] And in the vestibule of the gate were two tables on either side, on which the burnt offering and the sin offering and the guilt offering were to be slaughtered. . . .

[44] On the outside of the inner gateway there were chambers for the singers in the inner court, one at the side of the north gate facing south, the other at the side of the east gate facing north. [45] He said to me, "This chamber that faces south is for the priests who have charge of the temple, [46] and the chamber that faces north is for the priests who have charge of the altar; these are the descendants of Zadok, who alone among the descendants of Levi may come near to the LORD to minister to him." [47] He measured the court, one hundred cubits deep, and one hundred cubits wide, a square; and the altar was in front of the temple.

[48] Then he brought me to the vestibule of the temple and measured the pilasters of the vestibule, five cubits on either side; and the width of the gate was fourteen cubits; and the sidewalls of the gate were three cubits on either side. [49] The depth of the vestibule was twenty cubits, and the width twelve cubits; ten steps led up to it; and there were pillars beside the pilasters on either side.

41:1 Then he brought me to the nave, and measured the pilasters; on each side six cubits was the width of the pilasters. [2] The width of the entrance was ten cubits; and the sidewalls of the entrance were five cubits on either side. He measured the length of the nave, forty cubits, and its width, twenty cubits. [3] Then he went into the inner room and measured the pilasters of the entrance, two cubits; and the width of the entrance, six cubits; and the sidewalls of the entrance, seven cubits. [4] He measured the depth of the room, twenty cubits, and its width, twenty cubits, beyond the nave. And he said to me, This is the most holy place.

[5] Then he measured the wall of the temple, six cubits thick; and the width of the side chambers, four cubits, all around the temple. . . .

[13] Then he measured the temple, one hundred cubits deep; and the yard and the building with its walls, one hundred cubits deep; [14] also the width of the east front of the temple and the yard, one hundred cubits.

[15] Then he measured the depth of the building facing the yard at the west, together with its galleries on either side, one hundred cubits.

The nave of the temple and the inner room and the outer vestibule [16] were paneled. . . . [17b] And on all the walls all around in the inner room and the nave there was a pattern. [18] It was formed of cherubim and palm trees, a palm tree between cherub and cherub. Each cherub had two faces: [19] a

human face turned toward the palm tree on the one side, and the face of a young lion turned toward the palm tree on the other side. . . .

[21] In front of the holy place was something resembling [22] an altar of wood, three cubits high, two cubits long, and two cubits wide; its corners, its base, and its walls were of wood. He said to me, "This is the table that stands before the LORD." . . .

We are now presented with a report of the main temple courtyards and in particular of the inner sanctuary, the most holy place (41:1–4). Once again the ordered geometric pattern is noticeable, with a marked emphasis on the square pattern of one hundred cubits forming a kind of pure, or whole, space (40:47; 41:13; etc.). The provision of tables and facilities for the preparation and slaughter of the burnt offering and the sin and guilt offerings (40:38–43), and the way in which they are mentioned as a primary feature, indicates that special emphasis is placed on them.

This was not simply a matter of practical necessity, although skill and care were needed to ensure hygienic conditions, the humane slaughter of the animals, and careful manipulation of their blood and carcasses. It was also a matter of theological attention, since the new temple was to be supremely the place where atonement was made for the sins of Israel. Obviously, this was not a wholly new feature; atonement sacrifices were a feature of the Jerusalem temple from its first foundation. Nevertheless, it does appear that these particular classes of sacrifice, and their role in worship generally, were to assume a new prominence once the restored temple came into use in 516 B.C. We know from the sacrificial rules of Leviticus 1—7 that there were many and varied types of sacrifice, but henceforth those specifically aimed at removing the consequences of sin will take overall priority. The listing by Ezekiel of the provision of facilities for these specific types of offerings as of first importance is therefore significant.

Although Ezekiel cannot have intended to achieve such a result, it is possible to discern here a growing curtailment and restriction of sacrifice, taking it progressively out of the hands of lay persons. This prepared the way for the increasing remoteness and priestly distancing of sacrifice from ordinary men and women that eventually led to its demise. When we read the letter to the Hebrews and consider the fact that many Jews of the time of Jesus would rarely have witnessed an approved Jewish act of sacrificial slaughter, save at Passover, we can see that sacrifice was undergoing a great and deeply significant change. From being a crude physical act of bloodshed and slaughter, it was increasingly interpreted in terms of submission to God and self-denial before the divine holiness.

In this fashion, it is possible to see that Ezekiel is not really in fundamental disagreement with the criticism of earlier prophets who denounced the slaughtering of many sacrificial animals as a piece of religious sham (so Amos 5:21–24; Hos. 6:6; Isa. 1:10–17), which achieved nothing of spiritual value when unaccompanied by deeds of justice and righteousness. With Ezekiel, obedient submission to God and remorse for past sins became essential features of the meaning of sacrifice, so much so that, after the temple was again destroyed by the Romans in A.D. 70, formal sacrifice ceased in Judaism and the inner intention of surrender to God replaced the outward form.

The figured decoration of the paneling of the temple described by Ezekiel is now elaborated further by the inclusion of cherubim and palm trees (41:18–20). We learn that the cherubs are portrayed with two faces, one of a human being and one of a young lion. This helps explain Ezekiel's complicated description both of the heavenly throne chariot that came to him at his call and the departure of God's glory from the temple. Such mixed-form creatures were widely used in the decoration of royal and sacred buildings in the ancient Near Eastern world, most especially in Egypt, where several of the gods were portrayed in the guise of hybrid animals.

Obviously the symbolism was designed to express intelligence (human faces), power (lion faces and bodies), and mobility (eagle's wings). The life-giving fertility of the bull was also very important (Ezek. 10:14). All this helps us understand why seeing and visionary images were so important to Ezekiel. He pictured God, rather than listing a series of divine attributes (as in modern theology). Increasingly, and no doubt in reaction against the overuse and grotesque abuse of such images in pagan religions, Judaism and Islam came to shun their employment in worship. Christianity has shown a more mixed response to their historical significance. Nevertheless, in the present image-laden society of modern Western culture, the theological debate is emerging with renewed vigor. Horror images, designed to portray evil and forbidden powers, were clearly a deep affront to Ezekiel (and later to the medieval church), whose tirades against idolatry we have noted extensively. False and threatening images may be as damaging and hurtful as false doctrines! Contrastingly, good images can open up an understanding of truth.

THE PRIESTS' APARTMENTS
Ezekiel 42:1–20

42:1 Then he led me out into the outer court, toward the north, and he brought me to the chambers that were opposite the temple yard and opposite the building on the north. . . .

13 Then he said to me, "The north chambers and the south chambers opposite the vacant area are the holy chambers, where the priests who

approach the LORD shall eat the most holy offerings; there they shall deposit the most holy offerings—the grain offering, the sin offering, and the guilt offering, for the place is holy. [14] When the priests enter the holy place, they shall not go out of it into the outer court without laying there the vestments in which they minister, for these are holy; they shall put on other garments before they go near to the area open to the people."

[15] When he had finished measuring the interior of the temple area, he led me out by the gate that faces east, and measured the temple area all around. . . . [20] He measured it on the four sides. It had a wall around it, five hundred cubits long and five hundred cubits wide, to make a separation between the holy and the common.

If we had not been told from the outset that Ezekiel was brought up as a priest in Jerusalem, we could readily infer the fact from his prophecies. This priestly connection was certainly important, since prophecy lacked the formal institutional rigidity and continuity that the priesthood enjoyed. Probably overall, the Old Testament is more favorable to prophets than to priests, who are often portrayed as clinging to their privileges and assumed status but lacking in religious intensity. Yet true spiritual vitality requires both steadfast continuity and bold originality. The fact that Ezekiel combined priestly training and upbringing with a prophet's characteristic creativity is of primary importance. His prophetic authority enabled him to bring changes to the administration of priestly rules and privileges that would otherwise have been impossible. He was also able to provide a bridge of sacred ministry across the painful interval of time in which the Jerusalem temple lay in ruins, with sacrificial services either nonexistent or severely curtailed (as appears to be the case in Jer. 41:5).

Yet for all the boldness and spiritual originality we find in Ezekiel's message, there remains an underlying adherence to the world of priestly tradition and scruple. It is no surprise, therefore, to find that his vision of the new temple focuses attention on where the priests of the new temple ministry will live and the orderly provision of accommodation and facilities for them. It offers us details that are wholly lacking regarding the arrangements in the old temple that Solomon built. The details may appear to the modern reader to be scrupulously tidy and orderly in their layout. Nevertheless, a significant feature comes to the fore in the explanation given for the plan: The court of the priests is holy (42:13, 14, 20). It is true that it was not regarded as quite as holy as the sanctuary of the main temple complex, which was most holy (41:4), but it was certainly distinct from the everyday world that ordinary citizens inhabited. Therefore, a careful distinction had to be made, and the priests even had to undergo a change of clothing before they mixed with the common people (v. 14).

Such semiphysical ideas of holiness were widespread in the ancient world, and Ezekiel's prescriptions present an interesting aspect of the entire notion of holiness of the special sphere of the sacred. Many scholars have found this feature of Ezekiel's teaching to be restrictive and even backward-looking in its implications. Where prophets earlier endeavored to emphasize the point that holiness is concerned with goodness and righteousness (as in Isa. 5:16), Ezekiel appears to reestablish a more formal and blatantly physical understanding of the concept. When more widely adopted, it was a feature of Jewish development in the second-temple period that was to cause difficulties for the temple authorities (in keeping out foreigners who were judged to be unclean). Concern about holiness and its opposite—that is, the profane and unclean—came to be a cause of provocation and tension between Jews and Gentiles in a larger setting.

It is impossible to feel at ease with what Ezekiel has to say about holiness, seen against the backdrop of later Jewish and Christian teaching on the matter. We are compelled, nevertheless, to recognize the importance of his position as a bridge builder between the old order and the new. It does appear that there were already circles in Israel who regarded holiness as a difficult and unhelpful term that failed to make clear the strong moral demands of allegiance to the Lord as God. It is noteworthy that the teaching of the sages makes only infrequent use of the idea, preferring rather to emphasize loyalty and right-dealing as the primary demands of God. It is unlikely that such a view was shared among the priesthood or that any priest who ignored the demands of holiness could have retained respect and authority. It may even be the case that the very emphatic manner in which the issue is underscored in Ezekiel's renewal program makes rather more of the point than Ezekiel, simply acting as a prophet, would have done. The destruction of the temple by the Babylonian armies drew attention to the issue in a powerful way.

It is interesting to reflect that the very well organized and beautifully arranged quarters for the priesthood of the new temple that Ezekiel envisages contrast markedly with the crude and makeshift features of life in a Babylonian encampment. More than one passage in the book indicates that the prophet instinctively shrank from actions and practices that brought him deep inner feelings of horror and defilement (for example, in 4:14). The visionary attention to the practicalities of life as a priest in the new temple was an important feature in the sense that a new beginning and a new seriousness of priestly endeavor that were to mark its activities. Priests would be free to arrange their way of life and activities in a manner befitting their high calling.

THE MEANING OF THE NEW TEMPLE
Ezekiel 43:1–12

> 43:1 **Then he brought me to the gate, the gate facing east. ² And there, the glory of the God of Israel was coming from the east; the sound was like the sound of mighty waters; and the earth shone with his glory. ³ The vision I saw was like the vision that I had seen when he came to destroy the city, and like the vision that I had seen by the river Chebar; and I fell upon my face. ⁴ As the glory of the LORD entered the temple by the gate facing east, ⁵ the spirit lifted me up, and brought me into the inner court; and the glory of the LORD filled the temple.**
>
> **⁶ While the man was standing beside me, I heard someone speaking to me out of the temple. ⁷ He said to me: Mortal, this is the place of my throne and the place for the soles of my feet, where I will reside among the people of Israel forever. The house of Israel shall no more defile my holy name, neither they nor their kings, by their whoring, and by the corpses of their kings at their death. . . .**
>
> **¹⁰ As for you, mortal, describe the temple to the house of Israel, and let them measure the pattern; and let them be ashamed of their iniquities. ¹¹ When they are ashamed of all that they have done, make known to them the plan of the temple, its arrangement, its exits and its entrances, and its whole form—all its ordinances and its entire plan and all its laws; and write it down in their sight, so that they may observe and follow the entire plan and all its ordinances. ¹² This is the law of the temple: the whole territory on the top of the mountain all around shall be most holy. This is the law of the temple.**

"The glory of the Lord filled the temple" (v. 5). So the purpose and meaning of the vision is brought to a close with the divine presence reentering and reclaiming the building that is to be built again. Because Ezekiel was brought up in Jerusalem, in the temple precincts, the destruction of the temple was for him the removal of a symbol by which the whole of life could be valued and understood. It would have been for him an act of total profanation and senseless vandalism, had he not been given reasons why, in the divine scheme of things, such destruction was necessary. For him, it was God's own people, by their sin and idolatry, who first profaned and abused the temple. So the divine glory departed from the building, leaving an empty and useless edifice that could then be left to its destroyers. Only when the temple was rebuilt and the glory returned would Israel be whole again and the blessing of the temple once again available to the reborn nation.

With this doctrine, we can see a careful theological plan to the visionary features of Ezekiel's book (v. 3). First, God's presence is assured to Ezekiel in Babylon by the coming to him of the divine throne chariot at his call (chapters 1—3); then, in his vision of the departure of the glory from the temple (chapters 8—11), the abandoned state of Jerusalem and Judah is made known. Finally, in a vision of the new temple (chapters 40—43), the prophet is assured that a new temple will make possible the blessing and protection that Israel's sins denied to the old building.

That Ezekiel's followers found this doctrine difficult to believe and accept is suggested by the reinforcement of the doctrine of the unique holiness of the temple in verses 6–9. Our attention is struck by the fact that a new issue is raised here that clearly did not bother Israel earlier but was of growing significance. The royal burial ground had been established immediately adjoining the temple, since the royal palace and the temple proper were part of a single complex. It has even been suggested that, in Solomon's original plan, the temple was little more than a royal chapel. This is certainly an overstatement, but it indicates how closely the civil and religious aspects of the old Israelite state were intertwined. Quite clearly, Old Testament records show how extensively the royal court controlled affairs in the temple, thereby weakening the authority of the priesthood.

Ezekiel wished to see things done differently in the future, and this is undoubtedly a marked feature of Jewish development after Ezekiel's time. The civil and religious aspects of government were still to work together, since they had need of each other. Nevertheless, a much higher profile was to be accorded to priests in the future, and the new civil ruler was to submit to many restraints that the temple authorities demanded. Certainly, a great many factors contributed to the political arrangements that pertained to Judaism in the period of the second temple and differed from those of the first. Ezekiel's strictures here are no more than a symptom of the changing pattern of relationships, born in part of a deep awareness that the monarchy showed a tolerance for idolatry and contributed a large share of misjudgment in bringing about Israel's downfall. Increasingly, the trend toward a strict priestly integrity, separate from political interference, was successful in the future in enabling Jews to live with good conscience under varied political regimes.

A final command to Ezekiel to report the contents of his vision to the people (vv. 10–12) summarizes the purpose of the prophet's experience and helps explain why we have a book of his prophecies. Future generations would know that the rebuilding of the temple originated with divine authority, revealed to Ezekiel and committed to writing by him (v. 11). The command to "write it down" is of special interest, because there are only rare indications among earlier prophets that they themselves put down their messages in written form. With Ezekiel, it is different, and the form of many of his reports, taken together with the character and circumstances of his message, makes it highly likely that most of his prophecies were personally written by him. It seems likely also that literacy and the art of writing were skills that would have been especially nurtured among some if not all priests, who underwent a long apprenticeship.

It is important to keep such features in mind. In spite of many records of the widespread activity of prophets and diviners in the ancient world, only sporadic and occasional evidence survives of detailed prophecies recorded by them. Prophetic books or scrolls, as such, are virtually unique to the Bible. Prophecy clearly had a special importance for Israel. It is remarkable to find that even the central foundation of Judaism's organized religion, the Jerusalem temple, came to rest its authority, after the disaster of 587 B.C., on a prophet's written testimony that this was the purpose of God.

THE NEW ALTAR AND ITS INAUGURATION
Ezekiel 43:13–27

43:13 **These are the dimensions of the altar by cubits (the cubit being one cubit and a handbreadth). . . .**

18 **Then he said to me: Mortal, thus says the Lord GOD: These are the ordinances for the altar: On the day when it is erected for offering burnt offerings upon it and for dashing blood against it,** 19 **you shall give to the levitical priests of the family of Zadok, who draw near to me to minister to me, says the Lord GOD, a bull for a sin offering.** 20 **And you shall take some of its blood, and put it on the four horns of the altar, and on the four corners of the ledge, and upon the rim all around; thus you shall purify it and make atonement for it.** 21 **You shall also take the bull of the sin offering, and it shall be burnt in the appointed place belonging to the temple, outside the sacred area.**

22 **On the second day you shall offer a male goat without blemish for a sin offering; and the altar shall be purified, as it was purified with the bull.**

23 When you have finished purifying it, you shall offer a bull without blemish and a ram from the flock without blemish. 24 You shall present them before the LORD, and the priests shall throw salt on them and offer them up as a burnt offering to the LORD. 25 For seven days you shall provide daily a goat for a sin offering; also a bull and a ram from the flock, without blemish, shall be provided. 26 Seven days shall they make atonement for the altar and cleanse it, and so consecrate it 27 When these days are over, then from the eighth day onward the priests shall offer upon the alter your burnt offerings and your offerings of well-being and I will accept you, says the Lord GOD.

We now leave the realm of the vision proper and move into the first of a series of regulations related to how the new temple is to be furnished and laid out. We have noted in the introduction to the vision that these regulations were probably incorporated as a supplement to the original report in order to fill in details and avoid disorder. If, as was suggested, these further details became necessary when the work of temple rebuilding was undertaken in the years between 520 and 516 B.C., we can understand that it was because many administrative problems arose. Most obvious is the point that Ezekiel's vision was preserved and promoted by descendants of the large body of influential priests who had been taken to Babylon along with Ezekiel in 598 B.C. It cannot have been easy for these leaders after such a long interval to move into a position that would have placed them in charge of affairs in Jerusalem once again. Clearly, more local figures would have sought to keep control of what was to take place on the former temple site. The historical evidence we possess suggests that conflicts and strong disagreements over policy emerged, and it is significant that the final achievements were completed with support and approval from Persian-backed leaders.

We need not be concerned here with the historical problems, but their existence is relevant for understanding why a written program of temple restoration and community reorganization was needed. Thus, Ezekiel's vision of how it would be in the new Israel became a basis for appeal and guidance.

The altar was a supremely important feature of the temple complex. Traditionally it was especially holy. Careful design and particularly stringent services of purification and consecration were required to inaugurate its use. The fact that the former altars of the old building had been desecrated made the task both all the more urgent and the subject of careful scrutiny. We read in 2 Kings 23:16 how the ancient altar at Bethel was deliberately defiled by the burning of human corpses on it, and it is quite possible that similar acts of deliberate defilement were carried out in

Jerusalem. At all events great care was needed, so the assumption was made that a wholly new structure had to be built and new acts of consecration conducted. It was believed that defilement here could affect the efficacy of all subsequent rites of atonement carried out there. We cannot be surprised, therefore, that after the basic vision this is the starting point of a new set of detailed regulations aimed at turning the prophetic vision into historical reality.

THE RULES OF THE PRESENCE
Ezekiel 44:1–14

44:1 **Then he brought me back to the outer gate of the sanctuary, which faces east; and it was shut.** [2] **The LORD said to me: This gate shall remain shut; it shall not be opened, and no one shall enter by it; for the LORD, the God of Israel, has entered by it; therefore it shall remain shut.** [3] **Only the prince, because he is a prince, may sit in it to eat food before the LORD. . . .**

[4] **Then he brought me by way of the north gate to the front of the temple; and I looked, and lo! the glory of the LORD filled the temple of the LORD; and I fell upon my face.** [5] **The LORD said to me: Mortal, mark well, look closely, and listen attentively to all that I shall tell you concerning all the ordinances of the temple of the LORD and all its laws; and mark well those who may be admitted to the temple and all those who are to be excluded from the sanctuary.** [6] **Say to the rebellious house, to the house of Israel, Thus says the Lord GOD: O house of Israel, let there be an end to all your abominations** [7] **in admitting foreigners, uncircumcised in heart and flesh, to be in my sanctuary, profaning my temple when you offer to me my food, the fat and the blood. . . .**

[9] **Thus says the Lord GOD: No foreigner, uncircumcised in heart and flesh, of all the foreigners who are among the people of Israel, shall enter my sanctuary.** [10] **But the Levites who went far from me, going astray from me after their idols when Israel went astray, shall bear their punishment. . . .** [13] **They shall not come near to me, to serve me as priest, nor come near any of my sacred offerings, the things that are most sacred; but they shall bear their shame, and the consequences of the abominations that they have committed.** [14] **Yet I will appoint them to keep charge of the temple, to do all its chores, all that is to be done in it.**

The priestly mind possessed a range of assumptions that controlled everyday thinking about places, persons, and actions. Its fundamental conviction—as much emotional as rational—was that holiness meant difference and separation. This was a very physical idea of the nature of holiness and divine power, but it shaped priestly activities and set invisible boundaries that had to be observed. On the positive side, we can understand that separation promoted a sense of order and established routines and conventions that brought discipline and familiarity. But it also possesses a negative side, since it brought exclusions and aversions that left many persons outside the boundaries of acceptance.

We recognize many of these consequences in the modern world, where a range of distinctions and discriminatory attitudes, both religious and secular, can still bring great hurt and harm. The rules of holiness can also lead to a whole class of unconscious or unintended infringements of their demands, which may bring about deep feelings of guilt and shame. We must therefore view the rules that are reinforced in Ezekiel's program of renewal with considerable reserve and caution. They were to be implemented with urgency and seriousness in the new temple, but they almost immediately caused friction and distrust. The annals of the following centuries bring to light a number of celebrated incidents in which the rules of exclusion and the restriction on the entrance of foreigners into the temple area caused suspicion and conflict.

From the perspective of the New Testament, it is noteworthy that it was the breaking down and subsequent removal of such discriminatory rules by Christians that served strongly to necessitate the break between Jews and Christians. The apostle Peter's address in Acts 10:34–35 reveals several important aspects of this, as also do the charges that were raised by the Jewish authorities against the apostle Paul (Acts 21:26–30). Ezekiel's program, therefore, however well intended in its context, marks a restatement of an attitude to holiness that was to cause increasing difficulties for Jews and that now appears archaic in its historical setting. There are, nevertheless, several important features.

Three issues are dealt with here. First, the east gate of the sanctuary is to remain permanently shut, as a sign that God's glory has entered by it (vv. 1–3). Only the civil ruler, the prince, is to use it, for the purpose of eating certain sacred meals. Second, foreigners are to be excluded from entry into the sanctuary proper because they are uncircumcised, both physically and in their attitude, and will threaten the holy nature of the sacred building (vv. 4–8). This marks the development of an older concern to restrict membership of the worshiping community of Israel to those who were truly committed to its faith and traditions (as in Deut. 23:1–8). It also appears likely that, in the earliest period of Israel's temple worship, use was made of foreigners to perform some of the most menial and unpleasant tasks. Such employment of foreigners in the temple is now prohibited.

In line with this, the third of the regulations, set out in verses 9–14, makes a clear distinction between priests, who are to perform the primary religious duties concerning sacrifice and the conduct of worship, and Levites. Levites are to provide a class of second-rank temple servants who are barred from entry into the most holy place (v. 13). Instead, they are to act as servants of the building and "do all its chores" (v. 14).

We can well recognize that such rules were appropriate, given the strong emphasis on the avoidance of idolatry and all unseemly activities in the temple that characterizes Ezekiel's condemnation of Israel's past mistakes. They ensured that only well-trained and wholly committed families of priests would handle temple affairs, a great privilege and a great responsibility. In their own way, however, and as the life of the rebuilt temple eventually unfolded, these restrictive rules were to become obsessive and divisive. Not least, they failed to define with adequate clarity who was and who was not to be classed as a "foreigner." Both broader and narrower interpretations of rules became possible as a result. In a similar fashion, some rules might be inadvertently broken or insufficient allowance made to ensure that they were observed. So we can understand how a fundamental delight in observing the rules of holiness could lead some into an overscrupulous concern not to infringe on them. The law could become a burden.

Seen in retrospect, Ezekiel's program stands at an identifiable halfway point between the older Israelite worldview, in which ideas of holiness and uncleanness provided clear-cut and decisive patterns of behavior, and a more reasoned and heart-searching stage of development, in which conscience and intention became paramount concerns. The final shaping of the Old Testament owes much to the efforts at reconciling and holding together these twin concerns for ritual purity and individual moral responsibility. This was to lead to demands for a whole new rethinking of the nature of good and evil, with many old taboos being dropped or reinterpreted.

THE DISTINCTION
BETWEEN PRIESTS AND LEVITES
Ezekiel 44:15–31

44:15 But the levitical priests, the descendants of Zadok, who kept the charge of my sanctuary when the people of Israel went astray from me, shall come near to me to minister to me; and they shall attend me to offer me the

fat and the blood, says the Lord GOD. [16] It is they who shall enter my sanctuary, it is they who shall approach my table, to minister to me, and they shall keep my charge. . . . [23] They shall teach my people the difference between the holy and the common, and show them how to distinguish between the unclean and the clean. [24] In a controversy they shall act as judges, and they shall decide it according to my judgments. They shall keep my laws and my statutes regarding all my appointed festivals, and they shall keep my sabbaths holy. . . .

[28] This shall be their inheritance: I am their inheritance; and you shall give them no holding in Israel; I am their holding. [29] They shall eat the grain offering, the sin offering, and the guilt offering; and every devoted thing in Israel shall be theirs. [30] The first of all the first fruits of all kinds, and every offering of all kinds from all your offerings, shall belong to the priests; you shall also give to the priests the first of your dough, in order that a blessing may rest on your house. [31] The priests shall not eat of anything, whether bird or animal, that died of itself or was torn by animals.

Ezekiel's vision of the new temple focuses primarily on its architecture and carefully planned structure. It is to be a place of beauty and reverence of God. Yet its influence and authority will inevitably be placed in the hands of those who perform and control its services—the priests and other temple servants who run affairs. We can readily correlate this ancient concern with more modern ones. Religion and faith have drawn heavily on a sense of place and of centuries-old buildings that point the way of God. Yet within the buildings, sanctuary servants whose commitment and care will inevitably affect the efficacy of all worship conducted there must work and plan. A later Jewish writer of the Greek period was to complain that the priests hurried through the services in order to free themselves to attend the latest sporting contests and displays (2 Macc. 4:13–17).

The concern for good order brought about the carefully worded and important distinction demanded here between priests and Levites. Only the former are to be true priests, with all the major responsibilities for the conduct of worship and the offering of sacrifice. The Levites are to carry out more menial and less religiously directed tasks, to keep the activities of the temple in clean and effective order.

From the careful historical study of the Israelite priesthood, it is clear that this firm distinction between priests and Levites is a relatively new one, at least in its rigid enforcement. The book of Deuteronomy allows all Levites to perform priestly tasks, although this may well not have happened in practice. The turmoil and confusion brought about by the destruction of the temple in 587 B.C., together with the earlier removal of many priests, like Ezekiel, to Babylon, made the need for an agreed policy an urgent one if there were not to be unseemly disputes about privileges and duties relating to the temple service. It seems certain that it was a major point of difficulty, when the time came to reinstate temple services in 516 B.C., to determine who was allowed to officiate and how the various duties were to be divided between groups. By this time, there must have been many seeking priestly status whose claims were uncertain or unprovable. With all the deep anxiety concerning priestly purity and separateness, it is evident that after an interval of more than half a century it may have been difficult to prove genealogical descent and personal integrity in such troubled times.

So we must understand that the rules for priestly behavior and the defining of their duties as set out in the renewal program are very much a restatement of policy. They serve to reaffirm duties and obligations that may have been forgotten or held in disregard. So priesthood meant a great responsibility, which had to be accompanied by certain rules of separation and distinction from the ordinary populace. The priesthood had to be different if it was to preserve its tradition of holiness with its accompanying respect. It also enjoyed great privileges, which are set out in verses 28–31. They guaranteed the proper welfare and support of the people, and at the same time they ensured that the priests remained participants in the economic life of the people. In times of plenty the priesthood shared in the bounty, while in times of hardship and famine, the priests were not exempt from deprivation.

THE SHARING OF THE LAND
Ezekiel 45:1–12

45:1 **When you allot the land as an inheritance, you shall set aside for the LORD a portion of the land as a holy district, twenty-five thousand cubits long and twenty thousand cubits wide; it shall be holy throughout its entire extent. 2 Of this, a square plot of five hundred by five hundred cubits shall be for the sanctuary, with fifty cubits for an open space around it. 3 In the holy district you shall measure off a section . . . in which shall be the sanctuary, the most holy place. 4 It . . . shall be for the priests . . . and it shall be both a place for their houses and a holy place for the sanctuary. 5 Another section . . . shall be for the Levites who minister at the temple. . . .**

6 Alongside the portion set apart as the holy district you shall assign as a holding for the city an area five thousand cubits wide, and twenty-five thousand cubits long; it shall belong to the whole house of Israel.

⁷ And to the prince shall belong the land on both sides of the holy district and the holding of the city. . . . ⁸ᵇ And my princes shall no longer oppress my people; but they shall let the house of Israel have the land according to their tribes.

⁹ Thus says the Lord GOD: Enough, O princes of Israel! Put away violence and oppression, and do what is just and right. Cease your evictions of my people, says the Lord GOD.

¹⁰ You shall have honest balances, an honest ephah, and an honest bath. . . .

This section deals with two major issues: the apportionment of the land, including the allocation of a large area for the use of priests and Levites (vv. 1–6), and the designation of a substantial section for the residence and use of the prince (vv. 7–8). Two concluding injunctions exhort the ruling elite to desist from oppression and reaffirm a definition of weights and measures (vv. 9–12).

The pronouncements give us some valuable clues as to what the problems of the time were and why the inclusion of such regulations was important. The prince was evidently in a position to take advantage of his office to acquire land that he found desirable. Weights and measures were a long-standing cause of grievance and an all too easy means of exploiting the poorer and less protected sections and members of society. In general, in antiquity it seems that it was very largely a responsibility of the rulers, and royal courts where they existed, to ensure that just weights and measures were employed in the popular markets. Abuse of the system was widespread; it is significant that both prophets and sages condemned this (Amos 8:5; Prov. 11:1, etc.), but with a realization that such abuse was difficult both to track down and to prevent.

It seems highly probable that the economic and property-owning situation in Judah that had arisen by the time the restored temple was inaugurated at the end of the sixth century was giving rise to a good deal of anxiety and anger. If the title of prince in this program refers to the governor who was appointed by the Persian imperial rulers, as was the case with Zerubbabel, it is probable that such men were either negligent or powerless to put a stop to cheating. The temple authorities and the civil government were jointly responsible for upholding honesty and straight-dealing in a wide area of commercial and economic life. After more than three-quarters of a century of weakness and turmoil, it is understandable that it was proving very difficult to put things right. Ezekiel's renewal program spells out many of the basic requirements for rebuilding the inner fabric of decency and honesty without which no society can thrive.

In issues relating to commercial and legal matters, it is significant to note the importance of the fundamental concern for holiness and respect for God. The temple was not simply a place in which worship could be performed, it was also a symbol of the spiritual meaning and godly foundation of the whole of society. It is in this area that the modern reader has most to learn from the perspective presented in this renewal program. Creation was seen as a single whole, and the priestly interpretation of holiness that is set forth embraced life in its totality. Matters of law, commerce, health, education, and personal happiness all came under the overarching concept of "a holy people." Some aspects of what is set out in Ezekiel's program look to be rather theoretical (for example, the geometric division of land without regard for actual geographical features), but it nevertheless states certain fundamental principles. Dishonesty was not only a matter of infringing certain laws or rights but was an affront to the divine order of holiness.

THE PROVISION OF OFFERINGS
Ezekiel 45:13–25

45:13. . . . **This is the offering for grain offerings, burnt offerings, and offerings of well-being, to make atonement for them, says the Lord GOD. [16] All the people of the land shall join with the prince in Israel in making this offering. [17] But this shall be the obligation of the prince regarding the burnt offerings, grain offerings, and drink offerings, at the festivals, the new moons, and the sabbaths, all the appointed festivals of the house of Israel: he shall provide the sin offerings, grain offerings, the burnt offerings, and the offerings of well-being to make atonement for the house of Israel. . . .**
   [21] In the first month, on the fourteenth day of the month, you shall celebrate the festival of the passover, and for seven days unleavened bread shall be eaten. [22] On that day the prince shall provide for himself and all the people of the land a young bull for a sin offering. [23] And during the seven days of the festival he shall provide as a burnt offering to the LORD seven young bulls and seven rams without blemish, on each of the seven days; and a male goat daily for a sin offering. [24] He shall provide as a grain offering an ephah for each bull, an ephah for each ram, and a hin of oil to each ephah. [25] In the seventh month, on the fifteenth day of the month, and for the seven days of the festival, he shall make the same provision for sin offerings, burnt offerings, and grain offerings, and for the oil.

Just as with honest trading in the marketplace, so also was the provision of offerings for the sanctuary a matter of wide public importance. This was to be a joint responsibility between the prince and "all the people of the land" (that is, landowners, v. 16). All too often in antiquity, the provision of offerings was a form of temple tax, which fell as a burden on people who could not readily afford it. So it mattered greatly to insist that, since offerings were intended to secure atonement for the well-being of the whole "house of Israel" (v. 17), the responsibility for providing them should fall on everyone. The prince was under a major obligation for ensuring this, but he was not alone.

It remains for us a matter of considerable interest and uncertainty to know what arrangements the priestly community who were exiled in Babylon made for the provision of offerings and the celebration of the major Israelite festivals. It may well have been one of the "happy accidents" of historical necessity that the group of deportees who were taken with Ezekiel to Babylon included a large group of priests. They would have faced an almost insoluble dilemma, since, as priests concerned for good order in worship, they could not have permitted the presentation of offerings willy-nilly at makeshift altars and by unqualified personnel. At the same time, they could not simply have ignored the major festivals, or reinvented the traditional times and forms of worship, without forfeiting all credibility to be maintaining the authorized religion instituted by Moses. Some changes and concessions had to be allowed, while at the same time as much of the tradition of the past was upheld as was practicable. We can see therefore that the restoration of the temple of Jerusalem remained at the top of the agenda for such priestly leaders, since this would remove a major difficulty.

In the outcome, it is clear that an eminently sensible balance was achieved between keeping the traditional emphasis on a centralized focus of worship at the approved sanctuary and allowing simpler forms of prayer and worship to be observed outside the formal sanctuary area. Jews living in foreign lands, far distant from the Jerusalem temple, could sing psalms, offer prayers and petitions to God, and meditate on the historic traditions of their national past. In many of its features, much of the genius of Jewish piety has consisted in its domestic reality: It could sanctify and consolidate the home and the family through prayer and meditation without infringing on the importance of a more formal central order of worship. The temple became the guide and guardian of a pattern of worship that extended far beyond its walls. It was a school of prayer through which a widely scattered mixture of devout communities could learn the disciplines of faith. The sacrifices of prayer and praise could supplement, and ultimately replace, formal sacrificial acts as such.

It is no surprise therefore to find that the renewal program effectively sets out a short summary of the basic festivals and offerings by which Jewish communities can once again consecrate the whole of their life after the years of turmoil and defeat that followed the destruction of the temple. We can well understand that opinions at the time of temple rebuilding were seriously divided over the necessity and value of this. When, for more than half a century, so many Jews had learned to practice their religion without recourse to the temple, they may well have argued that this experience proved the temple to be unnecessary. Others, in contrast, must certainly have frowned on continuing any forms of worship, however simple, outside the priestly control of the temple area.

The effective outcome appears to have been a carefully coordinated recognition that worship needs both a central temple-based focus and wider, locally centered meetings for prayer and meditation. The pattern of synagogue worship that was to become such an important and formative feature of Jewish life undoubtedly grew up in this context. It was not a rival or alternative to temple worship but rather an aspect of its extension and outreach. Judaism was not restricted to participation in one single pattern of ritual at a single sanctuary, yet such a central sanctuary, located in Jerusalem, provided the beacon through which all Jewish worship was to be enlightened.

This aspect of Ezekiel's renewal program makes it a significant feature of the Old Testament and marks a very real and lasting point where there took place "a parting of the ways." It recognizes that many Jews were living outside Jerusalem and had been scattered among the nations. Yet it focuses their faith and spiritual commitment firmly upon Jerusalem. Through its temple, it elevates the city to fulfill a role as the center of a divine order of life, interpreted through worship, that has meaning for all.

THE RULER AND HIS DUTIES
Ezekiel 46:1–18

46:1 **Thus says the Lord GOD: The gate of the inner court that faces east shall remain closed on the six working days; but on the sabbath day it shall be opened and on the day of the new moon it shall be opened. 2 The prince shall enter by the vestibule of the gate from outside, and shall take his stand by the post of the gate. The priests shall offer his burnt offering and his offerings of well-being, and he shall bow down at the threshold of the gate. Then he shall go out, but the gate shall not be closed until evening. . . .**

¹¹ At the festivals and the appointed seasons the grain offering with a young bull shall be an ephah, and with a ram an ephah, and with the lambs as much as one wishes to give, together with a hin of oil to an ephah. ¹² When the prince provides a freewill offering, either a burnt offering or offerings of well-being as a freewill offering to the LORD, the gate facing east shall be opened for him; and he shall offer his burnt offering or his offerings of well-being as he does on the sabbath day. . . .

¹⁶ Thus says the Lord GOD: If the prince makes a gift to any of his sons out of his inheritance, it shall belong to his sons, it is their holding by inheritance. ¹⁷ But if he makes a gift out of his inheritance to one of his servants, it shall be his to the year of liberty; then it shall revert to the prince; only his sons may keep a gift from his inheritance. ¹⁸ The prince shall not take any of the inheritance of the people, thrusting them out of their holding; he shall give his sons their inheritance out of his own holding, so that none of my people shall be dispossessed of their holding.

Chapter 46 deals with the duties of the prince, or leader of the community. It is evident, as we have already noted, that he is denied the title of king, and this was certainly by considered intent. There may have been some theological constraints, but the most prominent consideration must have been the limitations imposed by the Persian imperial authorities. It would also appear to be a matter of considered design that no mention is made that such a prince should be of Davidic parentage. Clearly, many in Judah and among the exiles would have welcomed this, but it is likely that it was an issue that was already causing problems. Zerubbabel, who was of the royal house and who took a major part in the temple restoration of the years 520–516 B.C. (as is shown by Zech. 4:8), seems to have caused difficulties, possibly because some of his followers expected too much (the prophecy of Hag. 2:23 seems to point to this, without explaining the details).

The duties specified for the prince are quite straightforward and simply concern his participation in worship at the proper festivals in the temple and his obligation to provide sacrificial animals for them. Significant social and economic issues are touched upon only in verses 16–18. The prince is not permitted to abuse his power by acquiring land and giving it to friends and supporters—a well-known ploy of corrupt abuse of office that has marred much social history. He can, however, pass on territory as an inheritance to his own sons.

Overall, the chapter is of interest to the modern reader because of the changing balance of authority it discloses between religious and civil leaders. The records of the building of Solomon's temple show that at that period the civil (kingly) authority exercised major control over the temple and its priests. Now the roles appear reversed. A note of concession and constraint affects what the prince is and is not allowed to do in the temple. He has responsibilities, but they are limited. Behind this changed situation lies an unmentioned third factor, which was undoubtedly very important. This concerns the Persian imperial power, which controlled Jerusalem at the time these regulations were to be put into effect. Their attitude was clearly favorable to allowing local traditions of worship to be upheld and much less favorable to reviving local traditions of civil rulership.

Since no mention is made concerning how the prince is to be appointed, we must take it for granted that this was to be by approval of, if not explicitly by, designation of the Persian imperial power. More information comes to us from the next century when we learn of the work of such men as Ezra and Nehemiah, who received their commissions from the Persian royal court. The portrayal of the work of the prince of Ezekiel's renewal program shows him to be placed between a variety of interests where he needed skill to negotiate. He was a civil ruler in a small provincial city of the Persian empire where religion was a matter of paramount concern. It was an achievement to have received imperial support for the rebuilding of the temple and the restoration of its activities. Without proper restraint the temple activities could easily become so heavily politicized as to arouse the suspicion and wrath of the imperial rulers. It is even possible that such overstepping of the mark occurred, since we lack information of much that happened during the first half of the next century. By that time, new initiatives were needed by Ezra and Nehemiah to put things right.

It has been argued that Ezekiel's renewal program should be regarded as a highly theoretical document—it was what a group of exiled priests wanted to achieve, whether or not they could actually do so. Yet this understanding is too critical; with some allowances for the rather stylized presentation of a number of details, the general character and aim are very practical and appear workable. The program was a key factor in putting matters of faith and spiritual renewal in the forefront of Jewish life after the catastrophes that had brought ruin to the old Israelite kingdoms. It sought to translate the prophetic vision of Ezekiel into a practical reality. It is not surprising that it had to skirt some issues, such as restoration of the monarchy, which the circumstances of the time rendered unattainable. But it succeeded very powerfully in recognizing that the rebuilding of a temple in Jerusalem would provide a light by which Jews, both in Judah and farther afield, could keep faith in the present.

Once again, it is worth remembering that throughout its long history Judaism learned to survive, and even flourish, under a variety of political systems, some of them more oppressive and some of them less so. Nor does the Bible prescribe any one political system, even though its spiritual values are clearly more conducive to some forms of government rather than others.

THE RIVER OF GRACE
Ezekiel 47:1–12

47:1 **Then he brought me back to the entrance of the temple; there, water was flowing from below the threshold of the temple toward the east (for the temple faced east); and the water was flowing down from below the south end of the threshold of the temple, south of the altar. 2 Then he brought me out by way of the north gate, and led me around on the outside to the outer gate that faces toward the east; and the water was coming out on the south side.**

3 Going on eastward with a cord in his hand, the man measured one thousand cubits, and then led me through the water; and it was ankle-deep. 4 Again he measured one thousand, and led me through the water; and it was knee-deep. Again he measured one thousand, and led me through the water; and it was up to the waist. 5 Again he measured one thousand, and it was a river that I could not cross, for the water had risen; it was deep enough to swim in, a river that could not be crossed. 6 He said to me, "Mortal, have you seen this?"

Then he led me back along the bank of the river. . . . 8 He said to me, "This water flows toward the eastern region and goes down into the Arabah; and when it enters the sea, the sea of stagnant waters, the water will become fresh. 9 Wherever the river goes, every living creature that swarms will live, and there will be very many fish, once these waters reach there. It will become fresh; and everything will live where the river goes. . . . 12 On the banks, on both sides of the river, there will grow all kinds of trees for food. Their leaves will not wither nor their fruit fail, but they will bear fresh fruit every month, because the water for them flows from the sanctuary. Their fruit will be for food, and their leaves for healing."

The original prophetic vision of Ezekiel put in the forefront of hope for the future the work of rebuilding the temple of Jerusalem. Yet this task was not to stand by itself but was to be the centerpiece of a much larger program of rebuilding the life of the people of God in their homeland. The importance of the temple is everywhere assumed, and this is now explained and reaffirmed in a remarkable visionary picture of what it will mean for the land and the people who reside there. It has sometimes been described as a piece of mythology, yet this is to underplay its originality and uniqueness. It can best be described as a piece of "pictorial theology," entirely in character with the strong visual emphasis of Ezekiel's prophecies and presenting, by a whole series of symbolic images, the meaning of the temple for Jewish life and well-being. It remains one of the most memorable and striking of all the biblical portrayals of the meaning and value of worship for human life. Its lasting significance is shown by the fact that it became the foundational text for elaboration in the New Testament in Revelation 22:1–2 as "the river of the water of life."

Certainly, there is an element in the description of Ezekiel 47:1–12 that is drawn from ancient mythology about the location of paradise, where a mysterious spring, or stream, rises from the earth (Gen. 2:6). Since water was so vital for survival and for the fertility of the land, its God-given origin was taken for granted. So in spite of the rather limited water supply of the city of Jerusalem, it is remarkable that in a number of biblical texts (for example, Psalm 46:4; Isa. 33:21) the temple area can be pictured as a place where a great river flows.

However, it seems likely that it is not simply the old mythology of paradise that helped shape the marvelous picture of Ezekiel 47. Babylon was a city of waterways, and the low-lying marshlands of the region must have presented a dreary and unhealthy landscape for the exiles there. The longing expressed in Psalm 137 must have echoed powerfully in many an exile's heart. The very fact that Babylon was a city of waterways, linked to the great river Euphrates, must have raised thoughts and images of Jerusalem as a city where the great "river of grace" flowed. Nor does it require more than elementary knowledge to recognize that the malaria-infected marshes "by the river Chebar" would have been experienced as threatening and disease-ridden.

To contrast this, however idealistically, with the healing waters of Jerusalem and the fresh life and vitality that will be found there is a very meaningful visionary image. So the picture that is painted of the guide to the new temple conducting the prophet along the course of the marvelous river is full of symbolism. It has a Bunyanesque character, where the various details permit imaginative interpretation as to their spiritual significance. The further the prophet progresses in the water, the deeper it gets (vv. 3–5), until he can swim in it. Not only will there be an abundance of fish but its banks will flourish with trees and vegetation, and the leaves of these trees will produce healing herbs (vv. 6–12). Strikingly, the New Testament develops this theme further, with its picture of the tree of life growing along riverbanks that brings healing to the nations.

Overall, the picture that is drawn in this vision is suggestive of the great importance of the temple to all life. It marks a prophetic recasting of a way of looking at life in which worship, and the fact that worship makes possible access to God, occupies a central place. The temple was a point of orientation. For those close enough to see physically, it would signify the center of Jewish life. Yet for those who were too distant to see the building directly, it would nevertheless be a source of life and vitality. It expressed hope and new life simply by the knowledge that it was there. It is no wonder that from this time on we find in Judaism the emergence of the practice of turning one's head in the direction of Jerusalem to accompany an act of prayer.

This visionary picture of the temple serves to sum up the central theme and spiritual perspective of the entire renewal program. At its heart we can sense a decidedly priestly character and origin. It regards the temple as essential to life, so that the restoration of the building in Jerusalem and its services heads the list of tasks that can turn hope into reality. It inevitably focuses much of its attention on the details of preserving the authority of, and public respect for, the priesthood. Yet it is not priest-ridden in any narrow or negative fashion, since it regards true worship as vital for all human life. Seen in the light of later Jewish and Christian experience, after the destruction of the temple in A.D. 70 has marked yet a further tragedy that nevertheless serves as a transforming feature of the biblical story, Ezekiel's program retains its special interest. The spiritualized service of prayer and submission to God were not yet able to replace the outward rites and physical symbols of worship. Yet events had shown that, without the former, the latter were meaningless.

THE TRIBAL TERRITORIES
Ezekiel 47:13–23

47:13 **Thus says the Lord GOD: These are the boundaries by which you shall divide the land for inheritance among the twelve tribes of Israel. Joseph shall have two portions. 14 You shall divide it equally; I swore to give it to your ancestors, and this land shall fall to you as your inheritance.**

15 This shall be the boundary of the land: . . . 17 the boundary shall run from the sea of Hazarenon, which is north of the border of Damascus, with the border of Hamath to the north. This shall be the north side.

¹⁸ On the east side, between Hauran and Damascus; along the Jordan between Gilead and the land of Israel; to the eastern sea and as far as Tamar. This shall be the east side.

¹⁹ On the south side, it shall run from Tamar as far as the waters of Meribath-kadesh, from there along the Wadi of Egypt to the Great Sea. This shall be the south side.

²⁰ On the west side, the Great Sea shall be the boundary to a point opposite Lebo-hamath. This shall be the west side. . . .

We have already seen that the breakdown of political life in Judah following the disasters of the Babylonian military campaigns left a long legacy of conflict and territorial dispute. Much of the factional and sectarian division that continued to mar Jewish history down to New Testament times began here. It clearly mattered greatly to seek to settle these problems, and it seems likely that the boundary lists set out here were intended as a contribution to this end. Without land, people had no economic base and no security. It is likely, therefore, that a major hindrance to all attempts to restore peace and good order in Judah by the end of the sixth century foundered on these difficulties. We know that by the middle of the next century the conflicts were so deeply felt that large-scale reforms under the new leadership of Ezra and Nehemiah were called for to try to settle them.

THE PEOPLE OF GOD
Ezekiel 48:1–35

48:1 These are the names of the tribes: Beginning at the northern border, on the Hethlon road, from Lebo-hamath, as far as Hazarenon (which is on the border of Damascus, with Hamath to the north), and extending from the east side to the west, Dan, one portion. ² Adjoining the territory of Dan, from the east side to the west, Asher, one portion. ³ Adjoining the territory of Asher, from the east side to the west, Naphtali, one portion. ⁴ Adjoining the territory of Naphtali, from the east side to the west, Manasseh, one portion. ⁵ Adjoining the territory of Manasseh, from the east side to the west, Ephraim, one portion. ⁶ Adjoining the territory of Ephraim, from the east side to the west, Reuben, one portion. ⁷ Adjoining the territory of Reuben, from the east side to the west, Judah, one portion.

⁸ Adjoining the territory of Judah, from the east side to the west, shall be the portion that you shall set apart, twenty-five thousand cubits in width, and in length equal to one of the tribal portions, from the east side to the west, with the sanctuary in the middle of it. ⁹ The portion that you shall set

apart for the LORD shall be twenty-five thousand cubits in length, and twenty thousand in width. . . .

23 As for the rest of the tribes: from the east side to the west, Benjamin, one portion. 24 Adjoining the territory of Benjamin, from the east side to the west, Simeon, one portion. 25 Adjoining the territory of Simeon, from the east side to the west, Issachar, one portion. 26 Adjoining the territory of Issachar, from the east side to the west, Zebulun, one portion. 27 Adjoining the territory of Zebulun, from the east side to the west, Gad, one portion. 28 And adjoining the territory of Gad to the south, the boundary shall run from Tamar to the waters of Meribath-kadesh, from there along the Wadi of Egypt to the Great Sea. 29 This is the land that you shall allot as an inheritance among the tribes of Israel, and these are their portions, says the Lord GOD.

30 These shall be the exits of the city: On the north side, which is to be four thousand five hundred cubits by measure, 31 three gates, the gate of Reuben, the gate of Judah, and the gate of Levi, the gates of the city being named after the tribes of Israel. 32 On the east side, which is to be four thousand five hundred cubits, three gates, the gate of Joseph, the gate of Benjamin, and the gate of Dan. 33 On the south side, which is to be four thousand five hundred cubits by measure, three gates, the gate of Simeon, the gate of Issachar, and the gate of Zebulun. 34 On the west side, which is to be four thousand five hundred cubits, three gates, the gate of Gad, the gate of Asher, and the gate of Naphtali. 35 The circumference of the city shall be eighteen thousand cubits. And the name of the city from that time on shall be, The LORD is There.

To what tribe do you belong? The question sounds strange and lacking in relevance to today's Western ear. Yet it was of vital importance to most communities of the ancient world and still remains so for millions of people in present-day Africa. Paul was proud to recall that he belonged to the tribe of Benjamin (Phil. 3:5), even though he had been brought up outside the territory of Judah where the old tribal settlement areas had once had meaning. It is the awareness of tribal belonging as a badge of identity that makes this concluding list of tribes and their territories in the book of Ezekiel a document of interest. It is certainly one of the most theoretical and impractical parts of the entire program, and we are puzzled at first by what it is doing in the document at all. At the time of the Babylonian attacks on the cities of Judah, tribal belonging was already becoming outmoded for the people of God.

We find when we read the book of Genesis, and the narrative of the land allocations after the initial conquest under Joshua, that in those days tribal identities and distinctions were of vital importance. Both Jacob and

Moses uttered long-remembered prayers of blessing for the various tribes that made up Israel (Genesis 49; Deuteronomy 33). Yet the changes in agricultural practice, the growth of cities that housed an increasing proportion of the population, and the rise of international trade meant that tribes lost their influence and authority as local civil leaders enhanced theirs. Society was undergoing major changes, among the most radical that have taken place throughout all of human history. Reliance on the extended family became weaker as conditions changed. Neighbors became more relevant for support and help as the larger family groups began to split up and separate.

It is in the light of this that the allocation of tribal territories and the retention of old tribal family names in Ezekiel's renewal program show their distinctiveness. From a social perspective, they were backward-looking and archaic, not to say impractical and theoretical, as the geometrical divisions of territory reveal. Nevertheless, they were certainly not without significance, and their inclusion has much to say regarding the biblical understanding of community.

Various factors serve to explain the inclusion of such details. In the forefront lies the awareness that the return from exile was to mark a new beginning, so that just as Joshua allocated the original tribal territories after the first acquisition of the land, so was there to be a fresh start and a fresh opportunity for each tribe to recommence its life. Obviously, for those thrown unwillingly into the misery of life in Babylonian exile and for the many thousands of other citizens of the old lands of Israel and Judah who had been scattered among the nations, belonging to a tribe and possessing a tribal land holding were ideals of a lost past. Yet as Paul's later comment reveals, tribal affiliation remained a very important badge of identity for Jews, a meaningful standard that could not and should not be thrown away. The Bible has much to say about the way in which spiritual ideals may constitute an inheritance that can never simply be abandoned.

It also seems to be important to this concluding prescription for land allocation as a part of the renewal of Israel after the exile that it focuses especially upon ownership of land. If there is to be a genuine fresh start to life in the restored Israel, there has to be a renewal of opportunity for each member of the people to share in the promised prosperity.

The idealized and theoretical nature of going back to first principles, as though a new Joshua could divide up an unoccupied land to members of each tribe with no attention to existing conditions, is easily recognizable. Nevertheless, we can appreciate the good sense in affirming that those who were to share in the new life of God's people needed a firm and secure economic basis for doing so. To offer the promise of a new beginning but to deny the means whereby that new beginning can be made a practical reality would be an empty hope. So, for all its archaic strangeness this concluding allocation of land, which brings to an end the great prophetic vision of the rebirth of Israel, serves a purpose. It draws from the tradition of the past a stylized picture of what new life really means— not simply as a new feeling of well-being but as a new opportunity to develop God-given gifts for prosperity and human fulfillment.

The final comment, which provides a new name for the rebuilt city, sums up its spiritual significance: The Lord is there!

For Further Reading

Allen, Leslie C. *Ezekiel 20–48*. Word Biblical Commentary. Dallas: Word Books, 1990.

Brownlee, William H. *Ezekiel 1–19*. Word Biblical Commentary. Dallas: Word Books, 1989.

Eichrodt, Walther. *Ezekiel: A Commentary*. Old Testament Library. Richmond: Westminster Press, 1970.

Greenberg, Moshe H., *Ezekiel 1–20*. Anchor Bible. New York: Doubleday. 1983.

Klein, Ralph W. *Israel in Exile: A Theological Interpretation*. Overtures in Biblical Theology. Trans. Walter Brueggemann and John R. Donahue. Philadelphia: Fortress Press, 1979. Provides the reader with the general religious background of the prophet.

McKeating, H. *Ezekiel*. Old Testament Guides. Sheffield: Sheffield Academic Press, 1993. Provides the reader with a useful general introduction to the critical study of the book of Ezekiel.

Zimmerli, Walther. *Ezekiel*, 2 vols. Hermeneia. Minneapolis: Augsburg Publishing House, 1979–1983.